# Novell Certification Handbook

# Novell Certification Handbook

*Second edition*

## John Mueller, CNE
## Robert A. Williams, CNE, CNI

**McGraw-Hill**

New York   San Francisco   Washington, D.C.   Auckland   Bogotá
Caracas   Lisbon   London   Madrid   Mexico City   Milan
Montreal   New Delhi   San Juan   Singapore
Sydney   Tokyo   Toronto

## McGraw-Hill

*A Division of The* **McGraw·Hill** *Companies*

pbk    1 2 3 4 5 6 7 8 9 DOC/DOC 9 0 0 9 8 7 6

hc    1 2 3 4 5 6 7 8 9 DOC/DOC 9 0 0 9 8 7 6

**Library of Congress Cataloging-in-Publication Data**
Mueller, John, 1958–
      Novell certification handbook / by John Mueller and Robert A.
Williams. – 2nd ed.
         p.    cm.
      Includes index.
      ISBN 0-07-044364-5 (hardcover).  ISBN 0-07-044365-3
(pbk.)
      1. Electronic data processing personnel—Certification.  2. Novell
software—Study and teaching.  I. Williams, Robert A. (Robert
Allen)  II. Title.
QA76.76.C47M84  1996
004.6—dc20                                            96-5711
                                                           CIP

Acquisitions editor: Brad Schepp
Editorial team: Michael Christopher, Manuscript Editor
                    David M. McCandless, Associate Managing Editor
                    Lori Flaherty, Executive Editor
Production team: Katherine G. Brown, Director
                    Donna K. Harlacher, Desktop Operator
                    Jennifer M. Secula, Indexer
Design team: Jaclyn J. Boone, Designer
                    Katherine Lukaszewicz, Associate Designer

0443653
WK2

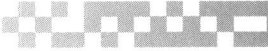

This book is dedicated to our families. Like the family of the network administrator who spends the weekend searching frantically for that broken cable, our families had to spend many weekends without us as we put this book together. We would like to thank our wives, Rebecca and Cyndie, for their endless support, tireless resolve to keep our homes together, and loving care when things didn't go well.

# Contents

# Contents

# Introduction

*Novell Certification Handbook* is the one source of information you need to prepare for, obtain, and use any of the certifications offered by Novell. This book concentrates on the elements that other certification books miss. We start by telling you why you need certification, proceed with educational requirements, tell you about testing requirements, and then help you come up with a workable plan to get the certification you need. We even tell you how to add your certification to your resume and how to present it to a potential employer. The book ends with a section on continuing education requirements.

In today's marketplace, many network administrators who need to get certification are unaware of the requirements or unsure of who to contact. This book provides all the answers you will need, by helping you in ten specific ways.

1 Learn the differences between the various certifications offered by Novell: CNA, CNE, ECNE, MCNE, and CNI. Many users are unsure what level or type of certification they need. Especially unclear are the differences between CNE, MCNE, and ECNE. This book helps you understand the differences and plan for the level of certification that meets your needs.

**2** Enhance your career by getting a Novell certification. Many people consider a Novell certification an extra responsibility they neither want nor need. *Novell Certification Handbook* helps you over this hurdle by showing you the benefits of certification. In many cases, a positive attitude could mean the difference between becoming and not becoming certified.

**3** Plan for the certification process. It's unfortunate, but many people start CNA or CNE training with no idea of what to expect or how to prepare for it. This book will help you prepare by understanding the requirements; it will also help you create various checklists tailored to your needs. For some people, writing down what they need to do is at least half the battle.

**4** Understand what support you can expect from Novell. Part of the benefit of becoming certified is the support that Novell provides. While the documentation provided with the certification package outlines some of the benefits, a mere list is not enough. This book helps people understand what they can do with these additional support items.

**5** Plan for continuing education requirements. Many people approach a Novell certification as they would a high school education. Once it's over, they peacefully go back to their old routine, never recognizing the need to continue their education. This book will help you avoid that trap by meeting all of Novell's recertification requirements, as and when they apply.

**6** Get all your certification questions answered in one place. One of the big problems in getting a Novell certification is that many prospects spend many hours searching for answers. This problem isn't new or unique; for example, consider at all the books that tell you how to get a GED or take an SAT test to get into a college or university. By comparison, there is no comparable guide for people who want to become a CNE, except for this book.

**7** Get your certification quickly and easily. This book provides tips and hints that will reduce your chance of failure when you take a test. This could shave days or even weeks from your certification schedule. Add to this the time you saved in researching the certification itself and you could end up saving a month or more.

**8** Learn what courses are available. Many people miss opportunities simply because they don't know what courses are available. *Novell Certification Handbook* provides an exhaustive list of classes offered by Novell. All you need to do is decide which courses you want to take (as long as they meet certification requirements), then do so.

**9** Get answers to your questions quickly and easily. This book provides a list of important phone numbers that will help you find the right person the first time you call.

**10** Find additional sources of information. There is no single solution to every problem, but this book provides a list of places you can go for additional help. This resource can be very important, to both novices and experts alike.

Overall, this book provides you with all the information you need to get your certification. However, if you would like additional help you might consider *The Novell CNA/CNE Study Guide* by John Mueller and Robert Williams (McGraw-Hill). Even though the book you are reading now provides sample questions you can use for studying, *The Novell CNA/CNE Study Guide* offers a wealth of additional study aids, including a disk containing at least 50 questions for every core and target exam, in Windows help file format. The same disk contains a game called *The Red Zone* that makes learning fun. You'll also find a copy of *Big Red Test*, a study aid that shows you how the actual Novell exams will look.

# ⇨ What's new in this edition?

This second edition of *Novell Certification Handbook* contains quite a few new materials. For example, we cover all the newest, most current requirements for becoming a CNA, CNE, MCNE, or CNI. Also all the tables, figures, and questions contain updated information that reflects Novell's changing certification requirements. For example, all the elective courses covered in Chapter 1 now include course and test numbers, in addition to the course names provided in the previous edition.

This book also contains information about two new certification routes that Novell provides. GroupWare is based on Novell's GroupWise offering. It allows workgroups to work together to accomplish specific projects. It still provides access to overall company resources through standard NetWare connections.

# Understand why you need certification

Many people don't understand what a Novell certification is, or why they need it. This includes employers as well as clients. Even if you understand why certification is important, presenting these facts to an employer or client might prove difficult. *Novell Certification Handbook* provides you with a full description of each of the certifications and explains why they are important. This not only increases your own knowledge, but helps you explain the different certifications to potential clients and employers as well. Having this information at your fingertips could mean the difference between getting a job or losing it to someone less qualified than you. It can also help you get the level of compensation you deserve for having a certification.

# Creating your own certification map

Every person needs to look at different aspects of the certification process. Rather than using a generic map created for someone else, you can tailor a certification map to your own specific needs. Of course, forging your own path takes more time and effort, but it pays in the long run because you'll know how to use your certification better.

This book helps you see what roadblocks you'll face and how to handle them. It also helps you create your certification map faster and more accurately. Mistakes cost time; let this book help you prevent those that could add weeks or even months to your certification effort. The checklists and other organizational aids help you get organized quickly.

# ➩ Learning how to use certification to increase your job opportunities

The bottom line in becoming certified is enhanced job opportunities, which includes getting jobs at higher pay and performing more interesting work. Why fill every day with boring repetitions of the same old work? This book shows you how to use your certification to make both life and work more interesting and profitable.

# 1

# Getting started

E VERYONE must learn the basics before they start a new task, and earning a Novell certification isn't any different. This chapter explains what types of certification Novell offers, what differentiates them from other certifications, and the criteria for earning each one. We will also discuss the duties and responsibilities associated with the various certifications. We even include a procedure for creating your own certification checklist, a must for anyone serious about obtaining this useful and beneficial credential.

Novell patterned its certification process after the credit system used by colleges and university. Each Novell exam that you pass earns you a predetermined number of credits. Two types of credits are available, *required* and *elective*. The required credits come from passing the *core* exams, while the elective credits allow you to pick exams in your field of expertise, (or exams that interest you). Each certification requires a certain number of both required and elective credits.

Novell offers five classes of certification: CNA, CNE, ECNE, MCNE, and CNI. The ECNE program is being phased out; you won't be able to become an ECNE, under the current guidelines, after June, 1996. The replacement program is the MCNE (master certified netware engineer) certification. Once you understand what each certification requires, you will be able to select the one best suited to your knowledge and experience.

# ⇨ What is a CNA?

The Certified NetWare Administrator (CNA) is Novell's entry-level certification. It is designed for the person who needs to administer a network on a day-to-day basis. Often the duties of this person include adding users, assigning security to the users, writing login scripts, backing up the system, installing applications onto the network, and managing the printing environment. Individual companies might assign this person other network administration tasks as well. The CNA is usually a full-time employee of the company and is often required to perform other duties besides managing the network.

Having the CNA certification assures current or prospective employers that you have a good understanding of the Novell operating system. It also certifies that you understand the different administration tools, and that you are familiar with the different aspects of managing a network.

The knowledge and information that you acquire by becoming a CNA can assist you in becoming a Certified NetWare Engineer (CNE). The CNA certification requires you to know the basic and advanced concepts of the Novell operating system, along with more than a basic understanding of microcomputers.

One of the first decisions you must make before pursuing the CNA certification is to select the operating system you want to work with. Novell offers four operating systems and one non-operating system as certification alternatives: 2.2 NetWare, 3.x NetWare, 4.x NetWare, or GroupWare.

➢ The 2.2 system is based on the Intel 286 microprocessor. This operating system is basically a modification of the 2.15 operating system, which was one of Novell's largest selling operating systems. This particular choice is already off limits for CNEs. Novell will probably phase out the CNA program in the future, so you won't want to pursue this option unless your company uses this particular version of NetWare.

➢ The 3.x operating system uses a completely different operating system kernel than that of 2.2. However, Novell has made the look and feel of it the same as past versions of NetWare.

➢ The 4.x operating system is Novell's latest version of these operating system(s).

➢ GroupWare is the second new offering for CNAs. It is based on GroupWise, a new workgroup offering from Novell, and is similar to other workgroup offerings, such as Lotus Notes.

Which certification option your choose should depend on which type of system you have in your office, or which system you have the most experience with. It could also depend on the particular type of business you intend to work in. For example, GroupWare certification would lend itself more to large businesses than to small ones. As with any of the different certifications that Novell offers, the more hands-on experience you have in the subject the better chance you will have of passing the exams.

The criteria for getting the CNA certification involves passing one competency exam, which covers the system administration for any of the following products: NetWare 2.2, NetWare 3.x, NetWare 4.x, or GroupWise. There is no separate exam, and no questions on the basic exam, about DOS and/or microcomputer concepts.

# What is a CNE?

CNE is Novell's certification for people who are more than system administrators. Many of those who obtain the CNE certification are consultants, system integrators, or employees of a company that needs a person with more skill and knowledge than a CNA, to help maintain the overall network.

CNE responsibilities include managing the network in day-to-day activities, repairing and upgrading the hardware at both the workstations and file server, troubleshooting problems on the network, and fine-tuning the network for maximum performance. In general, the overall job of the CNE is to make sure that the network stays up and running.

To obtain CNE certification, you should have a good general understanding of microcomputers and how they work. You should also have an intermediate knowledge of DOS. Other areas that you should be very familiar with include the NetWare system, network hardware, network cabling, and network diagnostic and troubleshooting tools. Even GroupWare certification requires you to know both DOS and NetWare.

*Important note:* While you could probably qualify for GroupWare certification by knowing NetWare 3.x, all the Novell documentation states that you must know NetWare 4.x to meet the requirements. The only exception to this rule occurs if you are currently a NetWare 3.x CNE in good standing, who also wants to obtain the GroupWare certification. If this is true for you, check with your CNE administrator to make sure you understand the GroupWare requirements.

Under the old system of CNE certification there was only one option, even though you might specialize in a particular operating system. The new program provides four different certification options, to reflect both the additional products that Novell offers and the increased complexity of the networking environment. Before you begin the CNE certification process, you much choose a certification option: NetWare 3.x, NetWare 4.x, or GroupWare. Notice that there is no longer a NetWare 2.x certification option for CNEs because Novell has stopped producing this product.

To become certified as a CNE you must pass a minimum of eight competency exams, to obtain a total of 19 credits, and you must then submit a formal application to Novell. The exams fall into three categories: core, target, and elective. The core exams consist of NetWare Service and Support and Networking Technologies. These will give you a total of eight credits.

The next category is the target exam, which contains four different exams. The actual contents of the exams depends on the certification option that you choose. Figure 1-1 shows the target exam requirements for each option. In all cases, the target exams are worth nine credits. The CNE elective exams are worth two credits. The electives you can choose depend on the certification option that you intend to pursue. Table 1-1 shows the electives available to the NetWare 3.x or NetWare 4.x CNE candidate. Table 1-2 shows the electives available to the GroupWare CNE candidate.

Novell places a time limit on getting all the CNE exam credits required for certification. From the time you take the first exam you have one year to complete all other requirements. If Novell changes the requirements, or adds additional requirements, while you are still in the certification process you must satisfy the new requirements.

Once you become a CNE you must maintain your certification by taking additional courses and/or exams, as required. New requirements are usually imposed if Novell releases a new or updated

Figure 1-1

### NetWare 3.x CNE

| | |
|---|---|
| NetWare 3.x Administration<br>Course 508<br>Test 50–130<br>3 Credits | NetWare 3.x Installation & Configuration<br>Course 802<br>Test 50–132<br>2 Credits |
| NetWare 3.x Advanced Administration<br>Course 518<br>Test 50–131<br>2 Credits | NetWare 3.x to NetWare 4.x Update<br>Course 526<br>Test 50–162<br>2 Credits |

### NetWare 4.x CNE

| | |
|---|---|
| NetWare 4.x Administration<br>Course 520<br>Test 50–152<br>3 Credits | NetWare 4.x Installation & Configuration<br>Course 804<br>Test 50–163<br>2 Credits |
| NetWare 4.x Advanced Administration<br>Course 525<br>Test 50–161<br>2 Credits | NetWare 4.x Design & Implementation<br>Course 532<br>Test 50–601<br>2 Credits |

### UnixWare CNE

| | |
|---|---|
| UnixWare Administration<br>Course 680<br>Test 50–150<br>3 Credits | UnixWare Installation & Configuration<br>Course 678<br>Test 50–149<br>2 Credits |
| UnixWare Advanced Administration<br>Course 685<br>Test 50–151<br>2 Credits | UnixWare OS Fundamentals<br>Course 220<br>Test 50–107<br>2 Credits |

### GroupWare CNE

| | |
|---|---|
| GroupWise 4.x Administration<br>Course 325<br>Test 50–154<br>3 Credits | GroupWise Async. Gateway & Remote Client<br>Course 326<br>Test 50–155<br>1 Credits |
| GroupWise 4.x Advanced Administration<br>Course 328<br>Test 50–604<br>2 Credits | NetWare 4.x Administration<br>Course 520<br>Test 50–152<br>3 Credits |

*CNE target courses for various certifications*

## NetWare Elective Courses Table 1-1

| Course name | Course # | Exam # | Credits |
|---|---|---|---|
| *Network management* | | | |
| Printing with NetWare | 535 | 50-137 | 2 |
| NetWare Navigator | 550 | 50-138 | 2 |
| NetWare Expert for NMS | 730C | 50-205 | 2 |
| LANAlyzer for Windows | 1125 | 50-105 | 1 |
| *Infrastructure and advanced access* | | | |
| LAN WorkPlace for DOS 4.1 | 601 | 50-104 | 2 |
| NetWare TCP/IP Transport | 605 | 50-86 | 2 |
| NetWare NFS | 610 | 50-87 | 2 |
| NetWare NFS Gateway | 625 | 50-119 | 1 |
| NetWare IP | 630 | 50-139 | 1 |
| NetWare NFS Services: Management and Printing and NetWare NFS Services: File Sharing (You must take both of these courses to gain the knowledge required to pass the exam.) | 640 and 645 | 50-160 | 2 |
| NetWare Connect | 718 | 50-114 | 2 |
| NetWare for SAA | 720 | 50-148 | 3 |
| NetWare for LAT | 725 | 50-140 | 2 |
| NetWare Global MHS | 750 | 50-108 | 2 |

## GroupWise Elective Courses Table 1-2

| Course name | Course # | Exam # | Credits |
|---|---|---|---|
| Soft Solutions 4.x Administration | 345 | 50-158 | 3 |
| Soft Solutions 4.x Advanced Administration | 348 | 50-159 | 2 |
| InForms 4.x Administration and Form Design | 335 | 50-156 | 3 |
| InForms 4.x Advanced Administration and Form Design | 338 | 50-157 | 2 |

product, or feels that CNEs should know about significant technology changes concerning networking. If this happens, Novell will notify you by mail. After being notified of the continuing requirements, you have six months to pass the proficiency exams. If you let your CNE certification expire by not following up on the continuing certification requirements, you will have to start the certification process from the beginning to become a CNE again.

# ⇨ What is an MCNE?

This is Novell's new *Master* CNE certification. It replaces the older Enterprise CNE (ECNE) program. The MCNE program is for people who need to specialize in a particular area of network management, besides providing the more general services that a CNE provides. There are three areas of specialization, within which the selections you can then choose from depend on the CNE option you chose initially. For example, a NetWare 3.x or NetWare 4.x CNE might become either a Network Management or Infrastructure and Advanced Access MCNE. A GroupWare CNE may choose only GroupWare Integration as an MCNE certification option. Most of the people who obtain the MCNE certification are consultants or system integrators. Large companies might also require a person with more skill and knowledge than a CNE to help maintain the overall network.

MCNE responsibilities include managing the network in day-to-day activities, repairing and upgrading the hardware at both the workstations and file server, troubleshooting problems on the network, and fine-tuning the network for maximum performance. Also, part of the overall job of the MCNE is to make sure that the network stays up and running. Besides these physical network management responsibilities, an MCNE will usually oversee the work of other network specialists, provide input to management on network-related requirements, and maintain control over his or her specialty area of the network.

To obtain the MCNE certification you must be a CNE in good standing. You should have an advanced knowledge of DOS and computer hardware. Other areas that you should be very familiar with are the NetWare system, network hardware, network cabling, and network diagnostic and troubleshooting tools. Even the GroupWare certification option requires you to know both DOS and NetWare.

To become certified as an MCNE you must pass a minimum of five competency exams, to obtain a total of 10 credits. The exams fall into three categories: core, target, and elective. The core exams consist of NetWare 4.x Design and Implementation, Fundamentals of Network Management, and Fundamentals of Internetworking. These required exams will give you a total of six credits.

The next category is the target exam. The Network Management specialty requires you to take the Network Management Using NetWare Managewise exam. The Infrastructure and Advanced Access specialty requires you to take the Internetworking with NetWare Multi-protocol Route exam. There is no target exam for the GroupWare Integration specialty; you need to take four credits of elective exams instead. The MCNE elective exams are worth two credits (four credits for the GroupWare Integration specialty). The electives you can choose depend on the certification option that you intend to pursue. Table 1-1 shows the electives available to the Network Management and Infrastructure and Advanced Access MCNE candidate. Table 1-2 shows the electives available to the GroupWare Integration MCNE candidate.

Novell places a time limit on getting all the MCNE exam credits required for certification. From the time you take the first exam you have one year to complete all other requirements. If Novell changes or adds to the requirements while you are in the process of certifying, you must comply with the new certification requirements.

Once you become an MCNE, you are required to maintain your certification by taking additional courses and/or exams. Continuing certification requirements are usually imposed when Novell releases a new or updated product, or feels that MCNEs should know about significant technology changes involving networking. If this happens,

Novell will notify you by mail. After being notified of the continuing requirements, you have six months to pass the proficiency exams. If you let your MCNE certification expire by not following up you will have to start the certification process from the beginning to become an MCNE again.

# ⇨ What is an ECNE?

This certification is a continuation of the old CNE program. If you earn the new CNE designation and then want to go beyond it, you will have to pursue the MCNE certification instead of this program. Because Novell will phase this program out by June, 1996, you should pursue the MCNE option unless you have already started the ECNE certification. Anyone who still desires to become an ECNE probably has some special requirements, or a particular interest, in certain advanced or specialized areas of networking. An example would be a consultant or a network administrator who needs to connect NetWare and UNIX using TCP/IP and NFS, or to create a wide area network using Novell's Dial-in/Dial-out products. Other examples include NetWare SAA or NetWare for Macintosh.

ECNE responsibilities include managing the network in day-to-day activities, repairing and upgrading the hardware at both the workstations and file server, troubleshooting problems on the network, and fine-tuning the network for maximum performance. Along with these responsibilities, the ECNE must also install, maintain and support the products and services that correspond to his or her ECNE specialty.

To become an ECNE you must first become certified as a CNE. You must also pass the 3.11 system manager and 3.11 advanced system manager exams. If you passed these exams en route to becoming a CNE, you will not have to retake the exams. After completing the CNE and the 3.11 operating system requirements, you are then required to obtain an additional 14 credits. These 14 credits can include the 2.2 system management and 2.2 advanced system management, the 4.0 system management and 4.0 advanced system management, or any of the other elective credits. There is no time limit imposed on getting the 14 credits. Every additional exam you take counts toward your ECNE certification.

Once you become an ECNE, Novell requires you to remain abreast of changes and enhancements with networking technology. All ECNEs are required to fulfill any continuing certification requirements offered by Novell. If Novell introduces any new or updated product, Novell might require you to demonstrate your proficiency with the product or technology, by passing the related exam. Novell notifies you by mail of any new exams you must take to maintain your certification. As with the CNE certification, you have six months to complete the requirements.

# What is a CNI?

CNI certification is for the individual who wants to teach certified NetWare courses. These courses are taught at Novell Authorized Education Centers (NAEC), or by a Novell Education Academic Partner (NEAP). The classes must use the Novell courseware. There are two basic types of CNIs: NAEC/NEAP-employed CNIs, and contract CNIs. The NAEC/NEAP-employed CNIs are employed full- or part-time by the NAEC/NEAP and teach exclusively for one education center. Often these CNIs are required to perform other tasks besides teaching. Such duties include installing systems, acting as technical support for other employees or customers, maintaining the computer network at the NAEC/NEAP, repairing and maintaining the equipment in the classroom, and teaching other non-Novell courses, such as applications.

Contract CNIs are normally not employed by any particular NAEC/NEAP. They are usually self-employed or work for consulting firms that broker their services. Contract CNIs can then be brought in by NAECs and NEAPs on a class-by-class basis. For example, while many NAECs/NEAPs employ full- or part-time CNIs to teach their scheduled classes, when extra classes need to be added the NAEC/NEAP might not have enough of its own CNIs available. NAECs/NEAPs also hire contract CNIs to cover classes when regular instructors become ill or go on vacation. Other NAECs/NEAPs do not employ any CNIs of their own; they use only contract CNIs. This eliminates the overhead cost of an employee and allows the NAEC/NEAP much more flexibility in scheduling.

The responsibilities of the CNI vary greatly. The basic responsibility is to present the Novell courseware in a professional and understandable format. The CNI must make sure that the classroom is properly set up, and that all necessary hardware and software are functioning properly. The CNI must also maintain current certifications and keep up with changing technologies that might affect the courses he or she teaches. Other responsibilities might include any other tasks that the company feels the CNI should perform.

# ⇨ CNI options

Before starting your CNI certification you should decide which area you want to specialize in. You have four main options: applications, networking, interoperability, and development. The applications area includes courses on products such WordPerfect and GroupWise. The networking area is most familiar to people who qualified under the older certification program. It includes all of Novell's network operating system products, such as NetWare. It also concentrates on connections to other types of machines, such as mainframes and the Macintosh. The development area is mainly for programmers. It concentrates on NetWare and AppWare programming issues.

Once you choose a specialty you must find an NAEC/NEAP to sponsor you. Then you must submit the following paperwork to your regional CNI program contact:

> ➢ A completed and signed CNI application form

> ➢ A signed CNI agreement

> ➢ A resume

> ➢ Three references, including one from an NAEC/NEAP manager

> ➢ Target course selection, indicating the first (and perhaps only) course you want to teach

The first two items on your paperwork list come directly from Novell. Call Novell Education at one of the numbers provided in Appendix A and they'll mail them out to you.

Next, make sure your resume reflects the experience required to teach the course you want to start with. Novell wants people who already have real-world experience, so if your resume doesn't show this they will probably turn you down. The three references must include either an NAEC or an NEAP manager. Make sure that the other two references come from professionals you have worked with. It also helps if these references are directly related to the courses you want to teach.

Finally, deciding which course you want to teach means deciding on a general area (applications, networking, interoperability, and development), plus a specific course within that area, *before* you start the paperwork process. You must choose an Instructor Performance Evaluation (IPE)-eligible course when you select the interoperability and networking areas, to become certified as a CNI. The four specialty areas for the CNI certification program allow a lot of flexibility as far as course choices go. These courses include:

➤ Applications
- WordPerfect 6.x for Windows
- WordPerfect 6.x for DOS
- InForms 1.x for Windows
- Networking (IPE-eligible):
- GroupWise 4.x Administration
- NetWare 3.x Administration
- NetWare 3.x Advanced Administration
- NetWare 4.x Administration
- NetWare 4.x Advanced Administration
- Printing with NetWare
- NetWare Service and Support
- Networking (additional courses)
  ~Introduction to Networking
  ~NetWare 3.11 to 3.12 Update Seminar
  ~NetWare 3.11 to 4.x Update
  ~NetWare 4.x Directory Services Design
  ~NetWare Navigator

~NetWare 3.x Installation and Configuration Workshop
~NetWare 4.x Installation and Configuration Workshop

➤ Interoperability (IPE-eligible):
- NetWare TCP/IP Transport
- NetWare NFS
- NetWare Connect
- NetWare for SAA: Installation and Troubleshooting
- NetWare Internetworking Products
- Interoperability (additional courses):
  ~Networking Technologies
  ~Fundamentals of Internetwork and Management Design
  ~LAN WorkPlace for DOS Administration
  ~NetWare FLeX/IP
  ~NetWare NFS Gateway
  ~NetWare/IP
  ~NetWare for LAT
  ~NetWare for Global MHS
  ~Administering NetWare for Macintosh 3.x
  ~Administering NetWare for Macintosh 4.x

➤ Development
- NetWare Programming: NLM Development
- NetWare Programming: Basic Services
- NetWare Programming: Directory Services
- NetWare Programming: Protocol Support
- AppWare Programming: Visual AppBuilder
- AppWare Programming: ALM Development

A CNI candidate can begin the certification process as soon as Novell accepts their application. The best way to start the process is to fulfill any prerequisite courses. The following lists provide you with the prerequisites for each general area.

➤ Applications
- DOS/Microcomputer Concepts for NetWare Users

➤ Networking
- DOS/Microcomputer Concepts for NetWare Users
- NetWare 3.x Administration or NetWare 4.x Administration

- NetWare 3.x, 4.x, or UnixWare Installation and Configuration

➤ Interoperability
  - DOS/Microcomputer Concepts for NetWare Users
  - NetWare Service and Support
  - NetWare 3.x Administration or NetWare 4.x Administration

➤ Development
  - No prerequisites

The CNI candidate must also attend a certified class for his target course, plus any prerequisites for that course. This course must be led by a CNI and the courses must be conducted at an NAEC/NEAP. The candidate must then mail or fax a copy of each course-completion certificate to Novell CNI administration. Also, the CNI candidate must pass the test for each course. (The only exception to this rule, obviously, occurs when there is no test for your target course.)

One of the more difficult parts of the CNI certification process is the IPE. Most candidates will want to gain some experience in teaching, or will at least want to attend a teaching course before they attempt the IPE. You must pass the IPE before you can become certified. Some cases involve special IPEs for developmental courses; specific requirements will be discussed later in this chapter.

Following this process helps you become qualified to teach one course in a particular area. You need to follow the same procedure for each additional course that you want to teach. Of course, Novell doesn't expect you to re-take the prerequisites each time. If you have already fulfilled those requirements all you need to do is concentrate on the new course, the corresponding exam, and the required IPE.

CNI certification is an ongoing process, so the CNI must continue to stay current with all new courses added to the category they are certified for. The CNI must also pay a yearly registration fee that covers, among other things, updates on courseware.

# Creating a certification checklist

Now that you have a basic idea of what each certification entails, you can create a checklist. This checklist will help you organize yourself to make sure you don't overlook any of the requirements. And, combined with understanding why you want or need the certification (to be discussed in greater depth in Chapter 2), it will help you maintain the proper focus to succeed.

Your checklist should include information about the certification that you will pursue; specifically, all courses and related exams. You should include dates of training courses, course numbers, dates of the exams, and exam numbers. You might also include the telephone numbers (and possibly the addresses) of your contacts at Novell, the NAEC/NEAP facility where you attend classes, the Drake or Sylvan registration office, and the Drake or Sylvan testing office. You might also want to include an area for reference material and another for notes.

Two very important contacts are mentioned in the previous paragraph. First, an NAEC is a training center that provides Novell-certified training, while an NEAP is an educational center, such as a college or university, that includes Novell-developed courses as part of its curriculum. The difference between someone who teaches Novell and an NAEC/NEAP is much like the difference between a non-accredited and an accredited college or university. You might learn something from either source of information, but people tend to view your credentials with less enthusiasm if you don't use an NAEC/NEAP. In fact, some people will disregard your Novell training altogether if you don't receive your training from an NAEC/NEAP. The level of training is often perceived as dubious (at best) from any other source.

The second contacts are the Drake or Sylvan Testing Centers. These companies provide testing for a wide range of certifications—everything from CPA to registered nurse. And candidates come from all over—the person sitting next to you during an exam might not even know very much about computers and might even fly planes for a living. Drake and Sylvan Testing Centers also appear in a wide variety of locations. You can find them in dedicated testing centers or borrowing space at a training facility, such as a college or university. In fact, you might even find one at your local NAEC/NEAP.

Drake or Sylvan Testing Centers always use people who are certified by them to administer the examinations you take. These people make certain that you do not have an opportunity to cheat on the examination. They also make sure that you have any required testing materials, and that your test environment is as quiet and comfortable as possible. You are required to follow any instructions they might provide, and they are the only ones you can talk to during the examination.

However, one thing these testing center administrators do not do is handle your examination. Drake downloads the examinations from the testing center on a daily basis and sends them to the appropriate places. Computers automatically grade the examinations after you take them, so your examination is untouched by any human hands but your own. If you fail, there is little chance that you will convince anyone that there was any problem except a lack of study on your part. On the other hand, if you do notice a flaw in an examination, make sure you point it out to the testing center administrator immediately. He or she can provide feedback to Novell, which might help you if you narrowly missed passing your examination. Reporting the problem will also reduce the risk that someone else will stumble over the same thing. You might also want to report the problem to your contact at Novell.

The following sample checklists will give you an idea of what you might want to include in your own. If you decide to use the checklists in this book, use a highlighter to mark the courses and exams you plan to use to obtain your required credits. Be sure to add any additional information that will help you reach your goals.

The checklist for the CNA certification is usually not as detailed as the ones for the CNE, ECNE, and MCNE certifications. The example in Fig. 1-2 lists the basic information.

Figure 1-2

## CNA Certification Checklist (Modified)

| Item description | | Date |
|---|---|---|
| Understand the responsibility of a CNA | | _____ |
| Complete goals worksheet | | _____ |

| Exam description | Exam number | Exam pass date |
|---|---|---|
| Certified NetWare 2.2 Administrator | 50-115 | _____ |
| Certified NetWare 3.x Administrator | 50-390 | _____ |
| Certified NetWare 4.x Administrator | 50-391 | _____ |
| GroupWise 4.x Administration | 50-395 | _____ |
| UnixWare System Administration | 50-392 | _____ |

*Other information:*

Phone number: _____

Date of exams: _____

_____

Location of test center: _____

Date paperwork sent to Novell: _____

Reference materials (books, software, etc.): _____

_____

Misc.: _____

_____

_____

*Sample CNA certification checklist*

Fill in the dates in the first two items when you are sure you
understand the responsibilities of a CNA and have completed the goals
worksheet. This is the preplanning section, which helps you focus on
what you are doing, and why.

The second area includes the exam description, exam date, and exam-pass dates. In the last section we provide a space for additional information, such as the phone numbers of the testing center and Novell. The form includes other areas for dates of exams and the location of the testing center. Make sure you include street address, cross streets, and any special directions about how to get to the testing center. The next line documents when you sent your paperwork to Novell. Also provided is space for any references that might help you prepare for the exams, and a space for any other comments or ideas that you might find important. Filling out each area of the checklist ensures that you complete each step necessary to become certified.

The CNE, ECNE, and MCNE checklists are a little more involved than the one for the CNA. All three certifications have a list of required and elective credits that you must keep track of. Notice that this form contains additional information designed to keep you on the right path. For example, in addition to the preplanning section, we include all of the required and elective requirements. This allows you to see all of the possible selections in one place. The sample checklist in Fig. 1-3 shows the requirements for the CNE certification.

**CNE Certification Checklist (Completely New)**                    Figure 1-3

| Item description | | | | | Date |
|---|---|---|---|---|---|
| Understand the responsibility of a CNE | | | | | _____ |
| Complete goals worksheet | | | | | _____ |

| Core requirements | Course number | Course date | Exam number | Exam pass date | Credits |
|---|---|---|---|---|---|
| NetWare Service & Support | 701 | _____ | 50-46 | _____ | 5 |
| Networking Technologies | 200 | _____ | 50-80 | _____ | 3 |

*Sample CNE certification checklist*

Figure 1-3

| Target requirements | Course number | Course date | Exam number | Exam pass date | Credits |
|---|---|---|---|---|---|
| *NetWare 3.x Track* | | | | | |
| System Administration | 508 | _____ | 50-130 | _____ | 3 |
| Advanced System Administration | 518 | _____ | 50-131 | _____ | 2 |
| Installation and Configuration | 802 | _____ | 50-132 | _____ | 2 |
| NetWare 3.x to NetWare 4.x Update | 526 | _____ | 50-162 | _____ | 2 |
| *NetWare 4.x Track* | | | | | |
| System Administration | 520 | _____ | 50-152 | _____ | 3 |
| Advanced System Administration | 525 | _____ | 50-161 | _____ | 2 |
| Installation and Configuration | 804 | _____ | 50-163 | _____ | 2 |
| Design and Implementation | 532 | _____ | 50-601 | _____ | 2 |
| *UnixWare Track* | | | | | |
| System Administration | 680 | _____ | 50-150 | _____ | 3 |
| Advanced System Administration | 685 | _____ | 50-151 | _____ | 2 |
| Installation and Configuration | 678 | _____ | 50-149 | _____ | 2 |
| UNIX OS Fundamentals | 220 | _____ | 50-107 | _____ | 2 |
| *GroupWare Track* | | | | | |
| NetWare 4.x System Administration | 520 | _____ | 50-152 | _____ | 3 |

*continued*

| Target requirements | Course number | Course date | Exam number | Exam pass date | Credits |
|---|---|---|---|---|---|
| *GroupWare Track* | | | | | |
| GroupWise 4.x Administration | 325 | _____ | 50-154 | _____ | 3 |
| GroupWise 4.x Asynchronous Gateway and Remote Client Support | 326 | _____ | 50-155 | _____ | 1 |
| GroupWise 4.x Advanced Administration | 328 | _____ | 50-604 | _____ | 2 |

| Elective requirements | Course number | Course date | Exam number | Exam pass date | Credits |
|---|---|---|---|---|---|
| *NetWare and UnixWare Tracks* | | | | | |
| Printing with NetWare | 535 | _____ | 50-137 | _____ | 2 |
| NetWare Navigator | 550 | _____ | 50-138 | _____ | 2 |
| NetWare Expert for NMS | 730C | _____ | 50-205 | _____ | 2 |
| LANAlyzer for Windows | 1125 | _____ | 50-105 | _____ | 1 |
| LAN WorkPlace for DOS 4.1 | 601 | _____ | 50-104 | _____ | 2 |
| NetWare TCP/IP Transport | 605 | _____ | 50-86 | _____ | 2 |
| NetWare NFS | 610 | _____ | 50-87 | _____ | 2 |
| NetWare NFS Gateway | 625 | _____ | 50-119 | _____ | 1 |
| NetWare IP | 630 | _____ | 50-139 | _____ | 1 |
| NetWare NFS Services: Management and | 640 and 645 | _____ | 50-160 | _____ | 2 |

*continued*

Figure 1-3

| Elective requirements | Course number | Course date | Exam number | Exam pass date | Credits |
|---|---|---|---|---|---|
| Printing and NetWare NFS Services: File Sharing (You must take both of these courses to gain the knowledge required to pass the exam.) | | | | | |
| NetWare Connect | 718 | _____ | 50-114 | _____ | 2 |
| NetWare for SAA | 720 | _____ | 50-148 | _____ | 3 |
| NetWare for LAT | 725 | _____ | 50-140 | _____ | 2 |
| NetWare Global MHS | 750 | _____ | 50-108 | _____ | 2 |
| *GroupWare Track* | | | | | |
| Soft Solutions 4.x Administration | 345 | _____ | 50-158 | _____ | 3 |
| Soft Solutions 4.x Advanced Administration | 348 | _____ | 50-159 | _____ | 2 |
| InForms 4.x Administration and Form Design | 335 | _____ | 50-156 | _____ | 3 |
| InForms 4.x Advanced Administration and Form Design | 338 | _____ | 50-157 | _____ | 2 |

*NAEC/Course information:*

NAEC name: _____

Phone number: _____

Contact name: _____

Location: _____

Course start times: _____

*continued*

Comments: _____

_____

*Testing information:*

Phone number: _____

Date of exams: _____

_____

Location of test center: _____

*Novell information:*

Date called Novell to order CNE application: _____

Date paperwork and picture sent to Novell: _____

Reference materials (books, software, etc.): _____

_____

Other: _____

_____

*continued*

The information contained in this checklist documents the preplanning responsibilities and goals as well as the certification courses and exams. The checklist is divided into sections to help you know which areas are required and which are electives. We also added space for the course/exam names along with the corresponding numbers, for easy reference. A note area allows you to keep track of any notes or comments about the subject. At the end of the checklist is a section for the phone numbers, addresses, contact names, and reference material. We even supplied space for any additional information that might assist you in your quest.

The ECNE checklist in Fig. 1-4, and the MCNE checklist in Fig. 1-5, basically follow the CNE checklist with just a few changes at their beginnings. Make certain you use the MCNE checklist if you haven't already started the ECNE program. Included in the change is an area to be filled out after completing the CNE certification. All the other modifications deal with differences between the various programs, as discussed at the beginning of this chapter.

Figure 1-4

### ECNE Certification Checklist

| Item description | Date |
|---|---|
| Understand the responsibility of an ECNE | _____ |
| Complete goals worksheet | _____ |
| CNE certification completion | _____ |

| Operating system 3.x & 4.x credits required | Course number | Course date | Exam number | Exam pass date | Credits |
|---|---|---|---|---|---|
| *NetWare 3.x Track* | | | | | |
| 3.x System Manager | 508 | _____ | 50-130 | _____ | 3 |
| 3.x Advanced System Manager | 518 | _____ | 50-131 | _____ | 2 |
| *NetWare 4.x Track* | | | | | |
| 4.x System Administration | 520 | _____ | 50-152 | _____ | 3 |
| 4.x Advanced System Administration | 525 | _____ | 50-161 | _____ | 2 |

Note

NetWare 3.11 and 4.0 are required for ECNE certification. If you select the 3.11 track, you can elect to take the NetWare 3.11 to 4.0 Update or the 4.0 Administration and 4.0 Advanced Administration. If you elect to take the 4.0 track, you can take the 3.11 OS Features Review or the 3.11 System Manager and 3.11 Advanced System Manager.

Note

Operating System and Electives must total 19 credits.

*Sample ECNE certification checklist*

| Elective credits | Course number | Course date | Exam number | Exam pass date | Credits |
|---|---|---|---|---|---|
| 3.x System Manager | 508 | _____ | 50-130 | _____ | 3 |
| 3.x Advanced System Manager | 518 | _____ | 50-131 | _____ | 2 |
| NetWare 3.x OS Features Review | 506 | _____ | 50-42 | _____ | 2 |
| NetWare 4.x System Administration | 520 | _____ | 50-152 | _____ | 3 |
| 4.x Advanced System Administration | 525 | _____ | 50-161 | _____ | 2 |
| NetWare 3.x to 4.x Update | 526 | _____ | 50-124 | _____ | 2 |

Note

The 3.x elective credits and the 3.x OS Features Review credits will not count as elective credits if the 3.x track was selected as the operating system credits.

| | | | | | |
|---|---|---|---|---|---|
| Product Info. for Auth. Resellers | 304 | _____ | 50-18 | _____ | 2 |
| Product Info. for Gold Auth. Resellers | 305 | _____ | 50-19 | _____ | 2 |
| NetWare 4.x Design and Implementation | 530 | _____ | 50-125 | _____ | 3 |
| LAN WorkPlace for DOS Administration | 601 | _____ | 50-95 | _____ | 2 |
| NetWare TCP/IP Transport | 605 | _____ | 50-86 | _____ | 2 |
| NetWare NFS | 610 | _____ | 50-87 | _____ | 2 |
| NetWare for Macintosh Connectivity | 615 | _____ | 50-93 | _____ | 2 |

*continued*

Figure 1-4

| Elective credits | Course number | Course date | Exam number | Exam pass date | Credits |
|---|---|---|---|---|---|
| LANtern Services Manager | 708 | _____ | 50-89 | _____ | 3 |
| NetWare Dial-In/ Dial-Out Connectivity | 715 | _____ | 50-112 | _____ | 2 |
| NetWare for SAA | 720 | _____ | 50-85 | _____ | 3 |
| NetWare Management System for Windows | 730 | _____ | 50-128 | _____ | 2 |
| NetWare 4.x Installation Workshop | 804 | _____ | 50-601 | _____ | |
| Btrieve: An Overview | 904 | _____ | 50-127 | _____ | 1 |

*NAEC/Course information:*

NAEC name: _____

Phone number: _____

Contact name: _____

Location: _____

Course start times: _____

Comments: _____

_____

*Testing information:*

Phone number: _____

Date of exams: _____

_____

Location of test center: _____

*Novell information:*

Date paperwork and picture sent to Novell: _____

*continued*

Reference materials (books, software, etc.): _____

_____

Other: _____

_____

*continued*

## MCNE Certification Checklist

Figure 1-5

| Item description | Date |
|---|---|
| Understand the responsibility of an MCNE | _____ |
| Complete goals worksheet | _____ |
| Complete required CNE certification (NetWare 3.x, NetWare 4.x, or UnixWare for the Network Management or Infrastructure and Advanced Access routes. GroupWare for the GroupWare Integration route.) | _____ |

| Core requirements | Course number | Course date | Exam number | Exam pass date | Credits |
|---|---|---|---|---|---|
| NetWare 4.x Design and Implementation | 532 | _____ | 50-601 | _____ | 2 |
| Fundamentals of Network Management | TBD | _____ | 50-xxx | _____ | 2 |
| Fundamentals of Internetworking | TBD | _____ | 50-xxx | _____ | 2 |

| Target requirements | Course number | Course date | Exam number | Exam pass date | Credits |
|---|---|---|---|---|---|
| *Network Management Track* | | | | | |
| Network Management Using NetWare ManageWise | TBD | _____ | 50-xxx | _____ | 2 |

*Sample MCNE certification checklist*

Figure 1-5

| Target requirements | Course number | Course date | Exam number | Exam pass date | Credits |
|---|---|---|---|---|---|
| *Infrastructure and Advanced Access Track* | | | | | |
| Internetworking with NetWare Multi-Protocol Router | 740 | _____ | 50-142 | _____ | 2 |

*GroupWare Integration Track*

There are no target requirements for this track. Select 4 elective credits worth of courses instead.

| Elective requirements | Course number | Course date | Exam number | Exam pass date | Credits |
|---|---|---|---|---|---|
| *Network Management Track* | | | | | |
| Printing with NetWare | 535 | _____ | 50-137 | _____ | 2 |
| NetWare Navigator | 550 | _____ | 50-138 | _____ | 2 |
| NetWare Expert for NMS | 730C | _____ | 50-205 | _____ | 2 |
| LANAlyzer for Windows | 1125 | _____ | 50-105 | _____ | 1 |
| *Infrastructure and Advanced Access Track* | | | | | |
| LAN WorkPlace for DOS 4.1 | 601 | _____ | 50-104 | _____ | 2 |
| NetWare TCP/IP Transport | 605 | _____ | 50-86 | _____ | 2 |
| NetWare NFS | 610 | _____ | 50-87 | _____ | 2 |
| NetWare NFS Gateway | 625 | _____ | 50-119 | _____ | 1 |
| NetWare IP | 630 | _____ | 50-139 | _____ | 1 |
| NetWare NFS Services: Management and | 640 and 645 | _____ | 50-160 | _____ | 2 |

*continued*

| Elective requirements | Course number | Course date | Exam number | Exam pass date | Credits |
|---|---|---|---|---|---|
| Printing and NetWare NFS Services: File Sharing (You must take both of these courses to gain the knowledge required to pass the exam.) | | | | | |
| NetWare Connect | 718 | _____ | 50-114 | _____ | 2 |
| NetWare for SAA | 720 | _____ | 50-148 | _____ | 3 |
| NetWare for LAT | 725 | _____ | 50-140 | _____ | 2 |
| NetWare Global MHS | 750 | _____ | 50-108 | _____ | 2 |
| *GroupWare Integration Track* | | | | | |
| Soft Solutions 4.x Administration | 345 | _____ | 50-158 | _____ | 3 |
| Soft Solutions 4.x Advanced Administration | 348 | _____ | 50-159 | _____ | 2 |
| InForms 4.x Administration and Form Design | 335 | _____ | 50-156 | _____ | 3 |
| InForms 4.x Advanced Administration and Form Design | 338 | _____ | 50-157 | _____ | 2 |

*NAEC/Course information:*

NAEC name: _____

Phone number: _____

Contact name: _____

Location: _____

*continued*

29

Figure 1-5

Course start times: _____

Comments: _____

_____

*Testing information:*

Phone number: _____

Date of exams: _____

_____

Location of test center: _____

*Novell information:*

Date paperwork and picture sent to Novell: _____

Reference materials (books, software, etc.): _____

_____

Other: _____

_____

*continued*

The CNI checklist, shown in Fig. 1-6, is modeled after the CNE checklist. However, it contains blanks that help you plan for many of the prerequisites that this program requires. The checklist also includes extra blanks for the other requirements of this certification program, such as the IPE. A CNI candidate will have to devote a lot more time than any of the other certification program candidates to planning for the certification process. As a result, the certification checklist provided here is a lot more complex than those provided for the other programs. The important thing for a CNI to remember is that, eventually, all the candidates for other programs will rely on you to provide them with the best possible level of training.

We have also provided you some ideas for creating your own checklist. Table 1-3 provides you with the reference list of all the courses and exams that Novell offers. The list includes course name and number, exam number, and credit value. We provided space at the end of the list to allow you room for course and exam additions.

**CNI Certification Checklist**

Figure 1-6

| Item description | Date |
|---|---|
| Understand the responsibility of a CNI | _____ |
| Complete goals worksheet | _____ |
| Complete CNI application form | _____ |
| Complete CNI agreement | _____ |
| Complete resume | _____ |
| Get three references | _____ |
| | _____ |
| | _____ |

| Prerequisite requirements | Course number | Course date | Exam number | Exam pass date |
|---|---|---|---|---|
| *Application speciality* | | | | |
| DOS/Microcomputer Concepts for NetWare Users | 1100 | _____ | 50-15 | _____ |
| *Networking specialty* | | | | |
| DOS/microcomputer Concepts for NetWare Users | 1100 | _____ | 50-15 | _____ |
| NetWare 3.x Administration or NetWare 4.x Administration | 508 or 520 | _____ | 50-230 or 50-222 | _____ |
| NetWare 3.x Installation and Configuration or NetWare 4.x | 802 or 804 or 678 | _____ | 50-232 or 50-226 or 50-149 | _____ |

*Sample CNI certification checklist*

31

Figure 1-6

| Prerequisite requirements | Course number | Course date | Exam number | Exam pass date |
|---|---|---|---|---|
| *Application speciality* | | | | |
| DOS/Microcomputer Concepts for NetWare Users | 1100 | _____ | 50-15 | _____ |
| *Networking specialty* | | | | |
| DOS/microcomputer Concepts for NetWare Users | 1100 | _____ | 50-15 | _____ |
| NetWare 3.x Administration or NetWare 4.x Administration | 508 or 520 | _____ | 50-230 or 50-222 | _____ |
| NetWare 3.x Installation and Configuration or NetWare 4.x Installation and Configuration or UnixWare Installation and Configuration | 802 or 804 or 678 | _____ | 50-232 or 50-226 or 50-149 | _____ |
| *Interoperability specialty* | | | | |
| DOS/Microcomputer Concepts for NetWare Users | 1100 | _____ | 50-15 | _____ |
| NetWare Service & Support | 801 | _____ | 50-218 or 50-253 | _____ |
| NetWare 3.x Administration or NetWare 4.x Administration | 508 or 520 | _____ | 50-230 or 50-222 | _____ |

*continued*

32

| Prerequisite requirements | Course number | Course date | Exam number | Exam pass date |
|---|---|---|---|---|
| UNIX OS Fundamentals (required for UNIX courses only) | 220 | _____ | 50-207 | _____ |

*Development specialty*

There are no prerequisite requirements for this specialty.

| Target course req. (select 1) | Course number | Course date | Exam number | Exam pass date | IPE date |
|---|---|---|---|---|---|
| *Application specialty* | | | | | |
| WordPerfect 6.x for Windows | No course required | | 50-xxx | _____ | _____ |
| WordPerfect 6.x for DOS | No course required | | 50-xxx | _____ | _____ |
| InForms 1.x for Windows | No course required | | 50-xxx | _____ | _____ |
| *Networking specialty (IPE-eligible course only)* | | | | | |
| GroupWise 4.x Administration | 325 | _____ | 50-254 | _____ | _____ |
| NetWare 3.x Administration | 508 | _____ | 50-230 | _____ | _____ |
| NetWare 3.x Advanced Administration | 518 | _____ | 50-231 | _____ | _____ |
| NetWare 4.x Administration | 520 | _____ | 50-222 | _____ | _____ |
| NetWare 4.x Advanced Administration | 525 | _____ | 50-223 | _____ | _____ |

*continued*

Figure 1-6

| Target course req. (select 1) | Course number | Course date | Exam number | Exam pass date | IPE date |
|---|---|---|---|---|---|
| Printing with NetWare | 535 | _____ | 50-237 | _____ | _____ |
| NetWare Service and Support | 801 | _____ | 50-218 or 50-253 | _____ | _____ |
| *Networking specialty (IPE-eligible course only)* | | | | | |
| NetWare TCP/IP Transport | 605 | _____ | 50-32 | _____ | _____ |
| NetWare NFS | 610 | _____ | 50-33 | _____ | _____ |
| UnixWare System Administration | 680 | _____ | 50-234 | _____ | _____ |
| UnixWare Advanced System Administration | 685 | _____ | 50-50 | _____ | _____ |
| NetWare Connect | 718 | _____ | 50-224 | _____ | _____ |
| NetWare for SAA: Installation and Troubleshooting | 720 | _____ | 50-241 | _____ | _____ |
| NetWare for Internetworking Products | 740 | _____ | 50-217 | _____ | _____ |
| *Development specialty* | | | | | |
| NetWare Programming: NLM Development | 930 | _____ | No test required (requires 930 IPE) | | _____ |

*continued*

| Target course req. (select 1) | Course number | Course date | Exam number | Exam pass date | IPE date |
|---|---|---|---|---|---|
| *Development specialty* | | | | | |
| NetWare Programming: Basic Services | 940 | _____ | No test required (requires 930, 940, 941, or 945 IPE) | | _____ |
| NetWare Programming: Directory Services | 941 | _____ | No test required (requires 930, 940, 941, or 945 IPE) | | _____ |
| NetWare Programming: Protocol Support | 945 | _____ | No test required (requires 930, 940, 941, or 945 IPE) | | _____ |
| AppWare Programming: Visual AppBuilder | 950 | _____ | No test required (requires 950 or 954 IPE) | | _____ |
| AppWare Programming: ALM Development | 954 | _____ | No test required (requires 950 and 954 IPE) | | _____ |

*NAEC/Course information:*

NAEC name: _____

*continued*

35

Figure 1-6

Phone number: _____

Contact name: _____

Location: _____

Course start times: _____

Comments: _____

_____

*Regional CNI Program Contact Information:*

Contact name: _____

Phone number: _____

Location: _____

Comments: _____

_____

*Testing information:*

Phone number: _____

Date of exams: _____

_____

Location of test center: _____

*Novell information:*

Date called Novell to order MCNE application: _____

Date paperwork and picture sent to Novell: _____

Reference materials (books, software, etc.): _____

_____

Other: _____

*continued*

**Course and Exam List** Table 1-3

| Course title | Course # | Course length | CNE/ECNE exam # | CNI exam # | Credits |
|---|---|---|---|---|---|
| Networking Technologies | 200 | 3 days | 50-80 or 50-147 | 50-81 or 50-247 | 3 |
| Fundamentals of Internetwork and Management Design | 205 | 2 days | 50-106 | 50-206 | 2 |
| Product Information | None | | 50-100 | | 1 |
| GroupWise 4.x Administration (CNA exam number is 50-395) | 325 | 3 days | 50-154 | 50-254 | 3 |
| GroupWise 4.x Asynchronous Gateway and Remote Client Support | 326 | 2 days | 50-155 | 50-255 | 1 |
| GroupWise 4.x Advanced Administration | 328 | 2 days | 50-604 | 50-604 | 2 |
| NetWare 2.2 System Manager (CNA exam number is 50-115)[1] | 501 | 3 days | N/A | N/A | 3 |
| NetWare 2.2 Advanced System Manager[1] | 502 | 2 days | N/A | N/A | 2 |
| NetWare 3.x Administration (CNA and CNE exams are the same number) | 508 | 4 days | 50-390 | 50-230 | 3 |
| NetWare 3.x Advanced Administration | 518 | 2 days | 50-131 | 50-231 | 2 |
| NetWare 4.x Administration (CNA and CNE exams are the same number) | 520 | 4 days | 50-391 | 50-222 | 3 |
| NetWare 4.x Advanced Administration | 525 | 3 days | 50-123 | 50-223 | 2 |
| NetWare 3.x to 4.x Update | 526 | 3 days | 50-124 | 50-224 | 2 |
| NetWare 4 Directory Services Design | 530 | 2 days | 50-125 | 50-225 | 2 |
| Printing with NetWare | 535 | 3 days | 50-137 | 50-237 | 2 |
| NetWare Navigator | 550 | 2 days | 50-138 | 50-238 | 2 |

Table 1-3                                    **Continued**

| Course title | Course # | Course length | CNE/ECNE exam # | CNI exam # | Credits |
|---|---|---|---|---|---|
| LAN WorkPlace for DOS 4.x Administration | 601 | 2 days | 50-104 | 50-204 | 2 |
| NetWare TCP/IP Transport | 605 | 2 days | 50-86 | 50-32 | 2 |
| NetWare NFS | 610 | 2 days | 50-87 | 50-33 | 2 |
| NetWare NFS Gateway | 625 | 1 day | 50-119 | 50-219 | 1 |
| NetWare IP | 630 | 1 day | 50-139 | 50-239 | 1 |
| NetWare Connect | 718 | 2 days | 50-114 | 50-224 | 2 |
| NetWare for SAA Installation & Troubleshooting | 720 | 3 days | 50-141 | 50-241 | 3 |
| NetWare for LAT | 725 | 2 days | 50-140 | 50-240 | 2 |
| NetWare Management System for Windows | 730C | 2 days | 50-205 | 50-205 | 2 |
| NetWare Internetworking Products | 740 | 3 days | 50-117 | 50-217 | 2 |
| NetWare Global MHS | 750 | 2 days | 50-108 | 50-208 | 2 |
| NetWare Service and Support | 801 | 5 days | 50-118 or 50-153 | 50-218 or 50-253 | 5 |
| NetWare 2.2/3.x Installation and Configuration Workshop | 802 | 2 days | 50-132 | 50-232 | 2 |
| NetWare 4.x Installation and Configuration Workshop | 804 | 2 days | 50-126 | 50-226 | 2 |

1 This course is no longer accepted for CNE, ECNE, Master CNE, or CNI certifications. You may still use it for the CNA certification, but the time to do so is limited.

# ⇨ Conclusion

As we have seen in this chapter, the CNA, CNE, ECNE, MCNE, and CNI certification processes take some planning. They involve much more than just calling Novell and asking for an application. You must know what the responsibilities and requirements of each one includes before you can choose the certification that best utilizes your knowledge and expertise.

The procedure for becoming certified might seem difficult if you do not preplan adequately. The list of exams is quite long, and there are many different ways to put together a certification program. By first deciding which certification you will seek and using the corresponding checklist, you can then decide which specific areas you want to pursue within that certification. Then you can highlight the appropriate exams and start filling in the missing data.

However, be aware that courses and exams are being added and removed as technology and products evolve. To get listings for the latest course and exam offerings, use the FAX-back number or the education number found in Appendix A.

# 2

# Understanding the certification process

T HE first chapter provided you with a better understanding of what each certification will help you accomplish. However, it answered only part of the question, "What can the certification do for my current company?" Everyone wants more from an educational experience than to simply fulfill a company requirement. Fortunately, a Novell certification can help you in a more personal way.

For example, it can pave the way to new jobs offering higher pay and more interesting work. It's not unusual for a consultant to double or even triple his rate after adding networking services. For example, a typical network consultant in California can get anywhere from $80 to $120 an hour.[1] A consultant could also go in-house, from a small computer-servicing business to running a full-fledged network with all the opportunities and work variety such a switch provides. One day might find you installing new applications. Another day might find you training users to use the network. A third day could find you installing new network hardware and testing it.

Staying with the same company can get you a larger salary as well, based on a new networking-based job title. It is unlikely that you will see an immediate large increase in pay, but many companies will allow smaller, incremental pay increases over time. A typical network administrator in California earns anywhere from $35,000 to $60,000 a year.[2]

The bottom line is that you get to do something more fulfilling than the work you used to perform, you gain the benefits that increased computer knowledge provides, and you still get paid more. Instead of helping the boss juggle paperwork all day, you can run your own department in a larger company with the right certification. Or, a certification can provide you the basis for starting your own networking business.

1 This rate is based on a survey of 100 network consultants in the state of California. The actual rate you can charge depends on a lot of factors, including the standard rate charged by other consultants in the area, your personal level of expertise, the type of client that your business services, and the number and type of services that your business offers.

2 This rate of pay is based on a survey of 70 network administrators in the state of California. Your rate of pay will vary by locale, level of expertise you can offer the company, local laws regarding pay rates, your company's pay policy, and the size and complexity of the network you administer.

This chapter helps you concentrate on how the certification helps you. It answers questions like "Why is certification important?" and "How do I obtain my personal goals as well as the company's goals?" Once you know the answers you can take an even more detailed look at the certification requirements. This will help the you complete the certification checklist you started in Chapter 1.

This chapter also helps you schedule the time required to complete the certification. Believe it or not, the major reason that many people fail to become certified is a lack of time. Certification requires a personal investment just like any other educational experience. You must schedule time to take the classes, study for the exams, and take the exams. What is more important, you must schedule time for continuing education. Many people attend classes, but cut a few because they don't quite have the time required to attend. Then they try to take the exams without studying. Finally, because they are totally unprepared to take the exams, they become frustrated after the first few questions and rush through the rest.

This is a sure way to fail. Even the people who do get certified can lose that certification if they don't attend to continuing education requirements. Certification, more than anything else, means that you must be willing to devote the time required to maintain a specific level of education and competency. The information in this chapter helps ensure your *continued* success.

# ⇨ Why do you need certification?

Many people look at certification as simply another sheepskin to hang on the wall. Certification is a lot more than some classroom study and a few exams. It is a commitment by you to maintain a specific level of training in order to perform a set of very specific tasks. It also involves the personal satisfaction of knowing that you have the skills to perform that job to the standards set by the industry.

Discovering exactly what certification will do for you is a big part of completing the requirements successfully. You need to keep your goals in mind as you choose classes and prepare for exams. Having goals in view also helps when you take the exams and set aside the time to maintain your proficiency. Figure 2-1 provides you with some ideas of how to create your own goals worksheet. You can use this worksheet to help you throughout the certification process.

Figure 2-1

**Novell Certification Goals Worksheet**

Name: _____

Certification: _____

Anticipated Date of Completion: _____

Goals: _____
_____
_____
_____

Profession Recognition: _____
_____
_____
_____

Network Skills: _____
_____
_____
_____

Industry Trend: _____
_____
_____
_____

Novell Support: _____
_____
_____
_____

Other: _____
_____
_____

*Novell certification goals checklist*

As you can see, the form is very straightforward. It contains blanks for your name, the certification you intend to pursue, and the date you plan to obtain it. Make sure you keep both the Certification and Anticipated date of completion fields up-to-date as you progress. Explanations of the Goals fields appear in the following sections. You should couple this form with the Certification checklist from Chapter 1.

The following paragraphs examine the reasons for certification in detail. Make sure you list the reasons that fit your situation on your goals worksheet. Listing the reasons you are doing something at the beginning of a project often helps you complete it. These reasons help you to focus on the goals you set at the start of the certification process, and emphasize your personal need to complete them.

# Professional recognition

Many people who would prefer to do something else are stuck in "dead end" jobs. Many administrative assistants or other semi-skilled personnel would prefer a job with a little excitement, rather than performing the same old work every day. A Novell certification can help you reach that goal. Even if you do have a fairly interesting job, a Novell certification can provide the variety that makes work more interesting. Instead of spending every day shuffling papers, you could spend part of that time working with the network.

Another group of people who really need Novell certification to gain professional recognition are consultants. How many times has a client asked why they should use you rather than Joe or Mary down the street? Have you ever had to lower your per-hour charge just to get the job? Wouldn't it be nice to have something you could show the client to settle the question in no uncertain terms?

These are all reasons why a consultant would want professional recognition, not only to increase self-satisfaction but to gain the respect of clients as well.

# ⇨ Network skills

No matter what you think your level of experience might be, certification training is always the best method for gaining network skills. While on-the-job training and keeping up with the latest news in the trade journals are viable ways of gaining some information, they do not give you the full benefit of certification training. When you go through network classes, the instructor provides you with information based on the input of hundreds or even thousands of other people. There is no way to gain this type of information in the comparative vacuum of on-the-job training.

And, even if you could gain the book knowledge, certification training provides you with at least one other valuable asset. You get to test this input in a laboratory environment. Your company won't let you test the knowledge you gain on the company LAN, but you can test it at a training center.[3] This ensures that you will really know how specific networking conditions normally look, and how to fully install all the features of the Novell Netware operating system.

In fact, you will probably spend as much time using your new skills as you will learning them. The instructor is there to help you fully comprehend what the manuals contain. How often have you read the manuals only to feel like you didn't know any more when you finished than when you started? Or, you might understand what the manual says but fail to implement the procedures correctly. Learning from an instructor through certification training helps you really know Netware, beyond the point of taking your best guess about what you think will happen.

Because every trainee begins with a different level of knowledge, it is important that you compare what you know when you start with what you expect to know when you finish. Once you determine what you expect to gain from the certification process, you need to write it down. Keep this goal in mind as you take each of your courses. Also

---

3 Some courses provide more hands-on training than others. See Appendix C for further details.

use it as a guide for helping you study. Concentrate on your weak areas before taking the exam.

# ⇨ Industry trend

Another reason to become certified is that certification is an industry trend. Novell plans to train approximately 115,000 CNEs in the near future to supplement the existing 65,000 CNEs, which results from industry's need for fully qualified individuals to manage networks. The number of new CNAs that industry will need is even greater—some analysts predict that one day there will be four to five times the number of CNAs as there are CNEs. Of course, the number of CNIs will increase proportionately to handle the influx of new certification candidates. And, even though the MCNE program is new and there is no way to gauge how many people will apply for this level of certification, you can be certain that many network managers will become MCNEs instead of CNEs. The industry's internetworking needs are just too great to ignore the benefits that the MCNE program provides.

So, what started this industry trend? Many companies do not want to trust the valuable information on their network to someone who doesn't possess the proper training. References are nice, but a certificate is just as good in many cases. Having a CNA, CNE, ECNE, MCNE, or CNI certificate will open many employment opportunities for you. Of course, having both experience and a certification makes you a sure winner at the negotiation table.

This is probably a good time for you to write down some of the ways that you can use your certification once you get it. Make sure you look at the various trade papers[4] to see how industry trends will help you in gaining the type of employment you want. You could write these trends down, or even take clippings from the trade papers to use for future reference.

---

4 See Appendix B for ideas on what trade papers you should read to find out what's going on in the networking industry.

Clippings from trade magazines and newspapers are especially important for consultants. They provide an extra level of credibility when you bid on a large networking job. Remember that the client is more apt to listen to what industry has to say than to simply take your word that certification is a good and necessary requirement for someone to install a network.

# ⇨ Novell support

Novell provides an added layer of support for people who become certified to use their products. It makes good business sense for them to do so. Novell uses several mechanisms to accomplish this.

> Special assistance on the Novell product support line. This is a forum on CompuServe in which you can discuss new advances in networking technology, or get help with an especially thorny problem. You can also use this forum to download new versions of drivers and programs.

> Use of the Novell logo for your price sheets, advertising pamphlets, business cards, and resume. Only a certified person may use this logo.

> One year's free subscription to the *Network Support Encyclopedia* Professional (NSEPro) edition, a software library crammed with information about Novell products. It also contains articles and papers describing how to overcome specific networking problems.

> Monthly Issues of *NetWare Application Notes*. This monthly magazine contains information about current product support problems and how to get around them. It also contains news about technological advances and new products. This is also the first place where most certification holders will hear about new product details. (The trade press normally provides the first look at a new product, but they seldom provide the information you will need to implement that new product prior to product release.)

The CNI gets a few additional support items. Most of these benefits reflect the CNI's need for additional information. Because CNIs spend the day in classrooms teaching other candidates, it's important that they receive the latest information as quickly as Novell can get it to them. The instructors often have information that supersedes what is in the manuals. The following list contains the items that a CNI gets above and beyond the other certification levels.

➤ **Ongoing Development and Distribution of Instructor Materials**. Even CNIs spend time going through the latest materials relating to their specialty. This allows Novell to provide other certification candidates with the best possible information.

➤ **Instructor Kit Updates**. This is the physical component of the new material that an instructor requires to remain up-to-date. It contains the materials CNIs will use to teach their class about advances in Novell products, changes in the certification program, or updates to educational programs.

➤ **CNI Update Training**. Sometimes an update to a manual or some additional materials will not get the job done. When that happens, the instructor needs to spend time with Novell representatives learning about new technology or updates to existing products. It is very important that Novell provide this updated information in the form of hands-on or classroom training to CNIs.

➤ **Informational Mailings (Including the *Novell Educational Bulletin*)**. A CNI requires constant input to remain current about his own trade and with the information he needs to teach others. Novell uses informational bulletins to help CNIs remain current about the requirements for maintaining their certification. The mailings also help CNIs improve their training approach, and provide them with new teaching methods. The *Novell Educational Bulletin* also provides information about new courses and test announcements.

➤ **CNI Support on NetWire**. This is support above and beyond the support that the other certification levels receive.

Novell's commitment to the certificate holder is just as great as the commitment you must make to become certified. The ability to receive special support from a company also works to both an employer's and a client's benefit. Your ability to provide better-than-average support because of your relationship with Novell could work to your advantage. You need to keep this support in mind when you attempt to sell your skills to a potential employer or client.

## ⇨ Other reasons

By now your head is probably buzzing with other ideas about how certification can help you. Make sure you write these ideas down while they are fresh in your memory. Because they can be so motivating they can help make the difference between failing and passing.

In addition, personalizing your goals list might provide the edge you need to gain an advantage over the competition. What if you decide to bid on a job that another certified person already bid on? Telling your client how your approach to networking differs from the competition can make the difference between getting the job or giving it to your competitor.

How about a job opening to which more than one certified person applied? Telling a potential employer how you view your certification might make them take notice. Make sure you let people know that you took the time and effort to get the most out of your certification training. Help them see you as someone who is willing to put a little more effort into doing the job right.

## ⇨ What are the certification requirements?

Now that you have a better idea of why you would want certification, let's consider how you can get it. The following paragraphs provide you with a detailed look at the certification requirements for each level of certification.

# ⇨ CNA

The Certified Novell Administrator (CNA)[5] is the lowest level certification you can obtain. The goal of this certification is to set a certain level of training for people who want to administer a specific type of Netware LAN. Five certificates are available: Netware 2.2 Administrator, Netware 3.x Administrator, NetWare 4.x Administrator, and GroupWise Administrator. Most people will want to avoid the NetWare 2.2 Administrator certification, because Novell has phased this product out and anything they learn will not apply toward a CNE certification. The requirements for this program appear in Fig. 2-2.

**CNA Certification at a Glance**

Figure 2-2

1. If you don't work with DOS on a daily basis, you may want to start your study with the DOS for Netware Users course. You will also want to take the Microcomputer Concepts for Netware Users course. Novell will not test you on this information, but you will need it for your certification specific classes.

2. Take the appropriate course. This consists of Netware 2.2 System Manager and Netware 2.2 Advanced System Manager for the Netware 2.2 Administrator certification, Netware 3.x System Administration and Netware 3.x Advanced System Administration for the Netware 3.x Administrator certification, Netware 4.x Administration and Netware 4.x Advanced Administration for the Netware 4.x Administrator certification, GroupWise 4.x Administration and GroupWise 4.x Advanced Administration for the GroupWare certification, or UnixWare System Administration and UnixWare Advanced System Administration for the UnixWare certification. It is very important to remember that there is only one exam for each CNA certification level that concentrates on the administrator, rather than advanced administrator, course.

3. Study the student manuals provided during the class. Make sure you study any weak areas in your knowledge skills. Check any notes you may have for information that does not appear in the manuals.

*CNA certification at a glance*

5 Novell changed this from Certified Netware Administrator in early 1995. All older materials still use this designation.

Figure 2-2

4. Schedule your exam by calling 1(800)RED-EXAM. Take the appropriate test: 50-115 Certified Netware 2.2 Administrator, 50-390 Certified Netware 3.x Administrator, 50-391 Certified Netware 4.x Administrator, 50-393 Certified UnixWare Administrator, or 50-395 Certified GroupWare Administrator.

5. Submit your paperwork to Novell. You can call 1(800)NETWARE to find out about the status of your paperwork. (Ask for the CNA administrator when you call.)

6. Subscribe to one more trade journals that allow you to keep up on industry events and advances in network technology. Examples of trade journals for this level of certification include PC Magazine and PC Week. Both periodicals include network specific sections on a regular basis. If you have a specialty area, you may want to pursue a magazine that leans toward that bias. For example, if you mainly work with database management systems, you may want to get a periodical like Data Based Advisor for the database specific networking tips.

7. Watch your mailbox for your certification papers and any other Novell sponsored information.

*continued*

As Fig. 2-2 shows, the certification process for CNA is fairly simple. Of course, the first step is to go to the appropriate course. (If you don't feel that you know enough about DOS you will want to take the DOS for Netware Users, and Microcomputer Concepts for Netware Users courses as well.) Many people feel that these courses are unnecessary. However, even if you have previous Netware experience, you will want to know the Novell way of maintaining the network. This is the most correct way to perform most tasks, based on the experiences of literally thousands of other administrators.

The next step is to study for the exam. Study your class notes and the student manuals thoroughly. This represents the best possible method for passing the exams. Make sure you spend the time required to study weak areas. You might even want to have someone else quiz you on various aspects of the material contained in the CNA manuals.

Once you feel that you know enough about Netware, schedule your exams. Try to schedule the exams when you are typically most alert, depending on whether you're a morning or an afternoon person. You might want to consider the day of the week as well, and schedule your exams for a day when you typically feel the least rushed. And incidentally, no books are allowed in the examination room.

Immediately after you complete your tests, make sure you submit your paperwork to Novell. Then, you will probably need to call Novell, later on, to check on the progress of your paperwork. Novell also issues you a picture identification card, so will need to provide them a photograph. You can obtain a suitable picture from any passport photo store.

While you wait for your certification papers to arrive, you might want to go to your local bookstore and browse for books and periodicals that pertain to networking. Make sure you get material you can understand. It doesn't matter how well the book or periodical explains networking technology if you can't grasp what it means. Most major bookstores (e.g., B. Dalton or Walden Books, and technical bookstores) also stock periodical stands. *PC Magazine* and *PC Week* both contain a wide variety of information that a network administrator needs to know, in both product reviews and networking articles. Periodicals often include Novell-supplied materials as well. You might even want to maintain a subscription to *Netware Connection* so you keep abreast of the latest innovations in Netware.

# ⇨ CNE

The Certified Netware Engineer (CNE) certification is one of the most common certifications. In many cases, this is the level of certification that a consultant would want. The revamped MCNE program makes this option very attractive if most of your clients use large networks or have special internetworking requirements. This is also the level of certification that an administrator of a large network should have.

Because this certification allows you to work with every operating system that Novell provides, it requires a lot more preparation and training than the CNA course. Of course, many of the points that we present in that section are equally applicable here. We assume that you have these particular skills and therefore don't discuss them again in this section. Figure 2-3 provides an overview of the CNE certification process.

Figure 2-3

## CNE Certification at a Glance

1. Take the appropriate courses. Chapter 1 provides a complete listing of the courses you can take. Make sure you take all the required courses and exams. You will want to spend a little time considering which elective courses to take. For example, you may want to take the Netware for Macintosh Connectivity course if you have Macintosh computers attached to your network.

2. Study the student manuals provided during the class. Make sure you study any weak areas in your knowledge skills. Check any notes you may have for information that does not appear in the manuals. Studying one student manual at a time may help reduce your confusion level when taking the associated exam.

3. Schedule your exams by calling 1(800)RED-EXAM. Table 1-3 provides a complete list of the exams required for the CNE certification. We also talk about these requirements in Chapter 1. Take the appropriate exams for both the required and optional courses you attended. Make sure you leave enough time between exams to allow for study. Don't rush the exams. However, you must make sure that you do take all the exams within the 12 month time frame allotted by Novell.

4. Submit your paperwork to Novell. You can call 1(800)NETWARE to find out about the status of your paperwork. (Ask for the CNE administrator when you call.)

5. You probably already subscribe to one or more trade journals like *PC Magazine* or *PC Week*. Make sure you also subscribe to one or more network specific trade journals that allow you to keep up on industry events and advances in network technology. Examples of trade journals for this level of certification include *LAN Times*. This magazine provides a much more intense view of networking than more generic magazines like *PC Magazine* do. If you have a specialty area, you may want to pursue a magazine that leans toward that bias. For example, if you mainly work with database management systems, you may want to get a periodical like *Data Based Advisor* for the database specific networking tips.

6. Watch your mailbox for your certification papers and any other Novell sponsored information.

7. Check with various printers about pricing for adding your new certification clipart to your resume, price lists, or advertisements. When your certification papers arrive, make sure you add the Novell logo to show that you've completed the required certification.

*CNE certification at a glance*

As Fig. 2-3 shows, the process for becoming a CNE is very straightforward. You go through about the same steps as a CNA, but at a much more intense level. Of course, there are more courses and tests to take as well. While the CNA takes only one exam, the CNE must take 19 credits' worth of exams. You might want to read through the explanation in the CNA section if you have any questions about the basic process for becoming a CNE.

There are other differences between the CNE and CNA certification as well. For example, as a CNE candidate you get to choose between several elective courses. Here, you can really hone your skills for the environment you intend to work in. For example, as shown in Fig. 2-3, you could pursue Macintosh connectivity as one of your electives, which simply reinforces our point that you must think about what you want to do with it before you actually begin the certification process.

One final place in which the CNE differs from the CNA is in the literature they read. We assume that you already read magazines such as *PC Magazine* and *PC Week*. The magazines you will need to consider subscribing to include *LAN Times* and *Network World*. These magazines really cover networking in detail and provide you with that added advantage in knowledge that you will need when talking with a client. Keeping yourself up-to-date in all the latest industry trends really makes a difference. For example, you might know of some new technology that works better and costs less than the old technology recommended by a competitor.

# ⇨ ECNE

ECNE is really an advanced form of CNE. It is for those who require a little more education to perform their work. In most cases this is the result of working with WANs or other large network situations. As shown in Fig. 2-4, you start as a CNE before you go to this program. Chapter 1 can provide you with all the details about the rights and responsibilities of this certification.

(Authors' Note: Novell is phasing out the ECNE program. We recommend that you start in the MCNE program if you have not already started in the ECNE program. There is a very good chance

Figure 2-4

## ECNE Certification at a Glance

1. Perform all the steps required to become a CNE (see Figure 2-3). Once you complete this step and feel comfortable with your skills as a CNE, you can go on to complete the requirements for ECNE.

### Note

You do not need to perform step 2 if you already completed 3.11 System Manager and 3.11 Advanced System Manager or 4.0 Administrator and 4.0 Advanced Administrator courses in pursuit of your CNE certification.

2. Complete the 3.11 System Manager and 3.11 Advanced System Manager courses. (As an alternative, you may complete the 4.0 Administrator and 4.0 Advanced Administrator courses.) Schedule, then take the 3.11 System Manager and 3.11 Advanced System Manager Exams.

3. You must obtain an additional 19 credits. Novell does not place any time limit on completing this step. The only requirement for these 19 credits is that you take courses and exams that you have not taken for the CNE certification. This includes: the 2.2 System Management and 2.2 Advanced System Management, the 4.0 System Management and 4.0 Advanced System Management, or any of the other elective credits.

4. Make sure you file the required paperwork after you take each exam. You can call 1(800)NETWARE to find out about the status of your paperwork. (Ask for the ECNE administrator when you call.)

5. Watch your mailbox for your certification papers and any other Novell sponsored information.

6. Check with various printers about pricing for adding your new certification clipart to your resume, price lists, or advertisements. When your certification papers arrive, make sure you add the Novell logo to show that you've completed the required certification.

*ECNE certification at a glance*

that Novell will require all ECNEs to become MCNEs sometime in the future, so changing your certification route now makes sense.

Figure 2-4 shows you how to become an ECNE. Notice that you must start as a CNE and work your way through the ECNE program. The main difference between this program and the CNE program is the 19 additional credits you must obtain prior to certification.

# MCNE

The MCNE is a continuation of the CNE program. It emphasizes various forms of connectivity. This is the certification for people who need to work with large networks or WANs. It is also the option that many managerial level candidates will take, because it provides a lot more information about network management versus administration. As shown in Fig. 2-5, you start as a CNE before you go to this program. You will find all the requirements for this program discussed in Chapter 1.

Figure 2-5 shows you how to become an MCNE. Notice that you must start as a CNE and work your way through the MCNE program. Again, the main difference between this program and the CNE

**MCNE Certification at a Glance**

Figure 2-5

1. Perform all the steps required to become a CNE (see Figure 2-3). Once you complete this step and feel comfortable with your skills as a CNE, you can go on to complete the requirements for MCNE.

2. Complete the MCNE core and target requirements for your selected area of expertise. Chapter 1 goes through the various specialties in detail.

3. Complete all required elective courses and exams. Make certain that you do not choose any courses used to complete your CNE certification. It is also important to select electives from your specialty. Chapter 1 defines the elective courses that you can take to complete the requirements for MCNE.

4. Make sure you file the required paperwork after you take each exam. You can call 1(800)NETWARE to find out about the status of your paperwork. (Ask for the MCNE administrator when you call.)

5. Watch your mailbox for your certification papers and any other Novell sponsored information.

6. Check with various printers about pricing for adding your new certification clipart to your resume, price lists, or advertisements. When your certification papers arrive, make sure you add the Novell logo to show that you've completed the required certification.

*MCNE certification at a glance*

program is the additional credits you must obtain prior to certification. Most of these are for courses that a CNE wouldn't take. They all deal with connectivity and other higher level issues that a MCNE will deal with. Remember that a MCNE usually supervises the network in some way, in addition to providing a much broader range of experience.

# ⇨ CNI

The CNI certification is far different from any of the other certifications we've discussed in this chapter so far. To become a CNI you must go through extra preparation and intense training. Unlike what you must do for the other certifications, you must attend the Novell classes to become a CNI. In addition, these classes must be taught by someone certified by Novell. Figure 2-6 provides you with an overview of the requirements for this certification.

Figure 2-6

**CNI Certification at a Glance**

1. Submit an application to become a CNI, a signed CNI agreement, and a resume to the Novell regional CNI program contact. Once you complete this task, you must convince a Novell Authorized Education Center (NAEC) or Novell Educational Alliance Program (NEAP) representative to sponsor you during the certification process. You must include an NAEC or NEAP reference with your application (along with two other professional level references). Contract CNIs do not have to actually maintain a relationship with the NAEC or NEAP, but Novell counts this lack of contact against you during the certification process.

2. Determine which target course you want to teach. (As part of this process you will select a specialty area.) You must provide this information to the regional CNI contact before your application will be approved by Novell. Chapter 1 contains a complete  list of available courses and divides them into specialty areas.

3. Take any prerequisite courses. Study for the required exams and pass them. You should complete the prerequisite requirements before you proceed to your target course. (Even though Novell does not require you to pass the exams in any specific order, passing your prerequisite exams first will enable you to pass the target exam a lot more easily.)

*CNI certification at a glance*

4. Attend the class for your target course at any NAEC, NEAP, or Novell training site. The training site must use CNIs for instructors and Novell course materials. (This may not be a requirement for some Applications specialty courses; check Chapter 1 for details.)

5. Study the student manuals provided during the class. Make sure you study any weak areas in your knowledge skills. Check any notes you may have for information that does not appear in the manuals. Studying one student manual at a time may help reduce your confusion level when taking the associated exam.

6. Schedule your target course exam by calling 1(800)RED-EXAM. Take the appropriate target course exam. Make sure you leave enough time between exams to allow for study. Don't rush the exams. However, you must make sure that you do take all the exams within the 12 month time frame allotted by Novell.

7. Obtain the required training for oral presentations.

8. Attend and pass your IPE. Make certain that you attend the IPE for your specialty and target course. This is especially important for some Development specialty target courses. Chapter 1 provides specific IPE numbers where required. Make sure you talk with your sponsor before you actually schedule the IPE time.

9. Submit your paperwork to Novell. Make sure you include the class certifications from each class you took. You can call 1(800)NETWARE to find out about the status of your paperwork. (Ask for the CNI administrator when you call.)

10. You probably already subscribe to one or more trade journals like *PC Magazine* or *PC Week*. Make sure you also subscribe to one or more network specific trade journals that allow you to keep up on industry events and advances in network technology. Example of trade journals for this level of certification include *LAN Times*. This magazine provides a much more intense view of networking than more generic magazines like *PC Magazine* do. If you have a specialty area, you may want to pursue a magazine that leans toward that bias. For example, if you mainly work with database management systems, you may want to get a periodical like Data Based Advisor for the database specific networking tips.

11. Watch your mailbox for your certification papers and any other Novell sponsored information.

*continued*

Figure 2-6

12. Check with various printers about pricing for adding your new certification clipart to your resume, price lists, or advertisements. When your certification papers arrive, make sure you add the Novell logo to show that you've completed the required certification.

13. Follow steps 2 through 9 for any other target courses that you want to certify for. You may skip any steps that you have already satisfied during a previous certification effort. Make certain that you do fulfill all the requirements for each certification.

*continued*

Novell greatly streamlined the CNI certification process over the past year or so, yet made it more flexible as well. Figure 2-6 shows the basic certification route. It is very important to note the various decisions you will make along the way. As with other designations, we discussed the various types of CNI certification in Chapter 1 so we will only cover the route itself in this chapter.

This certification begins with different requirements than the other certifications. You must get Novell's approval before you even start the process of becoming a CNI. This certification also requires you to obtain an NAEC or NEAP sponsor. There are also some paperwork requirements that the other certification levels do not have. And, you cannot immediately start this certification process by taking classes, as you can with other certifications. You must do a little preparation in advance.

In addition, one other requirement really differentiates a CNI candidate from all others. It is the IPE that you see in step 8. Passing the IPE is critical to your certification. However, the IPE is never really over. You get tested every time you step in front of the classroom. Your students will test your ability to teach on a daily basis. Their input after the course equates to the test results from the IPE. In fact, the IPE is so critical that Novell recommends you get some professional training before you attempt to pass it. Figure 2-7 provides you an overview of what will happen during your IPE. As you can see, it reflects a typical day in the classroom. However, this classroom is only a lab. Once you become certified that lab will become a daily experience.

**CNI Instructor Performance Evaluation (IPE) at a Glance**

Figure 2-7

*Day 1 Activities*

1. CNI Orientation—This is where you will learn about what Novell expects from you during the IPE. The head of the group evaluating your performance will talk about grading criteria and other IPE specific topics.

2. Assignments Given—The evaluation group will give you a teaching assignment. You will not know what this assignment is before you take the IPE. The whole purpose of this exercise is to see your performance during the entire teaching cycle.

3. Lunch—It isn't too difficult to figure out what you do now.

4. Candidate Preparation—You will spend the entire afternoon of the first day preparing for your assignment. It is very important that you fully outline everything you intend to present during the "test" class the next day.

*Day 2 Activities*

1. Presentations—This is where the real IPE begins. The evaluation group will judge you on all the criteria that you were told about the previous day. The criteria include the following items:

   **Presentation Characteristics:**

   • Confident when presenting the course materials
   • Modulate voice properly
   • Wear appropriate attire
   • Maintain eye contact with student
   • Enthusiastic about subject
   • Avoid filler words and other distractions
   • Present materials at an appropriate pace
   • Provide for student autonomy and security
   • Encourage class participation

   **Presentation Mechanics:**

   • Introduce section and identify objectives
   • Provide a verbal outline of the course topics
   • Talk about the relevance of each topic
   • Reference appropriate manual page for current topic

*CNI instructor performance evaluation (IPE) at a glance*

Figure 2-7

- Define new terms and acronyms
- Show proper preparation for actual topic discussion
- Talk about the topics in a logical order
- Reference the topics to subjects the student already knows about
- Use analogies to describe and illustrate the topic
- Use visual aids to help describe the topic
- Use questions to help the student remember the topic
- Promote class discussion
- Summarize the topic
- Avoid introducing new material during the summary

2. Lunch—This is the same as the day before.

3. More Presentations—The IPE evaluation group will use the remainder of the day to test any candidates they did not test in the morning.

*continued*

# ⇨ How long does certification take?

Some people look at the time required to gain certification as the number of hours spent in class and the time required to take the exams. But the certification process is ongoing and requires an ongoing commitment to maintain it. There are paperwork and continuing education requirements that you must consider in addition to the more obvious requirements. The following paragraphs will provide you with the information you need to take all these factors into account.

## ⇨ Training

The time you spend in training depends on the certification you plan to achieve. In most cases the courses are two to five days long. Chapter 1 contains a table that tells you the exact length of each class. However, the important consideration is not really the length of each class, but coordinating the class times. It helps to talk with your local NAEC/NEAP representative and get a listing of course availabilities and dates. Simply mark out the days for each course on a calendar to plan for the time you need to spend in training.

There is another way to look at the training time investment. It is very unlikely that time will allow you to schedule more than one class per week. As a result, you can simply count the number of classes you need to take and count this as the number of weeks you need to set aside for training. Of course, you will still have to set aside some time each week to complete your normal work.

# ⇨ Testing

As a practical rule, no one can tell you exactly how long testing will take. The problem is that, while the exam times are a constant, study time is not. Taking an exam without studying for it is likely to produce very frustrating results. You need to plan sufficient study time or you will fail.

A general rule of thumb is to plan at least two hours of study for each day spent in completing a course. If you took a four-day course you should plan eight hours of study time. Of course, you will not want to try to get all your studying done in one day. Plan for a maximum of three hours per day. Spending any more time in study during one day will reduce its effectiveness.

Make sure you include at least one hour, plus travel time, to take the exam itself. Also, you need to get to the testing center at least 15 minutes early.

# ⇨ Paperwork

The amount of time required to complete your paperwork is fairly flexible. It depends on the availability of resources to get the required documentation together, and the time required to communicate with Novell. A typical example would be six hours, which includes an hour at the photographer to take your picture, an hour to complete the paperwork itself, about half an hour to copy the required certificates, about an hour in communication time with the testing center/NAEC, and at least two-and-a-half hours talking with a Novell representative.

# ⇨ Continuing education

How much time should you spend on continuing your education once you obtain certification? It really varies by individuals. You must consider what you plan to learn about, what your current level of education is, and what the requirements of your company/clients are. A good rule of thumb is at least one hour of training time per day for CNEs without any special requirements, such as database management tasks. A CNA could probably get by with about half that investment, while a CNI might require quite a bit more.

Most CNIs will require a minimum of two hours of training each day, plus one full day of training per week. If you teach all week, then you will probably want to set Saturday aside for this task. You should plan on increasing your training time every time Novell introduces a new product. Make sure you spend enough time, in both reading and practicing, to feel comfortable with the level of your skills. Trying to learn at least one new item per day is probably a good idea, and overall, investing in yourself is good for both you and the company. Besides, you will never maintain your certification if you do not take the time required to train.

Also, make sure you spend a little time trying out new ideas with the network itself. Perhaps a different directory arrangement or a new menuing system will help improve overall system efficiency.

# ⇨ Conclusion

This chapter has provided you with information about three very important areas of certification. First, we looked at why you need to become certified at all. Second, we took a detailed look at the educational requirements for certification. Finally, we helped you plan the time required to become certified. When you combine all three of these elements you can come up with a single plan that will help guarantee a successful certification.

Remember that certification is not merely a decoration to hang on the wall. First, it proves to you and the programming community that you have the skills required to maintain a network. Self-confidence and the confidence of others are major requirements for a career in network management. Second, you can learn things in class that you will never learn on the job or from trade magazines. Third, people who hire network professionals are increasingly aware of the benefits of using a Novell-certified individual to manage their networks. Finally, you get Novell's continuing help in solving problems as part of your certification.

Make sure you understand the requirements for your particular certification. You cannot prepare for what you do not expect. Learn about all the requirements: classroom, study, exams, paperwork, and continuing education. Always list everything you need to do on your checklist and leave nothing to chance. Preparation is a critical factor in the certification process.

Time is also an important consideration after you become certified. Your investment does not stop after you pass the exams. You'll have plenty of paperwork and continuing education requirements to consider as well.

# 3

# Learning the trade

B Y this point you should have in mind the certification that best suits your experience and knowledge. It might be CNA certification, which you might plan to use as a stepping stone to CNE certification, which might then become a stepping stone to becoming an ECNE. Or, maybe you have most of the qualifications to become a CNE already.

Whatever the case, to reach the next level of certification you might need to expand your understanding of the theories, and your practical experience with some specific aspects, of networking. At the same time, many organizations will prefer that you have a certification like the Novell CNE before they will let you maintain the network, but if you want to advance into a higher position or into management the company will require you to have a college degree.

These increases in your understanding and experience might come about in a variety of ways. They might come via on-the-job training, through reading trade magazines, by attending seminars or lectures, or by the hands-on, trial-and-error method. Other ways might include formal education. Formal education could come in different ways, such as by attending Novell courses, through vendor training from companies such as Compaq or 3Com, or by obtaining a degree from a college or university.

In Chapter 2 we covered the requirements needed to become certified by Novell as a networking expert. In this chapter we will explore different ways to learn the trade. This will include the type of required training for your particular situation, but we will also consider whether it's even necessary. If training is in your future, what level of training will you need? Finally we will cover how to get the most from what you learn.

## ⇨ Is training really required?

The answer to the above question is YES. The level and amount of training depends on your situation. If you want to do more in this industry, and we assume that you do or you would not have picked up this book or even considered becoming certified by Novell, you will need more training. Besides, no one knows everything about networking (or even computers in general). Those who believe they are experts in everything are only fooling themselves, while cheating themselves out of any real chance to learn, grow, and become all that they can be in this business.

You now have an understanding, from Chapter 1, of the requirements and responsibilities of the different certifications. You have also completed the goals worksheet from Chapter 2, so you know exactly what certification you want to obtain and what it means to you. The certification process has been outlined as well, so you know what to expect and what you are trying to accomplish with your education. Armed with this information you can now decide if more education for obtaining the certification will be required.

To decide if you need education, take a look at the job duties. Or, if you are trying to advance in a company, look at the job description. If your education and experience meet the criteria, then you might not need to do any special learning of the trade. If you are not totally familiar with what's required for the certification or job description that you are applying for, then some form of training will be necessary.

# Deciding what training you need

The amount of training you will need depends on how comfortable you feel with the subject matter. You might only need a few hours of review with a student manual, or you might need to spend a few years developing the necessary skill(s). If your goal is to become a CNE and you now have a CNA certification or have been working with Novell NetWare for some time, chances are good that by attending the Novell courses given by an NAEC, and doing some studying, you will pass the exams.

On the other hand, if you have not had much hands-on experience with NetWare or do not know much about networking, you will have a hard time becoming certified. This is not to say that it is impossible. Many people have become certified by simply studying the student

manuals they borrowed from someone else. Unfortunately, once they get out into the workplace it became apparent that they were not qualified to service or administrate a network. These are the people who give certification a bad name. Luckily these people get weeded out in a short time.

To help you decide how much additional training you actually need, you need to know which certification you want and what level your skills are at. The chart in Fig. 3-1 will help you to gain an understanding of your skill level. The key to making these worksheets and charts work, though, is being truthful with yourself. It's normal to want to believe that we have more expertise or knowledge than we really have. Remember that only you will see this chart. No one else needs know how you rank yourself. Therefore, when you rank yourself, choose the lower level of the skill ranking if you have any doubts. This will help you to strengthen any weak areas you might have.

The chart itself can be separated into four areas. The first area lists the skills that an expert in Novell networks must have and can actually use in the field. This is only a general sampling of the different skills. You might find that, within a skill, you know some of the subtopics very well while other subtopics need improvement. Remember, the key is to be honest with yourself. Extra space is available at the bottom of the skill list so that you can add any additional skills you think are necessary. If you are a manager and are helping your employees become certified, you will want to include any unique or special requirements specific to your company, or that you feel are necessary for certification.

The second section within the chart is the ranking area. Here, you will rank yourself on a scale of 1 to 10. The rankings are listed from high to low, with 10 a high ranking and 1 a low ranking. Again, be honest in ranking yourself—this is for your eyes only and will be a study index. If you overrank yourself you might fail to study in an area that you are weak in. When selecting your ranking, place a check mark under the appropriate skill level. If you feel that you are between levels, place your check to the low side of the scale.

At the bottom of the skills chart is the third section, labeled "Areas Needing Improvement." Here, you should write down the specific

Figure 3-1

| Skills | Level High       Low | | | | | | | | | |
|---|---|---|---|---|---|---|---|---|---|---|
| | 10 | 9 | 8 | 7 | 6 | 5 | 4 | 3 | 2 | 1 |
| DOS | | | | | | | | | | |
| Microcomputer hardware | | | | | | | | | | |
| NetWare concepts | | | | | | | | | | |
| NetWare features | | | | | | | | | | |
| NetWare 2.x System Administration | | | | | | | | | | |
| NetWare 3.x System Administration | | | | | | | | | | |
| NetWare 4.x System Administration | | | | | | | | | | |
| NetWare 2.x Installation | | | | | | | | | | |
| NetWare 3.x Installation | | | | | | | | | | |
| NetWare 4.x Installation | | | | | | | | | | |
| Workstation Installation/Setup | | | | | | | | | | |
| Fine-tuning NetWare 2.x | | | | | | | | | | |
| Fine-tuning NetWare 3.x | | | | | | | | | | |
| Fine-tuning NetWare 4.x | | | | | | | | | | |
| System Back-up | | | | | | | | | | |
| Printing | | | | | | | | | | |
| Security | | | | | | | | | | |
| User/Group Accounts | | | | | | | | | | |
| Console Utilities (2.x, 3.x, 4.x) | | | | | | | | | | |
| Command Line Utilities (2.x, 3.x, 4.x) | | | | | | | | | | |
| NetWare Upgrading | | | | | | | | | | |
| Topologies | | | | | | | | | | |

*Skill level ranking chart*

Figure 3-1

Network Technologies

Others:

Prepared                    Areas Needing Improvement

_____          _____

_____          _____

_____          _____

_____          _____

_____          _____

_____          _____

_____          _____

_____          _____

*continued*

areas that you need to improve in. These will be both general topics from the skills section and specific subtopics from within the general skills. Be specific when filling out this area—it will be your basis for study. If you need more room to document your improvement areas, continue on another piece of paper. Do not shortchange yourself by leaving anything out. To become a professional networking person you must target your weak points, then concentrate on improving.

The last section is to the left of "Areas Needing Improvement." Here, write in the dates when you master the subjects listed as your weak areas. Keeping track of your milestones is important; it provides you with a feeling of accomplishment. By recording the dates on which you master your deficiencies you will feel at ease to move on to other topics.

Now compare your goals worksheet and your skills chart to determine the level of training you require. For example, if your goal is to become a CNE and you have been working as a network administrator, you might know the administration side of NetWare but you might never have installed or configured a NetWare file server. Instead of spending time in the system administration course, perhaps you should attend the service and support course. This might be much more helpful for you than taking every course or studying everything about NetWare. You might even find that no courses are necessary, but that some light review of the NetWare manuals is all you need. (You might want to find someone with a copy of the student manuals and study them as well. This could improve your chance of passing the exams.)

When you feel that you have completely prepared yourself for the exams, re-evaluate yourself again with the skills chart. This time, use a pen of a different color so you can compare your current skill level against what it was the first time you completed the chart. If you are still not happy about your ranking, find the areas that need improving and concentrate on them. Repeat this process until you know the topics cold. As you continue to find your weak points take whatever steps are necessary to become trained.

# ⇨ Obtaining the required financing

Financing your training is an important step in the certification process. Almost everyone can get financial support, but finding the best source for you takes time and effort. Before you begin, take time to figure out how much financing you need. Here are the important things to consider:

➤ Training costs

➤ Testing costs

➤ Travel expenses

➤ Lost work time

➤ Miscellaneous expenses

The first step is to add up all the costs of classes and testing. Also, take time to consider hidden costs. For example, you might need to factor in additional travel expenses if the test and training centers are farther away than your usual place of work. In some cases you might need to take time off work to attend classes. Some companies will not allow you to miss work to attend class; others will ask you to make up the time later. Try to think about all the possible problems and come up with solutions for each one, in advance, for example, if your company won't pay you for time spent in training you might have to arrange for vacation time.

There are a number of ways to get the money you need for certification training. The sources you will use depend on a number of factors, including who the training will benefit and what length of time will be involved. Of course, the most important consideration is whether you go to your company or simply rely on your own resources. Figure 3-2 provides you with some ideas on techniques you can use to get financial aid. There are at least three.

Figure 3-2

Some people save the money they need for education, then go to school. While this method does mean a delay in getting your training, it also reduces the after-training expenses you'll encounter. Consultants find this method ideal.

*Getting financial aid*

A common source of money for training is company sponsorship: you convince your company that it is in their best interest to supply the money required for training. This usually involves some type of payback period.

One option that many people don't consider is combining support from a number of sources. For example, your company could support half the cost; a loan could support a quarter of the cost, and savings could support the rest.

*continued*

Some people save for the training before they actually begin, so there are no costs to burden them after they graduate. Consultants, or people who plan to start their own businesses, often use this technique. However, trying to pay for your education and get a business going at the same time usually doesn't work very well. So, most people take a learn-now, pay-later approach to the whole process.

Company sponsorship is the method most people use to get certification training. Convincing your company to sponsor you might be relatively easy if they just installed a LAN or the network administrator recently left the company. The need for someone to manage the LAN is usually pretty obvious by the time all the hardware and software gets installed. Of course, convincing them that you're the right person for the job might prove a little more difficult. In this situation, you need to provide proof that you can not only do the job but do it better than anyone else in the company.

Other forms of sponsorship are also available as well. For example, you might get a state or federal government agency to sponsor you.

Other forms of sponsorship include everything from veterans programs to scholarships and grants.

There is always a small group of people who can't get total financial support from one source. These are the people who usually need to work a little harder to get anything done in their company; or, they might be part of a small business that can't afford the cost of training. In such a case you might need to spend time putting together a package deal. One or more sources help you get the training you need and reap the benefits of that training. To use this technique you spend time getting part of the support from one source, then use that source as a means to get other people to join in. For example, what if you are part of a small company? The company might recognize the need to obtain the services of a trained network administrator, but might not have the financial resources to pay for the training. If you could put part of your own money into the support fund, perhaps the company might provide the other part.

For another example, many military people can use their GI benefits. And, student loans and scholarships are also available. However, some of these will not be available to you because you don't qualify for one reason or another, so make sure you don't waste time trying to tap a financial source you can't possibly use.

Figure 3-3 shows you just a few of the sources you can use to pay for certification training and testing. These six sources are the ones most people use. The following paragraphs describe these options in detail. But don't be limited by our list—use your imagination and detective skills to track down other sources of potential financial support. Some jobs offer more potential sources of financial support than others do. Just remember, the opportunities are there—only a lack of research and motivation can prevent you from finding the financial support you need.

# ⇨ Company sponsorship

Getting financial support from a company is the most common method, though you usually need to provide proof that the company needs the services your training will provide, and that you are the best

Figure 3-3

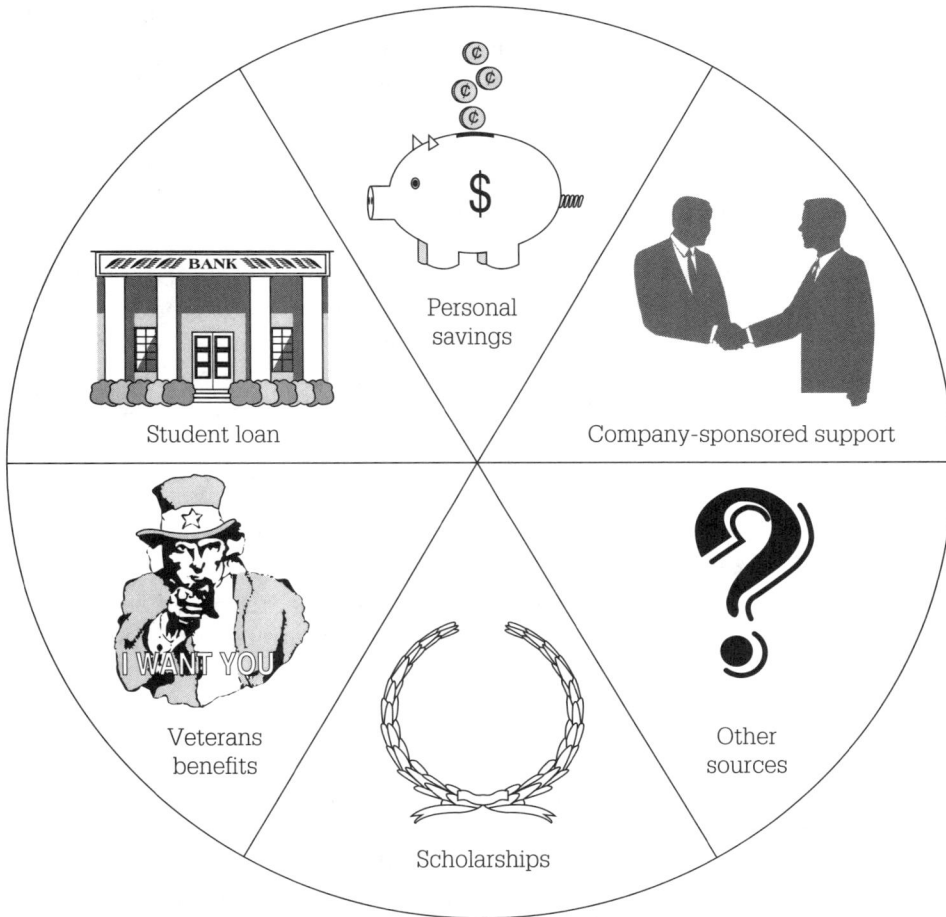

*Sources of financial aid support*

person for the job. In most cases, you must show a willingness to repay the company by promising to work for them for a specified period of time after you complete the training. In other cases, you might have to repay the company the money they spent if you fail to meet your goal. These are some of the things you need to consider if you plan to go this route.

At this point you might think that getting company support is an all or nothing proposition, but there are a lot of different possibilities when you attempt to get support from your company. You could offer to pay for half of your training (or get financial assistance from another source) and ask the company to pay the other half. This would show that you were willing to invest in your own future and might make it a lot more likely that the company would help. Some companies also offer interest-free education loans. Essentially, you take an advance against your salary to pay for the training.

Some people think that getting company support is only for full-time employees. Yet in many situations, a company might consider providing educational benefits to a part-time employee as well. Other scenarios include going full-time for a specific payback period or, in rare cases, showing that you will provide a huge benefit to the company via the training you get. Never limit your horizons by thinking small—all the company can do is say no if they don't like your proposal.

In your proposal you need to prove two things. First, you need to provide proof that the company needs a network administrator for their LAN. Second, you need to prove that you are the only person, or the most qualified person, to fill that role.

This book contains quite a few tools to help you on this proposal. The Novell certification goals worksheet in Chapter 2 (Fig. 2-1) helps you determine what you plan to achieve from your training. A goals worksheet can also show management that you are serious about obtaining it. It can further provide you with reasons why the company needs a network administrator. The skill level ranking chart in Fig. 3-1 can not only show personal weak and strong areas, but can also show why you are the best candidate for the job. Much of the material in Chapter 6 can also help you gather the information you need to create a convincing proposal.

Figure 3-4 provides a sample outline you can use to get started on your proposal. Of course, you'll need to modify it to meet any company-specific requirements, or to meet your own personal needs. Make sure you don't go to management empty handed or, worse yet, only half-prepared. Even if you don't write a formal proposal, you can at least prepare the answers to all the questions they are likely to ask. Make sure you are ready with the best possible responses.

Introduction

Figure 3-4

- A description of the proposal
- A synopsis of any relevant company rules, regulations, or benefits
- Definitions of terms and acronyms

How will this training benefit the company?

- Demonstrated need for a network administrator
- Cost/benefits analysis
- Resident LAN expert available at all times

What am I willing to provide the company in exchange for the training? Why am I the best person for the job?

- Existing skills
- Existing training
- Training goals
- Personality traits
- Other considerations

Conclusion

*Sample company financial aid propsoal outline*

As Fig. 3-4 shows, you need to include a number of things in your proposal. In the introduction, quickly summarize the reasons why you put the proposal together. Make sure you include any relevant company rules or guidelines. You also need to define any nonstandard terms you use within this section. Likewise, the conclusion summarizes the contents of the proposal. It should not contain a repeat of the information the proposal contains; instead, it should summarize the main points of your proposal. A manager should get a good idea of what you are trying to say by reading only the introduction and the conclusion. Then, if he or she wants more details he will read your entire proposal more carefully.

There are three main sections in the body of this outline, though yours might include more. The first thing you need to do is concentrate on the needs of the company. Show management that you are thinking of the company first, yourself second. The first part of the section tells them about their need to have a network administrator available.

Of course, one of the first questions that comes to mind is, why not use an outside consultant to perform this work? You need to demonstrate the need to keep a staff administrator. One way to do this appears in the second part of this section. Here you can show management that it is actually cheaper to maintain a staff network administrator. You can also cite other intangible benefits. For example, one is the security of knowing that no one outside the company has access to vital data. This information appears in the third part of this section.

The second area of the proposal tells management what you are willing to exchange for financial support. Standard items include a promise to stay with the company for a specific amount of time, and other concessions. Make sure you let management know that you are willing to negotiate. If you offer something they don't want and make it obvious that you are not willing to negotiate, your proposal will fail even if management is interested in having a trained network administrator on staff. Don't kill your chances by being inflexible or unimaginative.

The third area you must concentrate on is yourself. Tell management why you are the best person for the job. Here you can brag about your capabilities a little bit (Don't brag too much, though!). Initially you should concentrate on tangible evidence, such as your current job skills and training. Then, let management know about your training goals. Showing them the tangible parts of your plan makes it obvious that you want to succeed. Finally, tell them about the intangible benefits you can offer. For example, are you good at working with people? Make sure you offer management some evidence of this skill. Does your work record demonstrate that you're a hard worker? Make sure you let management know about this, too.

Writing a financial support proposal requires time but the results can be well worth the effort. Getting your certification can open up new opportunities that you might not otherwise get. To make it a little easier, some of the work you will need to do for the proposal is the same work you will need to do for certification, as explained in other sections of this book.

# ⇨ Student loans

There are many sources you can tap for student loans, even though most people look no further than their local bank. Of course, the number and type of sources vary by region of the country, and by personal situation. So, the first objective is to find out where you can get a student loan.

In most cases your local college or university can supply you with this information. Just look in their student catalogs or other brochures. Typically, these books are packed with great ideas for finding financial aid. (Obviously the college or university wants to make it as easy as possible for someone to attend; you're simply using this source of information for another purpose.)

You should also check with friends. You might be surprised at the bits of information you find out this way. Life insurance companies and other financial planning institutions also make good places to check for this type of information.

Once you determine where you can get a student loan, you need to know the criteria for qualifying. For example, any student loan will require that you provide evidence of income. A government loan might require that you fall below a specific income level, while a bank loan might require that you exceed a specific income level. The one loan that might require the least financial information is a student loan provided by an insurance company or a fraternal organization. In most cases you secure this type of loan with your insurance policy or another tangible asset.

You need to take other things into consideration with a student loan as well. For example, what type of payback period does the institution offer and how high is the interest? By shopping around you can usually optimize these features to your benefit. Especially important is the interest rate. Consider any other stipulations that the lender might have about the loan. For example, some lenders might require that you provide proof of schooling in the form of a graduation certificate. In general, you need to find out everything you can about the institution, what types of loans they offer, and what you can expect from them in the way of payment plans.

Of course, you also need to consider what you can afford. Unfortunately, some people find that they get into more debt than they can repay (as witnessed by the number of government student loans that remain unpaid). Make sure you aren't taking out too large a loan for your education. If you don't plan ahead, you might find yourself living on peanut butter and jelly sandwiches for a long time before you get the loan repaid. Even worse, you might end up filing for bankruptcy. Here, a little planning goes an especially long way.

# Scholarships

The number and variety of scholarships available to you are probably limited when compared with other forms of financing. Unlike your local college or university, it is doubtful that your local NAEC will have any type of scholarship plan available. Most scholarships are tied to a specific institution. A scholarship gets created when someone endows the university or college with the money required to fund it.

However, don't let the paucity of scholarships deter you from exploring this avenue of financial aid. Fortunately, there are a few other places to get them. For example, many life insurance companies and fraternal organizations provide scholarships. Some of these scholarships are aimed at technical schooling rather than more traditional subjects. Your local church might have scholarships available as well. In many cases, relatively few stipulations are placed on these scholarships by the people administering the fund. A check with the leaders of these organizations might reveal a scholarship that very few people know about.

Unfortunately, most such scholarships are fairly small and will pay for only one or two of the courses you require for certification. If you do go this route, plan on supplementing your scholarship funds with money from personal savings or other sources. The bright side is that, in many cases, a scholarship can offer just the right amount of additional funding to get company support for your educational needs. This is especially true of smaller companies that want network administrators but lack the funds for training. So even if the scholarship is small, it can make the difference between getting, and not getting, your education.

Once you do get a scholarship, make sure you understand all the qualifications. For example, many scholarships require that you pass the course before you receive payment from the scholarship fund. You need to supply proof that you passed the course in the form of a graduation or other type of certificate. If this is true, because most NAECs require you to pay for your classes in advance, you will have to pay some other way, then repay that money with the scholarship funds.

Some scholarships have other requirements; for example, the people who endowed them might restrict them to specific types of education. Make sure you understand all these requirements before you use the money you expect to receive from the scholarship. In some cases, failure to observe a specific requirement could result in a loss of scholarship moneys.

# ⇨ Veterans benefits

It's amazing how few veterans actually use their GI benefits to further their education, especially when you consider the time they spent in the service to get these benefits. Often, the perception is that veteran educational benefits are only for college, not for technical or vocational training. However, many forms of technical/vocational training can qualify.

You will need to do a few things to prepare if you plan to use veterans benefits. First, you can expect the usual amount of government paperwork to fill out. Make sure you talk to your local VA representative well in advance, to get all this handled. Also, check to make sure your specific training qualifies for VA benefits, because the requirements for these benefit programs change on an almost continual basis.

Once you determine that you and the training both qualify, and have all the paperwork filled out correctly, make sure your local NAEC will accept government payment. Some NAECs require payment in advance of the course. If so, you will need to work out some arrangement with the NAEC, because (as with some scholarships) the government pays only after you successfully complete the course. Unfortunately, they also pay the educational institution directly, making it more difficult to work something out.

# ⇨ Personal savings

All the previous approaches to the financial aspects of training had one thing in common: someone else paid the bills. While this might be the best way for you, it doesn't always work out that way. If you plan to pay for all or part of your training yourself, make sure you have enough to complete the process before you start. This is a good rule because it is all too common for someone to start certification training, only to drop out later due to a lack of funds. In fact, the best plan is to make sure you have all your bills covered, plus a little for emergencies, plus the total amount required for certification class and testing. Remember, paying for the classes isn't the end of your financial responsibility. You also need to set aside the money required for testing and continuing education.

There are other sources of personal income that you can tap besides your savings account. For example, some people have paid up life insurance policies they can borrow against. In many cases, the money contained in these policies can pay for the entire schooling process. The interest on such a loan is usually pretty small; almost always below the rate that you'll get from a bank or other financial institution. In essence, with an insurance loan you borrow from yourself.

You might also take money out of an IRA or other long-term savings account if you're willing to risk the penalties. Of course, you need to spend some time with your bank working out the details—the penalties and other legal considerations vary by bank and savings plan.

One final solution to get the last bit of support you need is to pay for part of your classes with a credit card. To pay the entire cost of certification classes and testing with a credit card you would need a fairly substantial line of credit. The big disadvantage to this method is the high interest rate you'll pay if you're not able to pay the bill(s) off within 30 days. On the other hand, you might need to get the training today rather than tomorrow to take advantage of an opportunity.

# Other programs

There are still other payment programs that you can try. For example, some states and the federal government have job-training plans for minorities (in addition to student loans or other forms of assistance you must repay). If you qualify for one of these plans, the money you receive might pay for all or part of your schooling. As with the veterans benefits mentioned earlier, there is usually a lot of paperwork involved with this approach. Make sure you know all the requirements before you sign up for any classes. In most cases you'll need to combine the money you get from these programs with some other type of financial aid. For example, your company might help pay for part if you can get government support for the other part. In fact, the personnel office of your company can be a good place to begin your search for aid programs.

You might be able to get grants from corporations or other organizations in exchange for some special consideration. For example, a consultant might get a grant from a company in exchange for free maintenance service for a specific time period. Though it takes time and effort to ferret out these sources of financial aid, you might want to consider the possibilities if all your other initiatives fail.

# ⇨ Who do you talk to about training?

Training comes in many different ways and from many different sources. The type of training that will best suit your needs will depend on your personal work and study habits. In many cases the best source of training will be on-the-job experience. In other cases the best training will come from a structured course. Other types of training include third-party lectures, videotapes, audio tapes, self-study manuals, instructor-led classes, and, of course, the trial-and-error method.

# ⇨ Hands-on training

On-the-job training can be the best way of obtaining information. It can also be the most time-consuming. While this type of training will teach you the most hands-on, real-world ways of performing tasks, the amount of time you must invest before you have enough experience for certification might take years. This is not to say that, if you do not have on-the-job training you cannot pass the certification, or, if you are working for an organization you will not become certified for a long time. It simply means that no matter how much knowledge you obtain from other sources, nothing can really replace knowledge acquired from on-the-job experience.

The best way to acquire on-the-job training would be, of course, to find a job related to your educational requirements, but this might not be a very easy task for most people. Many times, before you can get hired by a company, you must have the same skills you would like to learn. If this is the case, you might have to work out an arrangement with a prospective employer, to work at an entry level or at a reduced rate. Other times you might be able to work out an arrangement to assist in various projects at no pay, in return for hands-on experience. While this would not put any money in your pocket, you would get the training you were looking for. You could consider it a payment toward your education.

So where and how do you look for this job? First, check your personal resources. Many people might be in position to help you. They might include family members, friends, neighbors, or people you work with. Often these people will not be able to directly help you, but they might know of someone who might know someone. You will then have a warm lead and a name that you can use as a reference and an ice-breaker. The more people know what you are doing and what you are looking for, the better your chances of getting that warm lead. The more personal contact with a prospective employer, the higher the chances of obtaining a position.

Another area to turn to would be the help-wanted section of the newspaper. This will point you to employers that need some type of assistance. This is usually a tougher way to land a position than finding a warm, personal lead. Many people typically apply for the same position, and some of them will be better qualified or overqualified. You might need to find some type of angle to make your services more attractive. This might include working at a lower rate, or signing on with the company for a long time.

Other sources to look at for on-the-job training would be job services, job councilors, employment agencies, and headhunters. However, you will more than likely find that they will want someone with some type of experience, so you will again be caught in the loop of not being able to find a job without experience, and not being able to get experience without a job. The final way to find the on-the-job training you need would be to knock on doors. Look in the phone book for computer dealers and Novell dealers in your area, and then just visit them. The in-person approach will normally yield the best results. Present yourself to a possible employer so he can see what you are like, to talk face-to-face with you and get to know you. You will also to be able to present yourself in ways you cannot match over the phone. Remember, you must create a reason why they should hire or help you. You must create an incentive for the company to hire you.

# ⇨ Instructor-led training

The best way to get the training you need, and bring yourself up to speed, is to enroll in a professional education program. The courses will present you with much information in a class that lasts only a couple of days. The instructor will normally use a series of lectures, along with oral or written questions, lab exercises, and hands-on experience.

Instructor-led courses are available from a variety of different sources. These sources include Novell, Novell Authorized Education Centers (NAECs), colleges, universities, vendors, and different third-party educational facilities. The services offered by these facilities range from very general to very specific. The lengths of classes also range from just a few hours to four or more years. The cost can range from nothing to thousands of dollars.

To locate the different training institutes in your area, check the phone book, talk to your local chamber of commerce, and check with local computer dealers. Often, computer dealers will be able to tell you where the best place to get training might be. Because they are in the trade and see many of the qualified people working in the industry, they will know which institute has the best reputation.

The best place to obtain the required information for the Novell certifications would be from a Novell education center. Novell makes available excellent training for their certifications, as well as for their line of products. While Novell does offer some training directly, most of the training comes from the Novell Authorized Education Centers (NAECs). Novell authorizes the centers to teach their courses at a high level of quality, and inspects the centers for proper hardware and software, as well as the overall condition of the facility. NAECs are located worldwide, with the largest concentration in the United States. Some NAECs are quite large with several classrooms in one location. Also, a few NAEC companies maintain education centers in different parts of the country. The centers are all basically the same, because Novell must authorize each one.

Each center must use Certified NetWare Instructors (CNIs). The instructors must pass a series of competency exams and must attend special courses designed to make sure they meet the Novell standards for teaching each course. Nevertheless, what distinguishes the different centers from each other is the quality of the instructors. While each instructor is Novell-certified, many teach only what is in the Novell course manuals. While this is the base information required for the Novell certifications, the "extras" that the better instructors include usually come from years in the field, practicing what they teach. We have all had an instructor or a professor who really knew the book material, but ask them a question that was not in the manual and they would not have a clue. When selecting the education center that you want to attend, be sure to ask for references from past students. Talk to these people and get a feel for how the instructor handled the class, subject matter, and questions about related topics not included in the course material.

Other items that differentiate the NAECs will be the courses they offer. Many of the classes require the latest in computer technology, and some of the smaller NAECs cannot justify the expense of the equipment. These centers are then left teaching only the basic core classes. This is okay for the basic certifications, but if you want to become a CNE or an ECNE you will have to find an NAEC center that teaches the advanced classes.

The number and frequency of courses can also be important. If the class that you want to attend is offered only quarterly, you might have to wait a few months. Some of the larger NAECs offer most of the core classes on a monthly rotation, and the advanced classes on a four- to six-week rotation.

Whether you attend a large or small NAEC, you will receive quality training by some of the most credible institutes around. Novell has long been recognized by the industry for their proactive approach to training dealers, users, and technicians. You can always count on the course materials to be current with what's on the market.[1] To get a list of Novell Authorized Education Centers in you area you can call Novell directly at 1-800-NETWARE (1-800-638-9273), or the Novell FaxBack service at 1- 800-233-3382 or 1-801-429-5363. Both of these numbers will put you in touch with either the Novell education group or the FaxBack service. You can then ask for a list of NAECs centers. The list will be sent to your fax machine, free.

# ⇨ Self-study training

Novell—and other sources, too—offer self-study programs. The self-study programs are good for people who have both the time and self-discipline to study on their own. By using self-study programs offered by Novell and the NAECs you can save yourself a few dollars. The courses include the course manuals offered by Novell and some form of lab training. Most of the NAECs will send you all the course manuals so you can study them at a time convenient for you. After you have studied the manuals you can then attend some type of lab

---

1 Advancements in the industry are being made almost daily, so the course materials are maintained as current as possible.

session. A typical lab session is one week long, and a CNI is present. If you have any questions or problems during the exercises, the instructor will be more than willing to help.

The self-study programs are excellent ways to get training, hands-on experience, and knowledge needed to obtain Novell certification. They can save you money compared to the more expensive, instructor-led courses. But if you decide to participate in a self-study program, be sure you are 100 percent dedicated to reaching your goal. The biggest disadvantage of a self-study program is the amount of individual work it takes to prepare yourself. You will not have the luxury of a structured class and an instructor to lead you by the hand through each chapter of the manuals. You will have to devote at least two hours a day to studying the Novell manuals and researching any questions you have. Before you attend the lab session of the program you need to know the book material completely. The lab session will help you bring together all loose ends and answer any questions about the operating system, installation, software, hardware, operating concepts, or any other area related to networks.

To find out more about the self-study certification programs, contact your local NAEC, your local computer dealer, or call Novell. The programs will vary from education center to education center, so be sure to investigate what each has to offer.

# ⇨ Other types of training

Often, the standard approach to training such, as on-the-job training and attending classes, does not always fit into our schedules. For this reason, alternative forms of education are very popular. Such forms might include books, audio tapes, videotapes, and computer-based training (CBT) programs. These are all excellent sources of information that will help to augment your training.

For the experienced computer technician to the beginner, a bookcase with a wide variety of computer books will be a necessity. This library will be a great asset in your quest for advancement and will grow immensely in a short time. Many of your books will have just a few pages on subjects that concern you right now, but will provide a source of reference on other material in the future.

Many books about the Novell NetWare operating system are in the bookstores. Many of these are very general in nature, duplicating much of the material included in books supplied by Novell. In some cases they are more concise than the Novell books themselves. Most of these books go into great detail on how to install the operating system and how to manage the system once NetWare has been installed. If you attended the Novell courses, this will be a repeat of the information the instructor presented in class. On the other hand, Novell-specific books can be very helpful in teaching you about the system if you have not had any formal training on NetWare or any on-the-job experience. If you are new to NetWare these books will help supplement your knowledge.

There is another good reason to buy some of these general Novell books for your library. The Novell classes focus on the current operating systems. This is acceptable for learning about the latest systems, but many businesses still have old versions of the operating systems. Because the old version serves the business with everything that they need, they have no reason to spend money on a new one that will not provide them with anything they really require.

That's why, as a Novell expert, you will need to know about the early versions of NetWare and how they work. You should know the different commands and the different terminology that was part of old versions of NetWare. There are many differences in the versions of NetWare. Version 2.0a is different from NetWare v2.2 and NetWare v4.0. This is one reason why books written about the different operating systems will be an asset to you. It is sometimes difficult, if not impossible, to get books from Novell on older operating systems.

Meanwhile, don't ignore the general networking books. Many of these books have a lot of practical information about how to administer your network.[2] While these books might not provide Novell-specific

---

2 See *Hands-On Guide to Network Management* by John Mueller and Robert Williams (McGraw-Hill book number 4418) for more information on network administration in general.

information, they will help you gain a better understanding of networks in general. Even if you don't use this information immediately, you might find it essential later.

To find books on the Novell operating system (or networks in general) you do not need to go very far. Most bookstores carry at least a few. The large bookstore chains normally carry a good line of Novell books, written by many different authors. Many of the computer stores will usually carry one or two different ones as well. Also, many larger cities will have technical bookstores that specialize in computer books. Most of these stores will carry most of the books written about the NetWare operating system. You can normally find a list of those in your area in the yellow pages of your phone book. Another good idea is to talk to the Novell instructors from your area. They normally stay current with information on different computer-related topics. They also visit the more technical bookstores on an ongoing basis to help themselves stay current with technology. And, most of the more technical bookstores will supply you with a list of titles that they have access to, and will ship books anywhere in the world.

Besides books, another great source of training material is audio and videotapes. Both Novell and third-party companies make tapes that basically comprise the Novell courses. These tapes will supply you with a great deal of information about NetWare but are usually fairly expensive. While the cost puts them out of reach for many individuals, they are ideal for companies that need to train a few people in their organization. This allows them to buy one set of tapes and then let all their employees use them. This is a lot more cost-effective than sending all their employees to a certification class. (A note here for companies that might plan to do this: Unless you send at least one person to the certification course or have someone on staff who knows NetWare, you will find that the tapes present a lot of material but they will not be able to answer the questions that always arise.)

Novell itself offers a vast array of tapes on different NetWare topics. These include both basic and advanced topics. Novell prepares the tapes professionally and continues to update them as new products are released. You can order from Novell or from your Novell dealers. To get a list of tapes offered by Novell, call the Novell FaxBack service or your Novell dealer.

Novell also offers a computer-based training (CBT) program that will
help you train for both the certifications as well as just to get a better
understanding of NetWare. The CBTs are computer programs that
offer information, plus exercises that require input from the reader
(sort of a mini-exam that you can use to test your knowledge). These
are good programs that will help you understand the working of
NetWare, but will usually stimulate many other questions not
addressed by the program. The programs are also quite expensive for
the individual, but can be very attractive to companies that need to
train more than one person. To get a list of available CBTs and the
part numbers, refer to your Novell FaxBack information sheet or
contact your Novell authorized dealer.

# Getting the most from your training

As you have seen there are many different approaches to training to
become a certified Novell expert, and for general knowledge of the
computer industry. It is normal to feel a bit overwhelmed. The best
advice to help you obtain your certification will be to stay focused. By
using the goals worksheet presented in Chapter 2, and the
information presented here in Chapter 3, you will be able to formulate
your goals and obtain them. Keep your goals worksheet with you all
the time and look at them often. This will keep you focused.

To get the most from your training you will also want to take the
training one step at a time. It is very easy to get caught up in the
frenzy of trying to learn as much as you can as fast as you can. Take
one topic at a time and work with it until you feel that you know the
subject matter. Don't try to conquer all the other related subtopics at
the same time. You will find that every topic will have many other
related subtopics, and that each one will have many other subtopics as
well. Nevertheless, continue to take one item at a time and stick with
it until you are finished.

Another good way to get the most from your training is to take many
notes, both while reading and while in class. If you are in a class, do
not try to write down everything the instructor says, or you will miss

many things. You might not even catch enough of the discussion to ask questions. Try to write just the key words; then, after the class is over or at a break period, you can fill in some of the other information. Usually just the key words will start a thought process that will replay the lecture in your mind. Then you can write down as much information as you like.

Also, when reading books and manuals, use a highlighter and sticky notes for references. Many people highlight sections of the text that they know, but what you should be highlighting are the parts you don't know or the parts that you will need additional help on. Once you highlight the text, use the sticky note to mark the page for future use.

You will find that one of the best ways to study the course manuals is to break the process down into three parts. First, quickly read the material in a summary fashion. Don't spend much time; you only want to get familiar with the content of the book. For example, you might want to scan the headings and the first sentence of each paragraph. This will help you understand the author's intent in writing the book. Second, get a note pad, your sticky notes, and your highlighter. Then reread, making notes and highlighting the important information as well as the information that is new to you or that you do not understand. The third step will be to study your notes and marked pages and then research any areas that you do not understand.

Using this process will take a little more time than other techniques, but you will find that you will retain a lot more information. There is something special about converting the information from a thought in your mind to letters on a piece of paper. The final step in this process will be different for each student. Many times you will want to reread the manual and your notes again.

The secret to making this work and passing the exams will be to find the style, type of training, and studying technique that best works for you. This might take some time and you might have to change your approach, but be aware of what techniques work for you and which techniques produce the best results.

You will also find that short bursts of studying will produce better results than long periods of intense concentration. Remember the long all night cram sessions preparing for high school and college exams? All this did was put your mind in a state of exhaustion; more likely than not, you didn't retain much of the information you studied for more than a few hours. You will be able to concentrate longer and remember better if have a rested mind. You will find, too, that your exam scores will be higher if you take the test when you are rested and alert.

In terms of how long to study at a time, the best rule of thumb is to study until your mind starts to wander. The moment your mind starts to wander you aren't getting any real work done; it's time to take a break. Get up and walk around, get a drink or a breath of fresh air. You will find that your concentration will be much higher and your retention will also be better. If you just study for hours on end, your concentration is usually high at the start and near the end. Most of the information in between becomes diluted. The short burst prevents your mind from getting overwhelmed and tired.

Other study techniques include flash cards, posters, and recording your notes on a cassette tape, which you can play over and over again. Tapes are especially useful while you are driving. Like many others, you may find that by listening to your notes in your own voice your mind will retain more. You will also be able to reuse the tapes for different classes and different manuals. Also, use the tape recorder to record notes while in class. It then becomes possible to replay the course lectures at your convenience and at your own pace.

# ⇨ Conclusion

Learning the trade is much more involved than just reading some books, attending a couple of classes, and getting a little on-the-job experience. To be truly successful you must be better prepared than the average person who calls himself an expert or a CNE. Many so-called experts are nothing more than box movers or installers. What will separate you from them will be the extra education you pursue.

This education might come from upgrading your CNA certification to a CNE, an ECNE, or a CNI from Novell. It might come from obtaining a degree from a college or university. Or, it might come from on-the-job training, night classes, seminars, or vendor training.

The type of training that will best satisfy your needs and goals will be dictated by your job requirements and what you expect to accomplish in your career. Remember that to stay competitive with the average person in this industry you must do your homework. This includes reading the trade papers and working with the products. To be a real expert, wanted by all the companies, you must take the initiative. Decide what (and how much) education is right for you, make the investment, and follow through. The result will be well worth the effort.

# 4

# Taking the tests

## CHAPTER 4

T AKING tests is the least favorite part of any training experience; they seem to evoke the worst feelings from all of us. While general exams are difficult, professional examinations are more difficult than just about any other examination you can take. With most general exams you have a wide range of study aids available. If nothing else, you usually have a group of fellow students to talk with. Professional exams usually don't offer these aids; usually, only a small group of people with very specific interests (or job requirements) take them. Novell's examinations are no different. In addition to the general lack of third-party study aids, each exam is totally different. Therefore, you can't even rely on the input from fellow students to help very much.

The emotional pressures of a professional exam are a lot greater than those of a general exam, as well. This is easy to understand—the stakes are high and a career may be up for grabs. Every professional exam you take has the potential of helping your career if you pass it, or reducing your potential (or at least derailing you momentarily) if you don't.

However, learning to take an exam is just like any other skill; you gain the knowledge to perform the task, practice until you become proficient, then demonstrate your ability. To become a proficient test taker you learn how to study, how to think when taking the exam, and how to prepare yourself emotionally. This chapter takes a look at all these elements and more. It helps you prepare for the Novell exams, not only at the knowledge level, but the emotional level as well.

There is another event you have to prepare for as well. Even if you go through all the training courses, study hard, and take the proper approach to testing, there is a chance that you will fail at least one examination. After all, if failure were not a real possibility, would anyone want to become certified? The requirement of excellence, balanced against the potential for failure, helps differentiate between those who really want the professional recognition that comes with certification and those who don't.

This chapter helps you cover the three areas of testing by telling you how to study and what to study. It stresses the importance of assuming the Novell viewpoint when answering questions. Most important of all, this chapter helps you over the ultimate hurdle, dealing with failure. The better prepared you are to take the test, the more devastating the failure becomes. Helping you get back on your feet again is a very important feature of this chapter.

# ⇨ Gathering the information you'll need

The student guide you receive while taking the Novell courses listed in Table 1-1 is your most important asset in preparing for an exam, especially if you take good notes during class. There are two operative phrases here. First, you must take the Novell courses to obtain the Novell view of networking. Second, you must take good notes in class. Unless you do both there is a good chance that you will fail at least once for each exam. The reason for this failure is simple. While you might have a great understanding of networks in general, you need to know the Novell way of doing things to pass the exam.

# ⇨ The importance of the Novell courses

Your instructor is specially trained to help you understand networking from a Novell perspective. A Novell certification is a credential that tells the world you know what you're talking about when it comes to Novell networks. This implies that you know the Novell way of doing things. While you could argue that there are probably many other ways of performing a specific task, the certification implies that Novell has provided you with training in the Novell way of doing it.

It might seem that prescribing one way of doing things when there are many other equally correct ways is unnecessarily restrictive and oppressive. However, Novell cannot test everyone's methods of doing a task. Yet they must ensure that the methods used by the people they certify are correct. Any other course would make people ask, "Why should I trust anyone you certify to maintain my network?" But on the contrary, in this context, what might seem restrictive at first is simply a way of making sure that everyone can perform networking tasks in a way that works every time. It also ensures that someone certified by

Novell fully tests those techniques in a real-world environment. When people hire you based on your certification, what they are really hiring is someone who knows the Novell way of performing a task—an extension of Novell, if you will.

So how does this relate to test taking? Because Novell must test your ability to maintain a network, and because there is a logical reason for everyone's performing those tasks in the same way, it follows that Novell will test that single way of doing things. Therefore, if you walk into the examination room without a knowledge of Novell's specific methods, there is no way for you to answer the questions correctly. (The passing requirements are high enough to void just about any possibility of someone's guessing their way through the exam.) This is the first point you must remember. When you take a certification exam, you will be tested on your knowledge of Novell's way of performing a task, not on your networking knowledge in general.

# ⇨ Taking good notes

Before you can study for an exam you need a set of good notes. What makes the difference between a good note and a bad one? Actually there are no bad notes (with the exception of wrong information), but there are notes that help you study and notes that won't. While both convey information, one doesn't provide the correct type of input.

Notes are somewhat difficult to quantify until you actually need to use them. You might think something the instructor said is of the greatest importance during class, only to find that you never use that piece of information afterward. Keeping track of what kinds of information you use later on, as compared to what you don't use, is one way to improve your notetaking skills. Everyone differs in their ability to retain information. One person might need to write just about everything they hear down on paper or they will not remember later, while another person will fail to hear an important fact if they are too busy taking needless notes.

Part of the problem is levels of concentration. How well do you concentrate? Can you work on complex problems for hours without getting mentally tired? Do you remember what you read in trade journals long after the information is no longer useful? You might find that taking a minimum of notes and really concentrating on what the instructor has to say is your best method of retaining information. In fact, assuming the information to be covered comes directly from another written source, some people don't take any notes at all during class. They save that activity for after class, as a technique for going back over the information the instructor presented.

If you find that you can't remember anything without writing it down first, you might want to consider two other methods of taking notes. Some people use the outline approach. They write quick notes about what the instructor said as an outline on a separate sheet of paper. This allows the notetaker to concentrate on what the instructor has to say. After class these people fill in the outline. This helps reinforce what the instructor said during class.

Another group can actually concentrate on two things at once. They can write complete notes and still pay attention to what the instructor is saying. This is the same group of people that you find talking on the telephone while working away on their computer.

A final group of people need to resort to high technology to make sure they get all the facts. They simply take a tape recorder to class, record what the instructor has to say, and transcribe it later. This tends to reinforce the lessons but still allows the student to get complete notes. (Make sure you ask the instructor's permission before you start recording; some might object to the use of recording equipment in class.)

## ⇨ Complete your notes later

Never write down just a few words without filling the note out later. This is especially important if you use the outline approach to notetaking. Some people take good notes during class but fail to fill them out immediately afterward. When they try to use the note to study for an exam or part of their work later, they find the note is incomplete or indecipherable.

## ⇨ Take specific notes

Don't talk about generalities in your notes. Always make them as specific as possible. If the instructor provides an example in class, adding this example to the note can help you get the most out of it later. Making the note specific also helps trigger the memory process later. We tend to remember specific things best.

## ⇨ Don't take notes out of context

Always provide enough surrounding information so you can get the full meaning of the note. Never jot down a quick idea that you could misinterpret later. Always provide yourself with all the details. Did you hear about the guy who took notes about preparing a chicken for dinner? One of the notes said "Cut off head." So guess what he did! Don't cut off your own head; take complete notes that give you the whole story.

## ⇨ The test taker's study guide

A good study regimen does not mean spending a long time in study; it means studying efficiently. There are four major areas of concern: quality, environment, goals, and techniques. Working with each area will help you improve your study habits to obtain the best overall efficiency, in effect, to study faster and better.

The first part of this section will help you set time aside to study. Face it—everyone has a busy schedule and it's not always easy to get somewhere quiet to study. In fact, home and job probably consume more time and energy than you really want to admit. However, here is another fact to consider. If you are so busy taking care of other things that you cannot concentrate on what you want to study, then your retention rate will fall to near zero and there is no reason to even make the effort. This might seem a bit harsh until you really think about it. Why waste your time? Part of studying smart is to set aside a special time and place to study. Don't let anyone or anything interfere with it. Soon you will find that you can study for a lot less time and actually get more out of it. This will then help you free more of your time for those home and work duties.

The next area to look at is creating a good study environment. Some people try to study in the living room with both the TV and the radio blaring in their ears. This type of setup is hardly conducive to good study. Also, other seemingly unimportant things affect the study environment. We will look at such things as getting the correct materials together and making sure you have enough of the right kind of light. This section also looks at the physical requirements for study. Comfort is essential; for example, the type of chair you choose can greatly affect how much you get out of a study session.

The third part looks at setting goals for a study session. What can you expect to accomplish during any given session? Few people realize how much their minds can wander. Do you find yourself thinking about the work you need to get done tomorrow, while reading that test question? Setting goals keeps your mind focused. Conversely, failure to set goals might lead to random study that does not accomplish much. Consider how well you would do on the job if you didn't set and meet goals. You might not always meet those goals within the time frame you set, but you meet them to maintain your productivity. Studying is no different from any other human activity in this regard.

Finally, we look at study techniques. The technique that works best for you is a very personal thing. The same individuality that lends interest to life in general makes it difficult, if not impossible, to create a surefire study technique that will work for everyone. As a result, we will not even try to propose one standard way to study for your certification test. This part of the section looks at a variety of study techniques that you can choose from to create your own strategy. At least one of the methods will meet the needs of every reader who looks at this section. Ideally, you will use a variety of methods to make your study time most effective.

# Setting aside adequate study time

Time seems in shorter supply today than ever. Its use is closely guarded by all of us in our everyday dealings. In fact, many of us are even more careful with our time than we are with our money. Time is a quantity that you can never have enough of. This time shortage invariably extends into your studies as well.

Unfortunately, some people try to cram all the information they find in the student manuals, their notes, and third-party study aids into just one or two days of study. While this might work for a short course, it probably won't do much good for a longer exam. The average human being needs a lot more in the way of study to pass the certification exams. You will want to set aside at least a full week of study for each exam. Most people will require two weeks of study to really master what the exam requires.

Fortunately, there is an answer. You can do two things to get maximum benefit from your study time: control the starting time, and control the length of study. Controlling the starting time is important because that influences how you approach your study time. Controlling the length of study helps you maximize the results of your study time. The following rules of thumb should help you in both regards.

> **Always study when you feel well-rested; never study when you feel tired.** Not only are you apt to get facts confused when you feel tired, but you will remember them for a shorter length of time. Studying with a clear mind helps you retain the facts you learn for a longer time. Studying when you feel well rested also improves your attitude.

> **Try to study at the same time each day.** This helps you develop a study habit rather than forcing you to go through a perceived inconvenience. It also improves your ability to study. You will find that your body actually anticipates the demands of studying and prepares for it. Make your study time a treat instead of a dreaded job each day.

➤ **Choose a time of day when you are relaxed and there are few interruptions.** Trying to study right before or right after meals probably isn't a good idea in most cases. Most people are a little too relaxed right after a meal, or too hungry before. You will want to pick a time when your surroundings are quiet and you can spend some time hitting the books. This means that you won't want to study during your lunch hour at work. Trying to take care of the kids while you're trying to study probably won't work well, either.

➤ **Use an alarm or other timing device to keep yourself on track.** This will help reduce the chance that you'll spend more time watching the clock than you do studying. Decide how long you need to study for a particular session, set the timer, then forget about clocks until you hear the alarm. Of course, using this technique will also keep you from studying too long and losing the good results of your study time.

➤ **Never study more than two hours at a stretch.** Most researchers suggest that one hour of study is about all most people can tolerate. Have you ever gone to a seminar where they tried to cram as much as possible into two or three hours? Typically, after about an hour, people start leaving for places unknown or begin to fidget in their seats. As a person spends more time in study, his or her attention slowly drifts to other topics and finally gets completely away from the area he or she wanted to study. If you really want to study more than two hours, make sure you take plenty of breaks. One way to extend your study time is to study for an hour, take a fifteen-minute break to relieve the stress, then study for another hour.

➤ **Try varying your study technique.** You might try having someone quiz you one night, and some memorization another night. Another way to vary your schedule is to spend the first half an hour studying and the second half an hour having someone quiz you. Varying your technique can reduce the boredom that naturally occurs as study progresses.

Overall, it really helps if you can study without fear of interruption or of going to sleep. It also helps if you can maintain the most positive attitude possible; you want to study without becoming bored.

One technique that helps to prevent this is to read or study with a big bowl of popcorn. As you study, munch on the popcorn; the action of moving your hand from the bowl to your mouth will stimulate your other muscles just enough to keep you alert. (Make sure you don't douse your popcorn with too much butter; you don't want to complete your certification weighing 400 pounds.)

Variety is essential to meeting your nightly study goals. After all, this is your future livelihood. Why should you work at something that bores you? Give yourself *every* advantage; pick the times when you are best able to study; and make sure you study long enough but not too long.

# Creating the right study environment

Creating a productive study environment can prove daunting in the average home. No one wants to maintain a quiet environment after spending the day locked in a classroom or office. In addition, few homes contain a dedicated study area. More likely than not, you will find your study area located in the kitchen or a bedroom. Other possible areas you might want to use for study might include a public library, a park bench, the beach, or your own backyard. You need to find a place that satisfies at least the majority of requirements discussed in this section, even if that means studying outside your home. Figure 4-1 shows some typical study area needs.

Figure 4-1

Make sure you observe all precautions for using your computer. This includes sitting at least 30 inches from the screen and using a wrist pad to prevent carpal tunnel syndrome. Keep your display and other parts clean too.

*Creating a good study environment*

Go ahead and get relaxed, but not too relaxed. Remember, the whole idea is to study for your certification exam. Maintaining the correct posture and body position can help you focus on the job ahead.

Avoid study area distractions. A lack of light or the right of light can reduce your ability to see. Try to use indirect light. TV and radio can interfere with studies as well. Never try to study while doing chores.

*continued*

Notice that the requirements for a good study area are fairly simple. You can group them into three areas, as shown in the picture: optimum study environment, personal study needs, and a lack of distractions. Let's look at the requirements in a little more detail.

# ⇨ Optimum study environment

You have the greatest control over the study environment. It doesn't become tired or have a bad day. In addition, it usually stays in place once you set it up. As a result, this is the area you should concentrate on first. For example, a few dollars spent for a better computer chair today can continue to net results for many tomorrows. Also, because you will spend a lot of time in front of your computer studying for the certification exams, it really pays to invest in this area. Don't overlook things like an anti-glare screen if you need it. Many newer displays provide an anti-glare surface, but you might require more help.

One of the most important, yet often overlooked, requirements is the screen distance. If you can't see the screen at 30 inches without squinting, there is something wrong. Take the time to check for glare or dirt. You might want to change the size of your on-screen font to make it easier to see from a distance. Getting glasses specifically designed for computer work can help a great deal, as well.

A comfortable office chair, adjusted to fit your body, is also a must. Your calf and thigh should form a 90-degree angle and your thighs should be parallel to the floor. Also, check out your arms. Do you have to reach up to touch the keyboard? Your upper arms should rest against your body and should form a 90-degree angle with your lower arms.

Also, provide plenty of support for your wrists. A wrist rest is a very inexpensive tool for making certain that you don't end up with carpel tunnel disease, or another form of a repetitive stress injury.

## ⇨ Personal study needs

You can usually control the second area, your personal study needs, pretty well. Maintaining a positive mental attitude will help you get the most from your study. Trying to study while you are tired does not accomplish much. If you feel bad, take the night off. If you are too tense, then you will tire easily. You need to relax to go the distance during your study time. Of course, getting too relaxed will allow your mind to wander, and a wandering mind does not remember much.

# ⇨ Distractions

Distractions are the hardest parts of the equation to get under control. Don't try to study while performing chores around the house. One of two things always results. Either you will perform the chore with your usual flair and forget everything you studied, or you will end up frustrated because you cannot perform both tasks at the same time.

Avoid too much noise as well. A television or radio is a good companion when you work around the house, but they produce devastating results when you study. Do you ever find yourself singing a song on the radio instead of paying close attention to your studies? This is the natural result of noise in the study area. Of course, the same thing holds true for people who insist on talking to you while you study. Take the time to look away from your work, listen to what they say, take care of anything they need, politely ask them to leave you alone, and get back to work. Any other course will surely frustrate both of you.

Subliminal distractions are the worst of the group. Ever have a dripping faucet ruin a good night's sleep? The same thing happens when you encounter distractions that are almost beyond the range of your senses during your study time. The amazing thing here is the variety of forms that subliminal distraction can take. For example, you might need to remove the clock from your study area because it makes too much noise.

Even a source of light can provide a subliminal distraction. Try using indirect light instead of the direct light from a lamp while you study. You will probably feel more relaxed because you won't have light glaring in your eyes. Using indirect lighting also means that you can use the proper light level. Some people get rid of the glare by getting rid of the light. (The 500-watt halogen lamps that you get in most department stores provide the best possible level of indirect light and they don't cost very much; usually less than $30.00.) Taking time to eliminate subliminal distractions might not rapidly improve your test scores, but it will make your study time a lot more comfortable.

# Goalsetting strategies

Setting goals for each study session is *extremely* important. You need to decide where you are now, and where you want to be by the end of the study session. Using this technique will help you keep your mind focused on what you want to do.

Of course, it's equally devastating to rush through a study session simply to meet your goals. Think of your goals as the target that you want to hit. Get as close as possible to that target, but don't shoot yourself in the foot in the process. Rushing is one of the worst things you can do if you want to retain what you learn. Make sure you take the time to fully study each topic.

Above all, make sure you set a reasonable goal. After all, whom are you trying to impress? The following tips will help you set reasonable, yet worthwhile goals.

> **Check your actual progress from session to session.** Use this as a gauge for setting your goal for succeeding sessions. Then begin to set goals a little higher than what you might otherwise achieve. This will challenge you to do better, as long as you keep the new goal achievable.

> **Use the sample questions in this book (Appendix D) to measure your retention.** Make the first goal of each new session to test the amount of information you retained from the previous session. The score you obtain will tell you whether you are rushing or not. The combination of materials provided in your courses, plus the Novell manuals and third-party books, should enable you to retain a minimum of 70% of what you learn. If you do not retain at this level, consider slowing down and spending a little more time on each topic. If you still can't achieve a high enough retention level and you haven't taken any formal Novell courses, then consider taking classes at your local NAEC or NEAP.

> **Maintain a point system based on the goals you achieve each session.** Competing against yourself will make the study session more of a game and keep your interest level high. For example, you could assign each goal a point level: Hard (3);

Medium (2); or Easy (1). Add up the goal points for each goal that you accomplish during a session. Now, multiply this number by the test score you obtain at the start of the following session. For example, you achieved two hard, one medium, and one easy goal during an evening. You obtain a score of 80% on the test during the following session. Your score for the evening is: $[(2 \times 3) + (1 \times 2) + (1 \times 1)] \times 0.8$, or $9 \times .8$, or 7.2. Now you have an easy way to track your progress from day-to-day. Make sure you reward yourself for an above-average performance.

➤ **Set goals based on your ability and experience, not someone else's desires.** It is too easy to negate a study session if you try to live up to a boss' expectations or what a co-worker achieved. On the other hand, it is equally devastating to hold back your progress because you think you must spend a specific amount of time on each topic, simply because others have told you you should, when you're already familiar with the topic.

➤ **As suggested earlier, use a weekly test to check your overall retention level.** Don't fall into the trap of thinking that you are doing fine only to find that you don't remember the things you studied during the early part of your study sessions.

➤ **Set your goals based on your current work load.** If you have an easy week, then set higher goals. A stress-filled week might cry out for a lower goal level. Don't add to a burden by thinking that you need to maintain the same level of achievement every day.

As you can see, what looked like a difficult task at first might prove simpler than you think. Setting goals is easy. Checking to see that those goals are reasonable takes a little more time but is definitely worth the effort. Make sure you optimize your study time by optimizing your study goals.

# ⇨ Developing good study habits

Developing good study habits means a lot more than just getting into the right frame of mind or using good study practices. Using the right study *technique* can mean the difference between a boring study

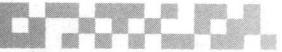

session and one that fully meets your objectives. For example, if you enjoy spending a lot of time with other people, a good study technique could include taking the time to converse with your peers about the topics that will appear on the test. You might even want to set up a group study session with others who are studying for the same exams.

Of course, you will surely fail if this is the only technique you use. You need to combine group study with individual study time and other study methods. Here are some additional ways to develop a comprehensive study strategy:

➤ **Have someone quiz you.** Make sure they concentrate on one test at a time, and that they vary the questions from one session to the next. Ask them to ask the same questions in different ways. This will help you center your thinking around question content rather than the format of the question itself.

➤ **Discuss the test and other study materials with your peers.** You can ask them about problem areas they have and identify your own problem areas. Having a group help you with your problem areas not only increases your chances of getting a great answer, it forces you to consider areas that you might not think about normally.

➤ **Make a game out of the test.** Try making your own flash card system or using some other game technique. You might even want to create a Trivial Pursuit or Jeopardy game for yourself.[1] These can put the test in a different light, making it more of a challenge and much more interesting.

➤ **Spend some time in concentrated book study.** Look over the Novell manuals in depth. Try to find at least one new fact during each study session. Go through the same process with your third-party books and the student manuals.

➤ **Try memorization.** Some people find this is an easy way to learn; if you think it might work for you, try to memorize as many of the facts in the Novell manuals as possible. Then recite them to yourself as you perform other network or application-related tasks.

1 *The Novell CNA/CNE Study Guide*, by John Mueller and Robert Williams, contains ready-made study aids of this sort.

➢ **Consider the hands-on activities in your student manuals and the Novell manuals as the basis for your own exercises.** Create your own case studies, based on your weaknesses and the guidelines presented in this book. Make sure you set a starting point and an ending point. Figuring out how to get from point A to point B is a good way to study. You can even use this in a group setting. Challenge one of your peers to a race. Each of you can set the starting and ending points for the other person.

➢ **Use association to study.** Take the time to associate the items you need to know for the exam with things you do every day. Some people even create acrostic sayings to learn various elements of the exams. For example, this works especially well when learning the security portions of an operating system, such as the different types of access or the attributes you can assign to a file. You can also use mnemonics for association. For example, to learn the names of the seven OSI model layers in order, try taking the first letter from each word of the saying "All People Seem To Need Data Processing." These equate to Application, Presentation, Session, Transport, Network, Data-link, and Physical.

➢ **Take notes as you read the Novell manuals and study the questions in this book.** Then, refer back to your notes and see if you can remember what you read. See how accurately your notes reflect what the manuals actually say. This can help you find and define problem areas. An alternative is to create an outline of the topics you study, then fill in the blanks later. This forces you to remember what you read and then reinforces it by having you write the information down.

➢ **Always study your weak areas first, then study the areas you feel more confident about.** If you have someone quiz you, make sure they quiz you about the weak areas first and the strong areas second. To help determine where your weak areas lie, make sure you look at your notes. If you spent the time to take notes about a particular topic, then you are probably weak in that area.

➢ **Study the appropriate student guide for the test you want to take.** Some people tend to race ahead or look at previously studied areas when they become bored with the current test material. Doing this can actually confuse you rather than help you study. For example, you might find that you start confusing the security rules for Netware 2.x with those used in Netware 3.x. Each exam tests only one specific course. Make sure you study for that course. If you find yourself becoming bored with the current material, take a short break. Get up and move around instead of racing ahead or looking at previously studied material.

➤ **Do not register for the exam until you feel ready to pass it.** Even though there is a limited time in which to take all the exams, you won't want to repeat one because you weren't prepared to take it. This is an especially important consideration if you are a self-motivated person who tends to rush things— make sure you are ready to take the test before you call to register.

➤ **Don't wait too long!** If you are a person who tends to procrastinate, you might want to register for your exam immediately after the preparation class is over. Try setting the date for two weeks from the time your class finishes. This will give you a goal to achieve and enhance your study efforts. Don't let your certificate pass you by; register now for the exam.

Of course, this is not the list to end all lists, you must develop your own list of study strategies that work for you. Use a variety of techniques to keep your study time from becoming boring. Following any or all of these suggestions might just make the difference between passing the exam and failing it.

# ⇨ Registering for the exam

Registering for the exam is one of the easiest parts of the process. All you need to do is have a credit card ready when you call the Drake or Sylvan Testing Centers. You can register for any test by calling 1(800)RED-EXAM. The person on the other end of the line will ask you a few questions. That's it.

Of course, you need to have a few pieces of information handy before you call. You will need the number of the examination you want to take (see Table 1-1), and the location of your nearest testing center. The person who registers you can provide a list of locations in your area, and directions to each one as well.

It's also a good idea to have several exam dates in mind before you call the testing center, in case your first choice is unavailable. Also, talk to your boss about taking the needed time off well in advance of the test. Make sure you don't schedule other appointments on your test day. Set this day aside for testing and nothing else, if possible.

# Taking the exam

Make sure you use all the time allotted to take the test; don't waste any of it on any other activities. Try to maintain your concentration during the entire exam. Don't allow interruptions to rob you of the chance to pass. Of course, time isn't the only thing you need to watch during the exam. The following hints should help you take the test faster and improve your chances of passing.

> **Look at the time indicator on your screen from time-to-time**. Make sure you pace yourself allotting enough time for each question. You might want to take a quick glance at the time indicator after each question and ignore it the rest of the time.

> **Read each question entirely.** Don't skip over small words such as "and" or "not." Small words can make a big difference. People often miss questions not because they didn't know the answer, but because they failed to read and interpret the question correctly.

> **Read all the answers.** Sometimes there is more than one "almost correct" answer on the screen. You need to pick the one *best* answer you find.

> **Remember to put on your Novell hat before you enter the testing area.** Novell bases all the answers in the exam on the student manuals. Even if there is more than one correct way

to perform a task, only the Novell way is the correct answer on the exam. Again, in some cases you might see more than one correct Novell answer to a question. Always pick the *most complete* answer.

➤ **Go with your first instincts.** Some people get so psyched out before an exam that they actually over analyze the questions. Going with the first answer that comes to mind is correct more often than not, especially if you took the time and effort to study.

➤ **Maintain your level of concentration.** Even though the exam center administrator tries to provide the very best testing environment possible, there are always distractions that can reduce your concentration level. Concentrate on the test; ignore any outside influences that tend to reduce your level of concentration.

➤ **Make sure you take care of your comfort needs before the exam.** For example, even though you don't normally need to eat breakfast, you might want to do so on the day of the exam to boost your energy levels. You will also want to wear comfortable clothing. Wear your glasses or contacts so you can see the screen without squinting.

Overall, the things you notice during the exam are really a matter of how well you prepare before you go into the testing center. For example, your body's energy level always affects your concentration level. It's also affected by all the environmental factors under your control, such as the ability to see the screen and wearing comfortable clothing.

Realizing the effects of environmental factors on your mind during an exam is very important. Some people go so far as to make out a schedule for the day of the exam. This can help you get from place-to-place without rushing. Make sure you allow plenty of time. Taking an exam while you feel relaxed is a lot easier than taking one after you have rushed around.

Figure 4-2 shows a typical schedule. Notice that our example contains little housekeeping notes on items such as calling work and placing the test results in a folder where you can find them later. These might seem like things you shouldn't have to write down, but writing them down can provide a certain peace of mind while you're taking the exam. You don't need to worry whether you took care of a specific item, because you have all the things you need to take care of listed on paper.

Figure 4-2

## Daily Reminders

*Call work and remind them of exam.*

*Drive to test center early - relax a little before exam.*

*Think a little about the exam, but don't study.*

*Take the exam, then get results from administrator.*

*Place test results in Novell folder for future reference.*

*Quickly write notes about missed questions (if needed).*

*Send Novell any required paperwork.*

*Sample exam day reminder list*

Once you do get into the test area, you will take one of two types of exams. The first type is the standard testing technique. This is the method that Novell originally used when their certification program started, and some tests still use this method. The second type of exam is called the adaptive testing technique. This is a new, knowledge-based method of testing. Here is how they work.

# Standard testing technique

The standard testing technique uses the same methodology as your instructor used for most of your classes in school. You'll receive an exam with anywhere from 60 to 100 questions. Novell creates a unique exam for each person by drawing a specific number of questions at random from a testing base. For example, you might get ten questions about printing from a test base of a hundred questions. Another ten questions might ask you about security.

Think about this testing method as the Chinese menu approach. You get so many questions from column A, so many from column B, and so forth. About the only thing you might be able to count on is getting a specific number of test questions in a specific area.

It is very important to study everything completely when you take a standard exam. You need an even amount of knowledge about all the testing areas to complete the exam successfully. However, you can do a few things to improve your chances of passing:

> **Talk to other people about their testing experience and the types of questions they saw**. Even though your chances of getting precisely the same questions as another individual are very small, you can build an overview of all the test questions if you ask enough people.

> **Make absolutely certain that your strong areas really are strong**. It is possible to have a weak area and still pass the exam. For example, you might find that you don't know printing very well, yet pass the exam by knowing security perfectly. Of course, having more than one weak area is still deadly; you need to answer enough questions correctly to pass the exam.

> **If you do fail an exam, make sure you write notes about your weak area as soon as possible**. Drake or Sylvan will not allow you to record any answers or take any other notes, but you can take the time to commit these facts to memory and write them down after you leave the testing center. It is very important to improve on your weakest areas for the next exam if you want to pass.

# ⇨ Adaptive testing technique

The adaptive testing technique is a different approach to testing. There is no way to predict how many questions you will get before you start the exam because everyone receives a different amount. In addition, there is no way to predict how many questions you will get in any one area unless you are really honest about your skills.

An adaptive test actually changes to meet your specific testing needs. For example, if you are very weak in printing, then you will get a lot of printing-related questions. Likewise, if you are very good when it comes to security you will see very few questions from that area. The adaptive test bases the next question on the results of the previous question. If you get a question wrong, you can be certain that you will see more of the same kind of questions during the exam. The adaptive exam will not continue to pound away at one area of knowledge, but it will give you enough questions to determine, one way or another, whether you know the information. Once it determines that you are weak in one area the adaptive exam will move on to another.

It might seem like Novell is making the exam process more difficult than it needs to be. On the contrary, in some situations an adaptive exam is actually easier to pass because you get fewer questions. Fatigue is a major problem with the standard testing technique. A candidate who answers a hundred questions is likely going to miss some of them because he/she is tired. This was one of the problems that led to the adaptive testing technique.

Even if adaptive tests are harder to pass in some respects, there are ways you can improve your chances of passing one. Since you know it will concentrate on your weak areas, it pays to study in your weak areas a lot more than in your strong ones. Because an adaptive exam will not give you any extra boost for knowing one area better than another, it pays to try to know them all equally well.

If you start seeing a lot of questions about a specific topic, then you know you are not doing well in that area. This means that you really need to slow down and take your time. Make sure you don't kill off your chances by rushing through the areas you don't know.

Novell will require you to provide some answer for every question. Because you can't bypass a question you really don't know the answer to, take the time to rule out the obviously wrong answers, then select that answer you think is correct. Novell still uses a policy of one absolutely wrong answer, one answer that is either a trick answer or has some minor flaw, an answer that is correct but less correct than some other answer, and finally, the most correct answer. Always choose the most correct answer from those presented.

# What do you do if you fail?

Even if you do fully prepare for an exam, there is still a chance that you will fail it. There is no means for you to take every variable into account in advance. For example, you might not realize that you even have a weak area. A cold or flu might strike on the day of the exam. An accident might delay you, forcing you to rush to the exam. Any or all of these reasons might prevent you from doing your best.

How you recover from a failure partially determines how you will react during the next attempt. It might even determine whether you even make another attempt. Many people try the exams once, fail, then give up on certification because the failure was too demoralizing. But remember, certification requires a lot of dedication and hard work. If certification were easy to get, the benefits would undoubtedly be a lot less. Don't give up after one attempt.

# → Understanding the mechanics of failure

Of course, nothing is more demoralizing than failing the same test twice. There are several things you should do after failing an exam to make sure it doesn't happen again. The following tips will help you pass the exam the second time around. Unlike the other tips in this chapter, these tips usually work for everyone. Make sure you try them all.

> ➤ **Write down the areas where you did well and the areas where you did not.** This will tell you where you need to concentrate before you take the next exam.

> ➤ **Maintain a positive attitude.** If you convince yourself that you're going to fail, you surely will. Literally thousands of other people have earned certification; there is no reason why you can't get it too, with the proper training and study. You need to keep this in mind while you study for the retake.

> ➤ **Don't overcompensate by studying too much.** Many people make the mistake of punishing themselves for failing by spending hour after hour at their desks, studying for the next exam. This is probably the worst mistake you can make. While it is important to study for the next exam and try to find the weak areas that caused you to fail the first time, studying too much can confuse you and cause you to fail again. Make sure you don't study more than two hours per day. (You might want to review the study tips in the previous section of this chapter.)

> ➤ **Try to remember specific questions that you might have had trouble with.** In fact, you should try to write these down while they're fresh in your memory. Even though it's unlikely that you will see the same questions on the next test, they might help you find weak areas in your study strategy. In some cases you might even see the same question worded in a different way. This is where reading the question and understanding what it says really helps.

> ➤ **Always study for a general exam, not the specific exam you took the first time.** Trying to study for a specific exam is

pointless because each exam contains different questions. Novell writes a new exam from questions in its database for each person.

# ⇨ Understanding the emotions of failure

Besides the mechanical methods for getting to the next exam, you must deal with the emotional issues as well. Failing an exam can lower your self-esteem and cause you to doubt your abilities. You need to find outlets for dealing with the disappointment. Some people perform some physical activity, such as bowling or tennis after a failure. The activity helps them release the frustration they feel over failing the exam. Other people work on crafts. A creative endeavor allows them to take their mind off the failure and put it to useful work. Whatever method you use to release the tension of failure, make sure you do it as soon as possible. Don't give yourself time to think about the failure too long.

You also need to convince yourself that you can still pass the exam. Remember, anyone with reasonable computer skills can pass the exams, with the proper training and the right amount of study. A positive attitude is one of your best weapons. Make sure you maintain a positive atmosphere as you study and when you retake the exam. Keep telling yourself that you can pass.

# ⇨ Conclusion

This chapter provides you with information about the three major aspects of taking a test: getting ready, taking it, and recovering from failure. The way that you approach these three areas can greatly affect the final outcome of your certification efforts.

We also looked at what you need to do to register for your exam. This is a fairly easy procedure, but you need to do some advance planning. Make sure you give yourself every advantage possible by taking the exam when you are best prepared to pass it.

# 5

# Finishing the paperwork

**T**HE job is never finished until the paperwork is done. This is a truism for Novell certification as well. Even if you finish all the required tests and training, you can still fumble around for several weeks, finishing all the paperwork, unless you take matters into your own hands.

Normally, Novell downloads your test scores from the testing center automatically. When you complete all the requirements for your certification, Novell automatically sends you the required paperwork.

However, everything doesn't always go as planned. You need to call Novell to make sure that nothing gets lost or overlooked—to maintain a line of communication between yourself and Novell to make sure your certification gets issued promptly.

This chapter provides you step-by-step instructions on filling out the paperwork and getting all the required documentation together. It also identifies the departments you need to talk with and tells where you need to send the paperwork. Finally, it tells you what kind of paperwork you should get back from Novell and how long it usually takes to receive it.

# Starting the paperwork

It is very important that you begin the paperwork process by getting organized. Make sure you can find the items you need to talk with Novell by putting them in one place. You might even want to create one folder for each course you attend, to keep notes, certificate, and test results for that course together. Whatever techniques you use, make sure you keep good records of all the certification items that Novell requires. You want to make it as easy as possible to find this information if you need it during a conversation with a Novell representative.

You will also want to make a list of the paperwork required for your certification (see Chapter 1). Make sure you keep this information in your folders as well. If you made a mistake in what you thought you required for certification, then you will want some basis to discuss the mistake with Novell. This might help them improve the amount and the quality of information they provide to other candidates in the future. It might also grant you some leeway on getting the required exams taken, or other certification requirements finished.

# ⇨ How long is too long?

The problem you face now is figuring out when to panic if you don't receive word from Novell regarding your certification. It is always a good idea to take a proactive approach. Novell downloads the data from the testing center about once a week. They compare the information they receive to their current database. If someone passes a test, they add it to their existing record. If Novell can't find your name on its lists, then it adds you to the database as a new applicant. People who complete all their requirements get issued a certificate. A computer performs all these database functions automatically, making the process nearly foolproof. There is little chance that your examination scores will get lost.

Based on this information, you will want to call Novell about 10 working days after you take your exam to make sure they received the results. Calling Novell ensures you will receive your certificate on time, and that your separate records (i.e., yours and theirs) are in synch. It also reduces the last minute rush you'll experience if you wait until you complete all the requirement to call Novell. And, if any mishap occurs, you can take care of it right away.

Then, once you complete all your requirements, call Novell again. Make sure you wait the requisite 10 working days after you complete your last requirement. Check to see that they received everything. Then ask your Novell representative how long it will take to receive your certification. His or her answer will tell you how long to wait for your certificate to arrive. Always allow a few days after the deadline before you call Novell again, to compensate for slow deliveries, especially during the holiday season.

# Maintaining a log of the paperwork

Keeping records is an important part of the certification process, though maintaining these paperwork logs might seem like a lot of fuss for nothing until something gets lost. Chances are good that you won't have any problems, but if you do, the time spent creating these logs will turn out to be invaluable.

Make sure you cover all the contingencies by keeping a record of what you do, when you do it, and how you do it. That way you won't have to rely on your memory if something goes wrong and you have to figure out what happened. You also want to maintain good contact with the Novell CNA/CNE/CNI administration department without making a nuisance of yourself. Maintaining these logs will help you maintain regular contact without calling too often. Remember, you are the one interested in certification. The Novell representative is only there to help you achieve your goal.

# Using the paperwork log

The time might arrive when you need to provide Novell with proof that you passed your certification exams. Because proof of completion is your responsibility, it really helps to keep a complete log of every certification requirement you complete, and when you sent proof of each completion to Novell. You will also want to make notes on what method you used to send the certification material. For example, did you fax the material or send it via overnight mail. (If you completed the requirement and simply relied on Novell to download the information from the testing center, make sure you record this information as well on the appropriate Chapter 1 form. The forms in this chapter are for emergency use only.)

Figure 5-1 provides an emergency log you could use for the CNA certification. Figures 5-2 through 5-4 provide the same logs for the CNE, ECNE, and CNI certifications. Use these logs to record any correspondence with Novell. For example, if Novell loses your paperwork, you would want to use these forms to record the time, date, and method you used to send replacement copies.

Name: _____

Figure 5-1

Date started: _____ Date completed: _____

| Requirement | Course number | Date sent | Method of mailing | Register number | Date received |
|---|---|---|---|---|---|
| Submit test results | _____ | _____ | _____ | _____ | _____ |

*CNA paperwork log*

Name: _____

Figure 5-2

Date started: _____ Date completed: _____

| Requirement | Course number | Date sent | Method of mailing | Register number | Date received |
|---|---|---|---|---|---|
| DOS/Microcomputer Concepts | _____ | _____ | _____ | _____ | _____ |
| NetWare Service and Support | _____ | _____ | _____ | _____ | _____ |
| NetWorking Technologies | _____ | _____ | _____ | _____ | _____ |
| System Manager | _____ | _____ | _____ | _____ | _____ |
| Advanced System Manager | _____ | _____ | _____ | _____ | _____ |
| Elective Credit 1 | _____ | _____ | _____ | _____ | _____ |
| Elective Credit 2 | _____ | _____ | _____ | _____ | _____ |
| Elective Credit 3 | _____ | _____ | _____ | _____ | _____ |
| Elective Credit 4 | _____ | _____ | _____ | _____ | _____ |
| Elective Credit 5 | _____ | _____ | _____ | _____ | _____ |

*CNE paperwork log*

Figure 5-3

Name: _____

Date started: _____ Date completed: _____

| Requirement | Course number | Date sent | Method of mailing | Register number | Date received |
|---|---|---|---|---|---|
| System Manager | _____ | _____ | _____ | _____ | _____ |
| Advanced System Manager | _____ | _____ | _____ | _____ | _____ |
| Elective Credit 1 | _____ | _____ | _____ | _____ | _____ |
| Elective Credit 2 | _____ | _____ | _____ | _____ | _____ |
| Elective Credit 3 | _____ | _____ | _____ | _____ | _____ |
| Elective Credit 4 | _____ | _____ | _____ | _____ | _____ |
| Elective Credit 5 | _____ | _____ | _____ | _____ | _____ |
| Elective Credit 6 | _____ | _____ | _____ | _____ | _____ |
| Elective Credit 7 | _____ | _____ | _____ | _____ | _____ |

*ECNE paperwork log*

Figure 5-4

Name: _____

Date started: _____ Date completed: _____

| Requirement | Course number | Date sent | Method of mailing | Register number | Date received |
|---|---|---|---|---|---|
| DOS/Microcomputer Concepts | _____ | _____ | _____ | _____ | _____ |
| Product Information | _____ | _____ | _____ | _____ | _____ |
| NetWare 2.2 System Manager | _____ | _____ | _____ | _____ | _____ |
| NetWare 2.2 Advanced System Manager | _____ | _____ | _____ | _____ | _____ |
| NetWare 3.11 System Manager | _____ | _____ | _____ | _____ | _____ |

*CNI paperwork log*

| Requirement | Course number | Date sent | Method of mailing | Register number | Date received |
|---|---|---|---|---|---|
| NetWare 3.11 OS Features Review (Optional) | _____ | _____ | _____ | _____ | _____ |
| NetWare 3.11 to 4.0 Update (Optional) | _____ | _____ | _____ | _____ | _____ |
| NetWare 4.0 System Administration (Optional) | _____ | _____ | _____ | _____ | _____ |
| NetWare Service and Support (category II only) | _____ | _____ | _____ | _____ | _____ |
| Networking Technologies (category II only) | _____ | _____ | _____ | _____ | _____ |
| NetWare 3.11 Advanced System Manager (category II only) | _____ | _____ | _____ | _____ | _____ |
| NetWare 4.0 Advanced Administration (category II only) | _____ | _____ | _____ | _____ | _____ |
| NetWare 4.0 Installation Workshop (category II only) | _____ | _____ | _____ | _____ | _____ |
| Specialty Course 1 | _____ | _____ | _____ | _____ | _____ |
| Specialty Course 2 | _____ | _____ | _____ | _____ | _____ |
| Specialty Course 3 | _____ | _____ | _____ | _____ | _____ |
| Specialty Course 4 | _____ | _____ | _____ | _____ | _____ |
| Specialty Course 5 | _____ | _____ | _____ | _____ | _____ |

*continued*

As you can see, each of the forms is for one of the certifications. Using this type of form helps you verify that you not only sent everything that Novell needed, but that you will know when and how you sent it as well. The first few fields of the form contain personal information, such as your name, the date you started the certification process, and the date you finished it. The table contains a list of the requirements you must pass to get the certification. Some of the information needed to fill in the blanks will come from the worksheets you completed in the previous chapters.

Notice that the course information is blank. This allows you to tailor the form to your specific needs. The course numbers you place in these blanks reflect your operating system specialty. The other fields in this form contain the date you sent proof of completing the requirement to Novell, the method used to mail the package, the registered mail number (you never want to send this information via regular mail), and the date Novell received it. You might even want to include the name of the person who verified that Novell did receive the package. (This information also appears in the telephone log described in the next paragraph.)

One good alternative to using the mail service is faxing your information to Novell. You might want to consider this alternative whenever possible. It is much faster than using the mail, and you can call Novell immediately after you send it to make sure they received it. Make sure you call and verify that you have the correct fax number, and tell them that you plan to send the information immediately. Once you send the information to Novell, verify that someone at the other end of the fax line received the material in good condition. If they did not, resend it right away.

## ⇨ Using the phone log

You should consider maintaining at least one other log. This is a record of your telephone conversations with people at Novell. Make sure you record when you call, whom you talked to, and a few notes about what transpired. Figure 5-5 provides a sample telephone log.

Date: _____ Time: _____ Contact person: _____    Figure 5-5

Phone number: _____ Ext.: _____

Topic: _____

Notes: _____

_____

_____

Problem: _____

_____

Resolution: _____

_____

_____

Date: _____ Time: _____ Contact person: _____

Phone number: _____ Ext.: _____

Topic: _____

Notes: _____

_____

_____

Problem: _____

_____

Resolution: _____

_____

_____

*Certification telephone log*

This log contains enough space for two entries per page. You might want to make a few copies of this sheet. However, maintaining the log on your computer might be more efficient, and will allow you to scan the records quickly during a telephone conversation. It also helps you ensure that no information gets overlooked while you talk with the Novell representative. Some database managers, such as AskSam or Folio Views, will allow you to enter this type of freeform information quickly. When you need to search for a particular topic, these database managers will look for phrases or whatever else you can remember about the conversation.

Notice that the telephone log contains space for the date, time, and contact person's name. The Notes field allows you to maintain a record of what each party said during the conversation. Reserve this section for conversation of a general nature. Be specific when taking notes. The more information you can include, the better your chances of resolving any difficulties. Make sure that you record times, dates, phone numbers, and any other names mentioned. If any commitments were made by either party, make note of them as well. Before you finish your conversation, summarize it from your notes before hanging up. This will help to prevent any miscommunications.

If you called about a problem, make sure you record it in the Problem field of the form. Use descriptive terms for this field. Don't write something like "Lost package in the mail." Provide exact details by writing, "Lost copy of the Advanced System Manager exam results in the mail." In addition to this information, you might want to record the registration number (if you sent it registered mail) and other important facts. If the field does not provide enough room, make a note about where you can find the information and record it at length elsewhere.

Record the resolution that you and the Novell representative talk about in the Resolution field. Again, document as much of the conversation as possible, immediately afterward. If you wait very long you might forget something. You can use the contents of the Resolution field to help make a To Do list later. Creating a To Do list ensures that you won't forget to follow through on your certification requirements. It also helps you remember when you need to call Novell to recheck the results of a problem resolution.

# Filling out the paperwork

There are two sets of required paperwork. The standard set applies to anyone who wants to obtain any of the certificates. The CNI set applies only to people who want to become CNIs. The following paragraphs explain these requirements in detail.

# Standard paperwork requirements

The paperwork required for certification by Novell includes the test scores, a release form, and a picture ID request. (Remember, you are responsible for maintaining a copy of your test scores.) As you complete and pass each test, the Drake Testing Center sends a copy of your test scores to Novell. CNE administration then enters that information into a database. If you are just starting the certification process, Novell adds your name and records to the database. As you take each test, Novell will add that information to your record. Once you complete all the exams, Novell will automatically register your certification. This applies to all the certification goals: CNA, CNE, MCNE, and ECNE.

The paperwork for the picture ID give you the specifications for the photograph. The picture ID is proof of your certification and is used as such by clients and employers. In most cases you can get this picture taken at any studio that specializes in passport or visa photographs. While color pictures are nice, Novell does not require one. Black-and-white photographs work fine. Just make sure that you provide Novell with the best picture you get. The photo studio normally takes four pictures, unless you request more. You might also want to dress in your normal work clothes and wear anything you normally wear on the job, such as glasses. This provides the client with a better idea of what you honestly look like when you present your certification card. It also makes it more difficult for someone else to use your ID.

# CNI paperwork requirements

The paperwork required for the CNI is about the same as for the other certifications. The only real difference is the initial application, and the additional requirement to send Novell copies of your course certificates. Remember that to become a CNI you must attend each of the classes that Novell certifies you to teach. After completing the courses, call the CNI administration department and tell them that you completed all your courses. They will then ask you to send them a copy of the course certification for each class. This can be faxed or mailed; you should also include a cover page with your name, address, phone number and why you are sending the certificate copies. Never send the original certificate; always send a copy. After you complete this step you are ready to take the CNI competency exams.

Once you complete the competency exams you will need to attend the Train The Trainer (TTT) classes. You must call Novell to register for the classes; at that point you will want to make sure that all test scores and passing dates are on your paperwork log form. After registering you for the TTT classes, Novell will send you a confirmation letter with the class dates, times, location, lodging information, and directions. Keep this information in you paperwork folder until the date of the class.

On the first day you attend, make sure you have the confirmation letter in case you have any problems or mix-ups. After completing the TTT course, you will want to retain this letter with your other paperwork for any future reference. Upon completion of the TTT class, Novell will send you a letter stating whether you passed the class. You will want to retain this letter with your other documents as well.

If you were successful in completing the TTT you will be eligible to teach the appropriate classes. At the end of each subsequent year Novell, will send you a recertification invoice. Novell applies the fee toward updating your manuals and provides you with the education bulletins and *Application Notes*. Again you will want to retain a copy of this invoice with your records.

# ⇨ Checking on the paperwork

Even though Novell will automatically register your certification, it is your responsibility to follow up. You can never take too many precautions; after all, you invested many hours and dollars to get this far. The last thing you want now is to have lost or misplaced paperwork hold up your certification or, worse yet, cause you to retake a test. After completing your last test, give Novell about seven to ten working days to process the paperwork. After that time passes, call the CNE administration to check on the status of your certification. The people in the CNE administration department will be very courteous and helpful when you call. Chances are very good that Novell will have processed your certification, and it might be on its way to you already. If Novell has not processed the paperwork yet, then you will be able to inform them of your standings and they can get the process moving.

Make sure you're armed with all the information you need, to talk intelligently with the Novell representative, before you call. This includes your logs and the actual documentation. The more information you can give the Novell representative, the faster and more accurately Novell can take care of your paperwork.

When you call Novell CNA/CNE/CNI administration, make sure you have a list of important telephone numbers as well. For example, if you work for a company, make sure you have a fax number that Novell can use to send you any required information, if necessary.

# ⇨ Victory—getting your certificate

The day of victory is the day your certificate finally arrives in the mail. Your certificate will arrive in your welcome aboard kit from Novell. There is nothing like the sense of accomplishment you will feel when you finally get to see the certificate you worked so hard to earn.

Now, spend a little time with your new credentials. Make sure Novell filled-in your name and other important information correctly. You might want to write down some of the vital information, such as your CNA/CNE/ECNE/CNI number as well. You can provide this number to your clients, employer, or potential employers for verification.

The welcome aboard kit contains many other items besides a certification certificate. These include your *Network Support Encyclopedia* (covered in Chapter 7) and some other paperwork. This paperwork includes a release form granting Novell permission to publish your name in the CNE section of *Netwire*. Another form instructs you to send a passport-style photo of yourself to Novell. The photograph is placed on your ID badge and then sent back to you. Once you receive your ID badge, display it to your customers or employers as proof of certification. Chapter 6 tells you how to use your new badge when you want to work for someone else. Chapter 8 will cover the use and purpose of the badge when you use it as a consultant.

You will also want to have your certification logo put on any brochures or sales literature. On the other hand, if you aren't a consultant and aren't in a retail business for yourself, you might want to put your logo somewhere on your resume. This might attract the attention of a future employer. You might also want to make some photo copies of the certificate and include it at the end of your resume.

Whatever situation you find yourself in, make sure you let everyone with whom you shared your dreams of certification know that you finally achieved your goal. After all, they supported you throughout the courses, long hours of studying, and the testing process. Also, frame your certificate and display it. Many companies and resellers will use your certification to add credibility to their organization. This is an important way to make your certification work for you.

# Conclusion

This chapter helped you process the paperwork required to get your certification. It began with a few simple ideas on ways to get the paperwork started and includes some pointers on making sure that Novell actually receives it. We also provided a few tips on ensuring you have all the required paperwork together before you mailed the package.

The next section of the chapter looked at some of the paperwork you need to maintain. It's important to maintain a log of the work you submit to Novell. This way you will have a simple list to refer to when you call Novell to check on the status of your certification. You can provide dates on which you shipped things to Novell, and tell them what shipping method you used. This might help you immensely if any items get lost.

We also looked at the actual process of filling out the paperwork. As with any other form, you must do it correctly to get correct results.

Finally, we looked at communication between you and Novell. It's important to verify that Novell has received all the paperwork you sent for their approval. You need to maintain communication to make it easy for someone to contact you regarding your certification.

The last section of this chapter deals with actually receiving your certification. After all the testing and paperwork, it's nice to see that certificate hanging on the wall. A Novell certification is more than just a piece of paper; it's verification of your ability to administrate or install networks. It tells the world that you have gained the level of knowledge required to make their network a joy to use.

# 6

# Using your certification to your advantage

# CHAPTER 6

**H**AVE you ever seen someone, who had all the advantages, lose out to someone else because they didn't know how to use what they had? It happens all the time in the movies. We find ourselves cheering for the underdog as he or she overcomes the vast resources of some villain to win out in the end. Of course, the movies don't truly reflect real life. In real life, the consequences of not using an advantage you might earn can be downright devastating. Imagine losing a job you really wanted to someone less qualified, simply because you didn't market your skills properly. Gaining access to a skill is only the first step in using it to enhance your career. You must learn to use your skills to your advantage in the marketplace.

This chapter focuses on the individual working for someone else. The trick to gaining the full benefit from your certification comes from marketing your new skills to a potential employer. This chapter helps you understand what you need to do to use the certification you acquire, to your benefit. We cover a number of topics, from advancing in your current company to getting a new (and perhaps better) job based on that training. (On the other hand, if you are a consultant, see Chapter 8 for specific information on how to use your Novell certification to best advantage in the marketplace.)

We cover two main methods of enhancing your career in this chapter. Either method will help you gain the full benefit from your certification, but use entirely different approaches. Section one covers the possibility of advancing within your own company. Many people are very happy with their job. If you fall into this category, there is absolutely no reason to move to a new company.

However, there is another group of people who take a job only for the short term, until they can get something better. In fact, some employers hire people knowing that they don't intend to stay. Moving from one company to another can help you gain the recognition you need, in addition (perhaps) to improving your benefits. If you want to make a change from your current company, it pays to follow the two-step plan outlined in section two of this chapter. The first step is preparing your resume; the second step is making the best possible impression during an interview.

We also spend some time talking about getting paid for what you do for the company. This is a big problem for some people. They get a brand new title and added responsibility, but very little recognition from the boss in the form of pay. Of course, it is always nice to be recognized for your contribution, and a change in title can help you find a better job later, but recognition alone does little for you now. You have to make sure that the time you spend getting your certification pays some dividend today. This third section of the chapter shows you how to get appropriate commitments from management before you even start the certification process.

# Advancing within your current company

There are lots of ways to advance within your current company. Your boss might get promoted or leave. If you demonstrate the abilities required to take over that position, your company might promote you.

Another method of advancing is to create your own position. Your company might want to get rid of an old method of doing something and replace it with a newer, more efficient method. If you provide your company enough reason to make the change, you might find yourself in charge of the group responsible for implementing it. After the change is made, you might find yourself in an entirely new position as head of the group.

Some companies will simply change your job title to match the work that you're doing. In some cases this includes additional pay or other benefits. Whatever method you choose to follow, you need to create an advancement plan. Don't wait for opportunity to knock because it seldom does. Create your own opportunities within the workplace.

The fact that your company chose to pay for your certification shows that there should be an advancement opportunity waiting for you when you return. Even if your company already has a network in place, there has to be some reason for them to train you. Therefore, your first task in getting a promotion or a new position is to know why you are getting the training. Finding out what plans your company already has might help you prepare. Use this knowledge as the basis for your advancement plan.

Of course this is only the beginning. You might have to do a lot of detective work before you work out a detailed advancement plan. Management often treats new network installations or the departure of a manager as closely guarded secrets. The following tips should help you start to formulate some advancement goals and strategies:

> **If your company already has a network, try to find out if anyone from that section is leaving the company.** You might fill their position if you demonstrate the proper skills to the company. Make sure you concentrate on ways of enhancing these skills. If your company doesn't have a network in place, you can be sure they will. The company would not train you for a position that will not exist. Try to become part of the planning process for the new network. Not only will the information you gain help you prepare for the new position, but it will show the company you have the dedication required for the position. Also, within some companies that provide training to their own employees, a CNE and a CNA might work together on a large network. The CNA might provide training services to free the CNE for the more technical network needs. If either one plans to leave, make sure your training will prepare you to take over the departing person's position. This would include training on all the applications they currently support. If your company does not currently have a training program in place, you might become the founding member of such a group.

> **Check to see if your company is increasing the size of the network or installing a new network.** If it is installing a new network, you might be chosen to maintain it. If it is expanding a network you might at least be in line for a title change.

> **Find out if your company is creating a new workgroup.** Some companies create splinter organizations when they want to introduce a new product, or when the current configuration becomes too unwieldy. If there are no plans to expand the current network, your company might want to create such a

splinter group. You might become the network administrator for the new workgroup.

➤ **See if your company recently won a large contract.** A company might create a small workgroup to deal with a specific contract. If so, your new position might last only through the term of the contract, but if you do a good job the company might make this new position permanent.

Unfortunately, there are also many problem situations in which you might find that your certification is more of a handicap than an asset. Here are some of the problems you might experience, together with strategies for dealing with them:

➤ In some cases a company will help you get your certification and promise you the sun, the moon, and the stars. But as soon as you get back to work you might find that, instead of a promotion, you simply got more work instead. Your company might feel perfectly justified in asking you to perform all your previous tasks, in addition to the new network administration tasks. Don't let this happen. If your company promises you anything to get your new certification, make sure you get the promises in writing. Verbal promises last only as long as you can hear the words.

➤ Your company might ask you to sign a contract promising to work for them a specific amount of time after you receive your certification. They might also ask you to sign a document promising to pay back the cost of certification if you fail to obtain it. Make sure you get some concessions in exchange for these guarantees. Never give your company something for nothing. Also, you might note that, in many states, it is illegal to hold you to such a contract or make you pay the employer back for education.

➤ You might find that the level of cooperation drops drastically once you complete a network installation. Without the proper tools and support, you will never maintain the network in peak operating condition. Make sure you talk to the company about these problems in advance. Don't make your new certification a source of problems.

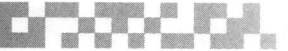

# Three ways to advance

Now that you have some ideas about the positive and negative aspects of getting a certification you can formulate a specific advancement plan. As the previous paragraphs showed, there are at least three different ways of getting a promotion within a company. The following paragraphs examine these three methods of advancing within your company. Of course, there are probably many other ways that you could pursue advancement. These methods simply provide ideas that you can use to create your own advancement plan.

## ✳ Advancement through promotion

Many people start at a particular company and stay there for their entire working career. They wait for the person ahead of them to either get a promotion or leave the company. As new positions open, these people try to fill them before someone else does. This is a perfectly good way to advance your career. Still, there are several different ways by which you can enhance your chances of getting each new position, based on your new certification and the longevity of your relationship with the company:

➢ **You can demonstrate an extensive knowledge of the company's ways of doing things.** This translates into a network administrator who is familiar with company policies. It means that you can do the job faster and more efficiently than someone hired from the outside.

➢ **Longevity also translates into a knowledge of the people in the company.** You probably have a better idea of who is working at the company, how long they have been there, what their job responsibilities are, and what you can do to help them. All this knowledge means that you will spend less time getting the network set up and maintaining it. It also means that you will probably make fewer mistakes.

➢ **That you have held several positions in the same company means that you can better identify with problem areas within the company.** You will have a greater understanding of why certain policies are in place, and what each person needs to complete their work, because of your hands-on experience.

> ➤ **The Novell certification you receive opens new doors of responsibility.** Your past job performance can help you get an advancement, based on cumulative proof that you can handle the added responsibility. If everyone in the company knows from experience that you are capable of doing the job, management will be much more willing to give it to you.

As you can see, ways of getting a promotion once a door of opportunity opens are there. Of course, simply because the door opens does not mean that management will put you in the new position. You must earn, which means you need to do other things as well. For one thing, you can't advance if you don't know where all the windows of opportunity exist. Figure 6-1 shows a typical organizational chart.

If you are Mary on the chart, the first thing you might think is that your next promotion opportunity is limited to Harvey's job. But in reality there are many other windows of opportunity waiting for you. For example, as you help administer the network you might find out about the tasks performed by Amy Hart or William Poe. You might even set your sights higher, by trying for the position held by Sedrick Barlow. Of course, your ultimate goal might include the vice-president's job. The important thing is to learn the organization of your company and look for opportunities to advance yourself, starting with a copy of your company's organizational chart, even if you have to make one of your own.

So how does this relate to your certification? Remember, there are many ways to use your certification as a key to future promotions. Don't limit your thinking to a single area, or one possible means of using it. You can use the information you obtain from administering the network to prove your worth in other areas of the company as well. Companies look for people who are willing to take charge; that show a real involvement in their work. They tend not to promote someone who simply does his basic work and shows no further initiative.

Figure 6-1

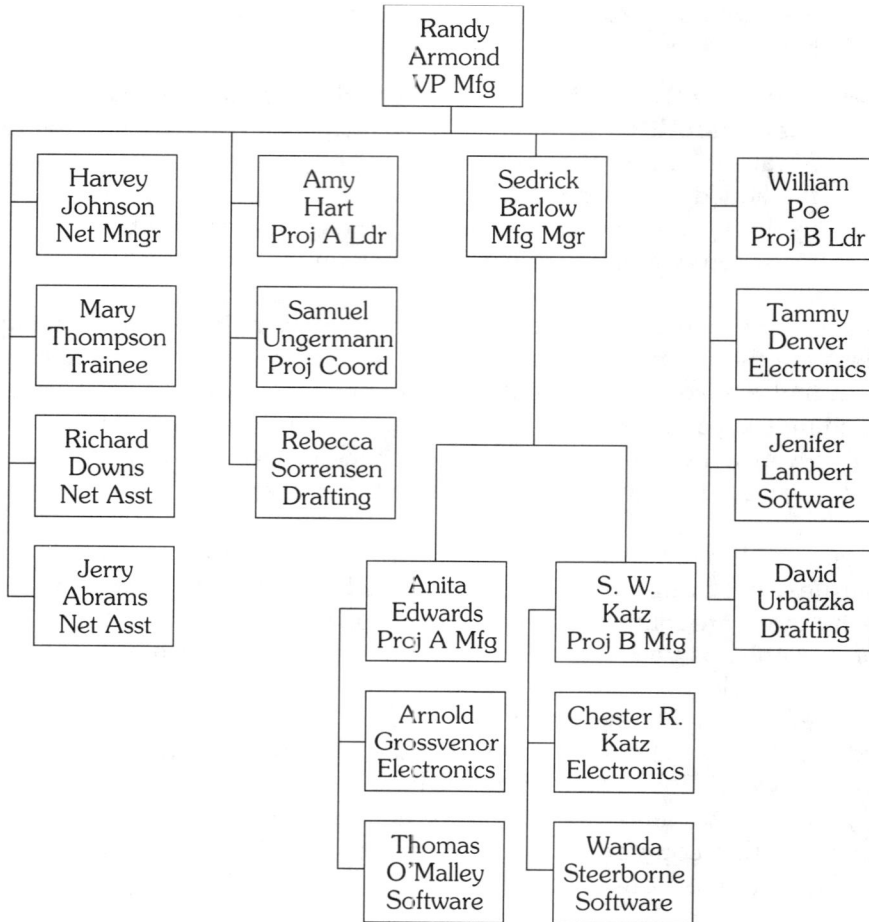

*Typical organizational chart*

Now it's time to combine everything you learned from the preceding paragraphs into a plan of attack. What we've discussed so far should provide you with all you need to know to fill out the advancement form in Fig. 6-2. It begins with a little self examination, by asking you to provide your current position and salary. This gives you a starting point; it shows where you are now. It also provides a reality check as you set your goals. Trying to reach president of the company in one step is probably not very reasonable, but moving to a management position from a technician's job might be a little more obtainable.

**Advancement Through Promotion Worksheet**                    Figure 6-2

Date: _____ Current job title: _____

Current pay rate: _____ Target pay rate: _____

1st Advancement goal: _____

Date of anticipation advance: _____

How will your networking experience help you attain your goal? _____

_____

_____

Experience needed to attain goal: _____

_____

Education needed to attain goal: _____

_____

2nd Advancement goal: _____

Date of anticipated advance: _____

How will your networking experience help you attain your goal? _____

_____

_____

Experience needed to attain goal: _____

_____

Education needed to attain goal: _____

_____

_____

*Advancement through promotion worksheet*

The next two sections of the form provide places for two goals. Here, list the positions you want to target as potential places for advancement. Make sure you pick realistic goals; also, picking at least two goals is an essential part of the process. To maximize your chances you must always look at more than one place for an advancement opportunity. Each goal area contains four sections.

**1** The first section asks you to define the goal itself. Make sure you include the title, pay, and any additional responsibility you would like to have as part of the advancement.

**2** Second, relate your networking experience to the position you want to attain. This serves as a reality check. It asks you to determine how you can use the experience you gain now to help in later promotions.

**3** Third, decide what other experience you need to gain to get to the next position. This is an important consideration, because it will allow you to grab opportunities to gain the experience you need. For example, when the boss asks for volunteers for a project you might get an opportunity to grab some experience.

**4** Finally, the fourth section asks you to determine what educational requirements the new position will have. Management is interested in both book knowledge and experience. Don't let someone fresh from college take your position from you. Make sure you prepare in both areas.

One final piece of advice for anyone who wants to advance in his or her current company. You need to grab opportunities because they seldom knock very loud. Always think about the best possibilities; don't stoop to reactive attempts at advancement. The proactive approach always yields some result; the reactive approach always yields stagnation. Of course, you need to think about the consequences of your plan before you present it. A proactive approach can have negative as well as positive results. Make sure you find opportunities that will yield positive results.

## ✳ **Advancing by creating a new position**

Some people still possess the frontier spirit. They go where no one else will go, and do the things that no one else ever thought about doing. Inventors and scientists commonly fall into this category. However, this same set of skills can work to your benefit in the corporate environment as well. Many people have made fortunes by inventing their own position and then showing management that the company couldn't survive without it. This is where the network administrator is today, at the forefront of technology with a real opportunity to break new ground and create a new position.

Of course, the network administrator doesn't always start with many benefits or recognition. Sometimes a network administrator starts as a grunt laborer, reporting to someone who doesn't appear to understand what the company needs and has no desire to learn. Many CNEs end up working as computer repair personnel instead of spending much time with the network.

If this happens to you, turn the situation around. Look at it as an opportunity to create a new position. Management is almost always interested in hearing about ways to improve work flow, but picking the optimum time (when they are really looking for ways to streamline the current setup) usually produces the best results.

Of course, the payment for failure to convince management of the benefits of the new position could be dismissal, though such a firing would probably be illegal. At the very least, your old boss might never trust you again, so this method of advancement is not without risks. But the risks can be worthwhile to someone prepared to take advantage of the results. Creating your own position means that you control how your job shapes up. It also means that your chances of being promoted to upper management are much better. If you prove that you are an idea person, someone capable of thinking on his own, management might sit up and take notice.

So how do you start planning for a new position? You must create a proposal that demonstrates the company needs the new position you want to create. More than that, you must demonstrate that you are the best candidate for the position. Just because you prove the company needs a new position doesn't mean that you'll get it. You must prove that you are the only person for the job, both through qualifications and in repayment to the company. Figure 6-3 shows a sample of what you can do to start the planning process.

Several interesting features are incorporated into this form. The first section asks you for a starting and ending date to accomplish your goal. Make sure you enter both dates, to give yourself a target. Here, procrastination is the worst trap you can fall into. However, don't be afraid to change the ending date if necessary; you'll want to prepare the most thorough presentation possible. Expect for the unexpected and remain flexible throughout the presentation. At the same time,

Figure 6-3

**New Position Worksheet**

Current date: _____ Planned presentation date: _____

New position title: _____

Reason the new position is important: _____

_____

_____

_____

_____

Cost of creating the position: _____

Potential cost benefit: _____ Payback time: _____

Intangible benefits: _____

_____

_____

Reasons you should take the new position: _____

_____

_____

_____

❑ Cost analysis                    ❑ Full presentation

❑ Time analysis                    ❑ Handouts

❑ Benefits analysis                ❑ Graphs and charts

❑ Requirements for the position    ❑ Presentation scheduled

*A sample plan for creating your own position*

don't put your presentation on hold while you attempt to anticipate every potential question in advance.

The next section of Fig. 6-3 talks about the position itself. It is very important to define a potential title by name, to explain the position is important, to conceptualize any potential costs and problems associated with creating the position, and to provide management with a projected payback period for their investment. Make sure you list both tangible and intangible benefits. Ideally, you will create a position that provides a payback in both areas. This does not mean that management will never consider a new position that provides only intangible benefits. However, you will likely find your job on the chopping block at the first sign of economic troubles if you take this approach. It is always better to show the company that you can make some money for them.

The third section states why you are the person to fill this position. You must write your reasons down and back them up with good arguments. Make sure you demonstrate beyond a shadow of a doubt that you are the right person. Of course, it helps that you are the one defining the new position. You can modify the job definition to make yourself the only person who can fill it, which actually provides another reality check. Once you completely define the job and your reason for filling it, make sure it still makes sense. Otherwise, you might find that management won't even talk to you about it. Don't try to create a position whose sole purpose is a promotion for you.

The final area is a checklist of items to complete before you make your presentation. This worksheet is for your benefit; the other items provide the information to management in an easy-to-understand manner. If you can't express your ideas to management, there is no reason to believe they will create the new position for you.

Now let's look at some of those additional pieces of information on the form.

➤ The first item is a cost analysis. You will want to create a full cost analysis showing exactly what it will cost the company to create the new position you propose. At the very least it will cost the company a pay raise (assuming you are not going through all this work for the sheer gratification of doing the work). Make sure you look for hidden costs as well. Consider items such as additional staff and equipment. Make sure you show how the company can amortize their investment over a period of time. Any friends you gain in accounting can probably help you in this area.

➤ Your next objective is to create a time analysis. As a minimum you need to create a milestone chart showing the goals you expect to meet by specific dates. Some of the more advanced project management programs could help you here. You might find a computer with one of these programs in the engineering or manufacturing areas of your company. Ask the supervisor if

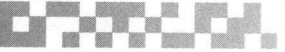

you can use the program, even if you have to come in after working hours to do it. Of course, you could use a standard drawing program to create the charts you need, but the project management software will help you look for potential scheduling conflicts. The project management software will also make it easy to incorporate changes in your plan.

The benefits analysis is one of the most important parts of your presentation. Management tends to focus on the negative element of any change, especially the costs of making it and maintaining it afterward. You need to focus their attention on the positive elements of what they will obtain from the change. Make sure you look at the company's interests when you write the list of benefits, not the elements that might be attractive only to you. For example, while you might find the increased responsibility interesting, management won't. However, they should find increased revenues or other company-related benefits interesting. One common way to make a case is to show that the new position will make the company more efficient. A more efficient operation usually means lower operating costs and higher income.

➤ Provide management with a complete listing of all the requirements for the position. This accomplishes two purposes. First, it defines the position and shows management that you took the time to think your idea through. It also helps you maintain your position later. One of the reasons that some new position ideas fail is that they are incompletely defined at the very start. This leaves the door for interpretation open. Second, you can use the requirements as part of your arguments later. For example, you can use the requirements to show management that you are the only person who can perform the job adequately. Make all the pieces of your presentation fit together into a well-coordinated whole.

➤ Create a full presentation for management. Include slides, charts, graphs, handouts, and anything else you can think of to make the presentation interesting. Remember, you are trying to sell an idea that many people in management will resist. In this situation you are not starting with an open-minded audience; you have to open their minds to the potential benefits of the new position.

- Handouts really help keep people interested if you use them correctly, but you need to observe three simple rules during the presentation. First, have someone help you pass them out. Second, don't provide all your handouts at once. Pass them out as you need them; otherwise, you might lose your audience to the handouts that were supposed to keep them interested in you and your presentation. Third, refer to your handouts frequently during the presentation. Otherwise, management will wonder why you took the time to prepare them.
- Charts and graphs can be extremely important parts of your presentation. Studies show that people can absorb information in graphic form much better and faster than they can when it's in printed form. The printed material is abstract; the graphic form is a lot more concrete. Rather than burden management with a lot of tabular data, present it in graphic form and offer to allow them to see the tables later. Make sure you make the actual data readily available, but keep your presentation interesting by using graphics first.

➢ When you schedule your presentation, make sure you get a specific date from management. A common problem is that management will want to see your presentation "sometime soon." But "sometime soon" is awfully vague, and they may keep putting the presentation off until (they hope!) you forget about it. To get their approval you might need to tell them about some aspects of your idea. Get management as excited as you are about this new position. Just make sure you don't tell them everything; keep some surprises for the meeting itself.

➢ Schedule a conference room for the meeting and avoid presenting your idea in someone's office. Reduce the chances of political posturing by holding the meeting in a neutral setting. This helps alleviate the problem of having to answer questions from someone who asks them only to increase his or her political stature in the company. In addition, holding the meeting in a conference room reduces the risk of interruptions. Then get everything ready for the meeting well in advance. Don't wait until the last minute.

As you can see, creating a successful presentation is a challenge in many ways. You need to do a lot of preparation before you will be able to present your idea to management. Take the time to research your company thoroughly. Make sure you can tell management everything they will need to know about your idea. Show them that you did your homework, that you're interested enough in the company to find out about it. If possible, you might want to spend some time viewing presentations made by other people in your company as well. Notice the ideas and presentation methods that seem to attract the attention of key management personnel. Make sure you write these ideas down to use in your presentation as well.

Of course, there are several additional ways you can use your certification to help establish a new position for yourself.

1 For one thing, as a network administrator you will meet many of the people you need to influence. This personal contact can make the difference between getting the new position approved and looking for a new job. Make sure you take the personalities of the individual members of management into account as you prepare your presentation.

2 You can also use your position to obtain information about the company and its operations. As network administrator you will have access to many areas of the company that many other people might not see. You will get a broad overview of all the jobs that people in the company perform. Your position will expose you to all the products that the company makes and will give you inside information about how these products could improve. The possibilities for gaining knowledge are almost unlimited.

3 Finally, your position as network administrator will give you a unique view of both management and the employees. You can use this view to gain unique insights and present some of the employee needs from a management viewpoint during your presentation.

## ✳ Advancement & recognition through a title change

After all you went through to get your certification, you'll want management to recognize that achievement. One of the best ways is to provide management with a reason to change your title. You might still work for the same boss at the same pay, doing about the same work, but the title change will show that you have made some improvements in your qualifications. More important, it could make a big difference if you leave your current company. The title change could show a potential employer that you made some effort to get a promotion, even if it didn't result in a pay raise (which, of course, might not come right away but might be awarded at your next salary review).

So what do you do to get this title change? First, you could simply schedule a meeting with your boss and ask for it. Your boss might then help you get the title change with no additional effort; after all, your title change could reflect favorably on your boss. It might show that he is doing his job by helping his employees make greater contributions to the company as a whole. You might even want to remind your boss of this—it never hurts to show the boss that you have his welfare in mind, too.

If this approach doesn't work, put your request in writing. Provide some reasons why the title change is so important. It will also provide your boss with something to pass up to his or her superior. The reason your boss didn't provide the title change could involve a lack of authority to do so. The following paragraphs provide some ideas on arguments you can use to get a title change:

➢ Because your job tasks have changed since you got your Novell certification, why not a title change to go along with it? Changes in job tasks should show up in job titles as well. An MCNE will want to pursue this reasoning, because MCNE certification usually involves some type of change to a managerial-level job. You could even argue that the job title change will help show that the company got value for the money it invested in your training.

➢ A new job title will help distinguish between the tasks you perform and those performed by other employees with the same title you currently have. This is especially important for government contractors, because the government usually looks to see that they have enough personnel to do the job in a given category before granting the contract. MCNEs will want to point out that government representatives usually want to deal with someone in a management position. Of course, this could be

important when you deal with other companies as well, especially when it comes time to impress visiting dignitaries.

➤ The new job title is a lot less expensive than a raise. (Of course, you can always argue later that your new title entitles you to a pay raise.) CNAs will want to look at this option, because their certification usually entails additional responsibility rather than an entirely new job.

➤ The new job title could even add to the company's prestige by showing they have an up-to-date networking system specialist on the staff. You would need to add some arguments that would show whom this would affect. It might also help to show how this new job title could help the company gain new contracts.

➤ Providing you with a new job title could enhance the way management views your boss. It would show that he or she had a wider area of responsibility than before. This could appeal to the his or her vanity, which is perfectly legitimate. It pays to use whatever will work.

Of course, these are just a few of the arguments you could use to convince your boss to grant you a new job title. The important factor is that you deserve the new title. If your current title is administrative assistant, it hardly reflects your new position as a network administrator. Even if you perform this job on a part-time basis, your job title should reflect your change in status.

There are several ways that a job title change can help you in the future, even if it doesn't appear to help you today. First, if you do decide to go to another company, the title change will appear as a promotion. Second, it could help you get a larger salary in your current company. When you demonstrate an increased level of knowledge, many companies are willing to pay for that increased knowledge. The only problem is that upper management will never know that your status has changed unless you get it down on paper somewhere. The change in title is one of the most efficient methods of doing so.

There are a few certification-specific, title-change issues to consider as well. What happens if you are already a CNE and work as a network administrator? In some companies, that is all you will ever need. However, a large company might need more than one network administrator. You might end up as one of many CNEs on staff. So, where do you go from there?

The MCNE program allows people who work in larger companies to advance to higher positions. Rather than act as one of several network administrators in a large company, getting some additional education and the MCNE certification will allow you to become a supervisor. Look at other areas of your company. It takes more than political power and astute powers of observation to create or advance to a supervisor position. You have to prove you are the right person for the job. Other managers in your company probably got their position because they had college degrees and proved their ability to get the job done. You need to do the same thing. Having the right certification (i.e., physical evidence of your knowledge) and job experience are the keys to getting to the managerial level in many large companies. Once you get this additional level of training and recognition, it is absolutely essential that you get the title change to go with it. Otherwise, you will end up with an MCNE certification that didn't really help you advance your career.

The same holds true for a CNA. What happens when you no longer want to work as an administrative assistant? If you got a title change when you earned your CNA certification, it will be a lot easier to convince management to support you in your attempt to get a CNE certification. This is especially important for growing companies in which CNAs might meet their needs to begin with, but which might grow until they really need CNEs to manage their networks.

Once you get your CNE certification, it is very important to get a title change that shows you have obtained a higher level of knowledge. And, you will probably need to talk about a new position at this point, because it is unlikely you will perform any administrative tasks after getting your CNE certification.

Getting a title change might not seem very exciting. In fact, it might seem as if you accomplished nothing at all. Of course, nothing is further from the truth. A title change might not dramatically affect your career today, but it could help a great deal in the future. Even if you don't want to get into management in your current company, it is very important that you gain the recognition you deserve for getting your Novell certification.

# Getting paid for what you do

How much of an increase in pay you can expect from a promotion or a new position is always a touchy subject. There are no hard and fast rules; the policy in your company and the conditions of the local economy make things even less definable. However, you can do several things to figure out what kind of increase you should expect. Tailor the following tips to your specific situation:

> **Check around the company for clues.** Some people will tell you what raise they got when they went to a new position. However, some companies will fire employees for even talking about salaries, so this might not be an option.

> **Talk to someone at your local chamber of commerce.** They track all kinds of business statistics, including local rates of pay. They might even provide information specific to your position. On the other hand, if you can't get this information in your own town, try the nearest large city.

> **Look through a local business magazine.** Just about every large community has one, although you won't necessarily see it on your newsstand but rather in a hotel lobby or other public area. Many local business magazines discuss current trends in business for your area, and some (as with the chamber of commerce) might even have salary surveys available.

> **Read the business section of your local newspaper.** This will give you some economic information for your area. It might also contain news about your company, or other information you can use.

> **Listen to the radio.** I was surprised when a local radio station revealed that the average pay raise in my area was running at three percent. Few radio stations will provide you with everything you need to know, but many will provide you with some clues.

➤ **Talk to people in your local user group.** If you don't belong to a user group, then join one. These people work in your area! So find someone who performs the same work that you do, and talk to them. What could be easier? However, ask them how long they have worked in your specific area, and take this into consideration when you look for a promotion.

There are a few absolutes that you should expect when it comes to pay. For one thing, you will always receive a salary instead of an hourly rate when working as a network administrator. The reason you get a salary is simple: no manager or supervisor in his or her right mind will pay you for the extra hours required when working these types of jobs.

You absolutely will not get the same amount of pay as a consultant doing the same work. There are a few reasons for this. First, your company provides you with benefits that a consultant does not receive. Second, the consultant pays business taxes and other expenses out of the money he or she earns, which you do not need to consider.

However, you can use the local consultant's fee as a point of reference for your pay. In most cases an employee will earn 25 percent to 33 percent of the fee charged by a consultant in the same area. Call at least three consultants in your area, average their hourly rates, multiply by 25 percent, then multiply by 40 hours to get your new weekly pay (or by 2080 hours to get your annual pay, which you can then divide by 52 to get your weekly pay; note that multiplying by 160 does not give you an accurate monthly rate). The difference between rates reflects the pay raise you might reasonably expect. Remember, though, this is only an estimate and not a hard and fast reality.

# ⇨ Moving to a different company

Some people work at a company to gain experience and a specific level of education, then move to another company. Sometimes (though not always) you can advance a lot faster using this technique. Of course, you give up quite a bit to use this strategy. For example, many companies will not provide you with any kind of retirement unless you stay there for a specific number of years (anywhere from 10 to 20). Companies offer other benefits as well. For example, in some companies you share in the stock program after you work there for five years. If you move from company to company in pursuit of a better position, you might never meet this requirement.

Once you weigh the consequences of moving around and decide that you want to improve your position more than you want to gain these other benefits, you need to consider how to present yourself to a potential employer. This includes both a written and a verbal presentation. The written presentation is commonly called a resume, while the verbal presentation is called an interview. The following paragraphs show you how to leverage your Novell certification as part of both processes.

# ⇨ Getting your resume together

Any good book on business writing or communication will show you how to write a standard resume and cover letter. That isn't the purpose of this section. What you need to know is how to modify these stock presentations to emphasize your unique qualifications. Here are several ideas:

➢ If you are currently a network administrator, place your experience first on the resume. Make sure you include detailed information about your network-related jobs. Provide one or two sentence summaries of other jobs.

➢ If you recently passed your CNA, CNE, ECNE, or MCNE certification tests, place your education first to emphasize your certification. Don't be afraid to use bold type for this credential to make it stand out from any others you might have. Add your date of certification to show that you are current.

➢ ECNE and MCNE certification holders will want to emphasize their CNE level experience as well as their education. It is vital to show a potential employer that you did not move from one certification to the next without getting the proper experience at the CNE level first.

➤ Place a reference to your certification in the first sentence of the cover letter. Many managers don't read past this point unless you say something to pique their interest.

➤ Always add your logo to both your cover letter and your resume. This will make them stand out.

Figure 6-4 provides you with a sample cover letter, which uses a Novell certification label in the lower left corner. This helps to differentiate the letter from others. Notice the white space; the letter

Figure 6-4

John Mueller
2020 Twin Palms Street
River City, CA 92104-3703
(619)881-7732 Business
(619)881-8833 FAX

26 August, 1995

Mary Jones
Engineering Manager
The Industrial Place
3288 The Place Street
Somewhere, CA 92112

Dear Ms. Jones

I recently saw your advertisement for a CNE in the California Job Times. According to the ad, you need someone with a minimum of two years experience and proof of certification. As you can see from the attached resume, I can meet both qualifications. I worked two years at Jobber Industrial and three years at Technical Stuff, Inc. I can provide my certification papers to you on request. (There is a copy of the certification attached to the back of the resume.)

The important consideration for you is that both of my former employers produced about the same products as your company does. In addition, according to your annual report, the corporate structure of all three companies is similar. These similarities mean that you will spend less time training me to fill the position at your company. Hopefully, these qualifications will allow you to consider my application in preference to others who applied.

Sincerely,

**John Paul Mueller**

John Paul Mueller

NOVELL®

*Sample cover letter*

does not look cramped or difficult to read. Make your letter as inviting to read as possible. The letter also contains the names and addresses of both parties; this is for your benefit as well of that of your future employer. The first paragraph tells your future employer how you meet the qualifications set by the advertisement. It also tells him where you saw the advertisement. The second paragraph tells the employer why he should consider you before someone else. This is an important part of the cover letter. You have to gain the interest of the person reading the letter or they will never read your resume.

We also spent some time looking at the things you should do to modify a stock resume to emphasize your certification. Let's look at an example or two. Figure 6-5 shows an experience-based resume. Figure 6-6 shows an education-based resume. Notice that each one provides a different perspective on the same information. Be flexible in tailoring your resume to your target employer's needs.

Figure 6-5

# John Mueller
## 2020 Twin Palms Street
## River City, CA 92104
## Home Phone: (619) 775-2123

**EXPERIENCE:**

**Network Administrator, Technical Stuff, Inc. (July 1990–August 1993)**

In charge of two assistants at Technical Stuff, Inc. The combination ethernet and token ring LAN supports 150 users and 4 file servers. There are eight servers attached to the network as well. Most of the print servers had two printers attached, one HP Laserjet III and a high speed dot matrix. All maintenance scheduling went through my office. In addition, I supervised the installation of a new DBMS (database management system) on one of the file servers.

**Assistant Network Administrator, Jobber Industrial (January 1988–July 1990)**

Assist the LAN Administrator in maintaining the company LAN (local area network). The LAN supports 40 users and 3 file servers. There are four print servers attached to the network as well. Part of my LAN responsibilities include installing and maintaining Windows. I also performed much of the hardware maintenance.

*Sample experience-based resume*

**Sonar Technician, US Navy (July 1976–September 1987)**

Maintained computer controlled sonar and fire control equipment. This equipment ranged from tube based technology, to solid state discrete circuitry, to modern CMOS circuitry. Learned to operate and maintain every type of data storage device available today. Most equipment was hybrid digital and analog circuitry.

Designed and was paid for a design change to audio recording equipment. Change decreased recording reproduction time by a factor of four, reducing the per recording cost to the government for a training tape.

Operated sonar equipment which included acoustic signal analysis equipment. Supervised work center personnel. Wrote six part training course using tapes and training books.

**EDUCATION:**

Technical Diploma in Electrical Trade, Milwaukee Technical High School, June 1976

Various Military Electronic Equipment Maintenance Courses:
- Basic Electronics and Electricity
- Sonar Specific Advanced Electronics
- Acoustic Analysis Schooling
- Fire Control System Maintenance/Operation Schooling
- Computer Controlled Sonar Maintenance/Operation Schooling
- Other Peripheral Equipment Maintenance Schooling

Bachelors in Computer Science, National University, June 1986
Artificial Intelligence Programming Course, Cubic Corporation, October 1986
Certified Netware Engineer Courses, VITEK Corporation, April 1991

**COMPUTER LANGUAGES:**

- Pascal—IBM PC knowledge only
- BASIC—IBM PC and Perkin-Elmer mainframe experience (Includes various Windows 3.1 dialects like Access BASIC and Visual BASIC)
- Assembler—IBM PC (DOS, OS/2, and Windows NT environments), Macintosh, and various military computers
- dBase III (Clipper, Force, and FoxPro)—IBM PC
- Prolog—Learning stages, IBM PC knowledge only
- Machine Code (Hex)—IBM PC, Macintosh, and various military computers
- C—IBM PC (DOS, OS/2, and Windows NT environments)

**NOVELL.**

*continued*

Figure 6-6

## Robert Williams
### 9845 Harbor Road Suite 22
### Some Region, CA 92112
### (619)234-7890

**CERTIFICATIONS:**

1991  LanAlyzer Basic and Advanced for Ethernet
      Network Technologies
      Novell 3.11 Advanced System Manager

1990  Novell Certified Instructor (CNI) Category I & II:
      Novell Certified to teach 286 System Manager
      Update & Advance features
      386 OS/Features and Review
      386 System Supervisor
      Service & Support
      Novell Enhanced Support Training
      Introduction to Data Communications

1989  Novell Certified Engineer (CNE)

**EDUCATION:**

1989  Novell Authorized Education
      System Manager
      Update & Advanced Features
      Service & Support
      Diagnostics & Troubleshooting
      Introduction to Data Communications
      Novell Enhanced Support Training
      Novell 386 Training

1987  Mt. San Antonio College, Walnut, Ca.
      Construction Estimating
      Elements of Construction
      4.0 G.P.A.

1977  Citrus College, Azusa, Ca.
      Industrial Engineering Technology
      3.8 G.P.A.

**EXPERIENCE:**

**Very Impressive Systems, Hard Rock, Ca. (1989–Present)**

Novell Authorized Distributor, Novell Authorized Education Center, Distribution center for major brands of computer equipment.

*Sample education-based resume*

Novell Certified Instructor: Duties include: Education of Resellers and end users in the use of the Novell Operating System. The classes include 286 system mgr., Update & Advanced Features, 386 OS/Features and Review, 386 System Supervisor, Service & Support, Introduction to Data Communications, Novell Enhanced Support Training, Basic and Intermediate DOS, Hardware Basics.

Other Duties include: Operate and maintain the Education Facility in San Diego Ca.

### Great West Computers, Hard Rock, CA (1988–1989)

Novell Authorized Reseller, Novell Authorized Education Center, Network Installations, Technical Support.

**SERVICE AND SUPPORT TECHNICIAN:** Duties include: Technical Support for customers, Education of customers on the use of the Novell Operating System, Network sales.

NOVELL®

*continued*

The first resume uses a lot of white space and bold lettering to draw the reader's attention to particular areas. This helps the manager read the highlights of your resume quickly, then concentrate on any important areas. The resume is slightly longer than one page, but all the information relates to the position offered by the company. The author mentions network experience twice in the experience section, and once in the education section. There is a special computer languages section that draws the manager's attention to the unique qualifications of this candidate. The resume writer does a good job of relating the special qualification back to networking in the first paragraph of the resume. (Knowing computer languages is a good asset for network administrators who need to administer large database management systems.) The writer also spells out each acronym the first time it appears in the document. This is important.

The second resume looks somewhat the same as the first. It uses the same amount of white space and the same bold letter. However, this resume places education first. Notice that the certifications appear in a category by themselves. This tells the reader that the certifications are of great value. The rest of the educational skills appear second to these all-important ones. Notice that the job information in this case is very short and concise. The emphasis here is on education supported by experience, not the other way around.

Again, modifying a stock letter and resume is essential if you want to use your certification to your advantage when getting a new job. You get two pages only to convince someone to hire you, one for the resume and another for the cover letter. It's your job to use those pages to good effect.

# Emphasizing your qualifications during an interview

Everyone knows the basics of an interview. You're supposed to get dressed up and present a clean appearance. Of course, breath mints and a good attitude are important too. All these things are a part of any interview. However, there are several things you can do to enhance your interview by leveraging your Novell certification. Here's how:

➤ Many Novell certificate holders receive lapel pins. Make sure you wear this pin during the interview. It serves to reinforce your qualifications every time your potential employer looks at you and sees it.

➤ Take your badge with you. Your employer might ask you to present proof of your certification.

➤ Prepare a listing of the hardware you worked on in the past. You can use this information during the interview.

➤ Create a list of questions you want to ask the employer. Every employer asks if you have questions during a successful interview. Make sure your questions are based on the company and what it does. This is your opportunity to impress the employer with your knowledge of his company.

➤ The interview is a two-way street—the company is interviewing you but you are interviewing the company as well. You need to make sure that this is the company you want to invest your time and effort in. Though your preliminary research on the company might come out okay, that doesn't necessarily mean they are a good company to work for. The only time you find this information out is during your conversation with your prospective boss.

➤ During the interview, make sure that you maintain eye contact, speak clearly, and portray confidence in yourself. If asked a question that you cannot answer, do not make something up. You can usually avoid looking like a dunce when this happens by showing interest in the topic. Phrases such as "I didn't know that!" go a long way toward making the interview a success. Make sure you show an interest in what the boss knows, and in what the company needs rather than irritation at not knowing the answer to a question.

# ⇨ Talking about a rate of pay

How much should you get paid for your qualifications? That's a tough question for a lot of reasons. Your past work greatly affects how people view your certification. Someone who has managerial experience in addition to certification should expect to receive a better job than someone who has only the certification. Likewise, someone with a computer-related degree will typically receive more than someone who does not possess this credential. The following tips should help you determine what type of pay increase you should expect.

➤ Always use a point of reference based on fact to compute your new rate of pay. You need to know that a change of company is worth the effort. One point of reference might be any proposed pay increase your current company offers. You can also talk to people at a local users group to find out what other companies pay for similar work. Finally, you can check statistical information contained in business magazines or other sources.

➤ Try to get a pay increase equal to at least twice the current average pay raise rate in your area if your new job title is about the same, or only one level higher than your old one. For example, suppose the newspaper in your area states that the average pay raise in your area is five percent and you currently make $24,000 a year. Simply multiple the rate by two, then add that percentage to your current pay. In this case you should expect a pay increase of at least $2,400 a year, or a salary of $26,400.

➤ Make sure your new company recognizes any supplemental capabilities you can provide. For example, if you have a degree in computer science there is a good chance you can perform some programming tasks in addition to your network responsibilities. A network administrator who also has training experience can provide a lot more than simple user assistance. Your new company will try to make use of these capabilities, so you should get paid for them.

➤ Be sure you consider any benefits your new company offers that your old company doesn't. For example, your new company might offer a dental plan when your old company did not. This benefit you can use even as a short-term employee. On the other hand, a stock option benefit might not be worth much if you don't plan to stay with the company. You also need to ensure that the new benefit is tangible. Use the value of these new benefits as part of the basis for the level of pay increase you're willing to accept.

Of course, these tips merely help you home in on a rate of pay. Here are some absolutes you also need to consider.

1 First, you always have to get more for a transfer to a new job than a promotion at your current company. There are a few simple reasons for this, but most of them have to do with a loss of benefits. Companies do not provide very many benefits to short-term employees. If your current company offers you a promotion, double the amount of the pay increase (not the pay itself) and add it to your current salary. This is what you need to receive from your new company to make the move worthwhile.

2 Second, almost no one ever got a pay increase for doing the same job at a new company. If you are a network training specialist with the current title of administrative assistant, then you should look for some type of network-related title in the new company—one that emphasizes your training skills. Your old title does not match your new job and you will not get the pay raise you deserve by using that

old title. The same holds true for other types of network specialties. If you previously had a title of maintenance technician, look for a new title of network administrator or assistant network administrator.

# ⇨ Conclusion

There are two ways to improve your position using your new certification. You can stay at your current company and get a pay raise or other tangible benefits, or you can move to a new company. Whatever course you pursue, the most important thing you need to do once you have your certification is to get some recognition. Your certification is important to you and it should be important enough to the people you work for that they will give you additional recognition.

If you can't get the recognition you deserve, it might be time to go out on your own. Chapter 8 provides invaluable information for starting your own business as a consultant. You might want to read this chapter even if you don't plan to make such a big move right now.

The next chapter looks at continuing education requirements. Everyone needs to keep his or her tools sharp and ready for use. The same holds true of the intellectual skills you developed for the certification exams. Following the advice in the next chapter can play a big role in helping you maintain that edge.

# 7

# Planning for continuing education requirements

Y OU have finally made it! The certification you so diligently worked for is finally yours! Take some time to feel good about yourself and your accomplishments. After all, you worked hard for it and you deserve it. Then, once you have had time to reflect on your accomplishments, you must begin to think about and plan for what it will take to maintain your precious certification. While yours at the moment, your certification is still revocable by Novell if you do not meet the continuing education requirements.

These requirements are not difficult and are not an every-other-month demand to squeeze more money out of you. Novell asks you to recertify only if there is a major change in networking technology. These requirements are a necessary request by Novell to keep your knowledge of the products current. You are Novell's best representative and salesperson, because you are on the front line with the customer. If your knowledge of the product is not current, or not accurate, Novell's credibility as well as yours might come into question. The last thing that we want is to have a customer think that Novell or our skills are not what they expected. If this customer is not comfortable with Novell's reputation or yours, they will most likely take their business elsewhere.

The process of planning for continuing education does not stop at what Novell requires of you. This only skims the surface. You must enhance your knowledge to maintain an edge in this industry. In this chapter we discuss your continuing education responsibilities for maintaining your Novell certification. Because the education process does not stop with the Novell training, we also cover topics that will help you remain current in the networking market, including where to find valuable information about networking. However, this chapter is only a beginning. As you gain experience and accumulate time in the networking business, you will find your own additional sources of continuing education to meet your particular needs.

# Looking for more information

Every real expert in this business, whether he or she is a system administrator, consultant, analyst, or instructor, always has a desire for more information. It's like an obsession. The more information and knowledge you have, the more you want. This is one of those unique industries in which, the more you learn about a topic, the more you find there *is* to know! It is also just about the only industry in which technology changes and advances so fast that the trade journals have a hard time keeping up.

The key to staying current is finding the information that pertains to your situation. The problem that faces most of us is information overload. The faster you absorb it the faster it seems to arrive. Every vendor wants you to know about his great new product; every magazine is the key resource you need to improve your business. The way to deal with the information overload is to know where your interests lie and concentrate there.

# ⇨ Filtering your input

Do not spend much time on topics of little interest to you. For example, suppose you are a system administrator of a small firm with 11 or 12 users, and you are using Novell NetWare v2.2 with no access or connections to a mainframe computer. Unless you are personally interested in mainframe computers and might someday need this information, spend your time gathering information about products and techniques related to Local Area Networks (LANs). This is not to say that all the other information sent your way is not worthwhile. But you need to remember where your priorities are. Make mental notes about other information for future reference, so you'll know where to look for it if you need it later.

Figure 7-1 helps you get a handle on information essential to your performance, by providing a survey of some of the things you need to read to maintain your network. Simply fill out the form and then look for those subjects in magazines and trade papers.

You can also use this survey in another way. Some people get so much mail and so many magazines that even a focused approach will not help them get through everything they need to look at. They often resort to clipping services, companies that send clippings from magazines and trade papers in specific areas of interest. A more

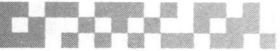

Figure 7-1

## Reading Interest Survey

Name: _____ Date: _____

Position: _____

*Hardware needs:*

❏ PC                                    ❏ Mainframe

❏ Macintosh                             ❏ Minicomputer

*Software needs:*

Word Processing: _____     Database: _____

Spreadsheet: _____         Accounting: _____

Communications: _____      Other: _____

*Peripheral devices:*

❏ Tape Drive                            ❏ CD-ROM/WORM Drive

❏ Sound Board                           ❏ Mouse

❏ MODEM

❏ Printers: _____     _____

❏ Other: _____     _____

*Network specific:*

Network Type: _____    Bridges/Routers: _____

Operating System Version: _____   Print Servers: _____

Other: _____    _____

*Sample reading interest survey*

cost-effective method of doing the same thing is to ask an administrative assistant or a secretary use the survey as a reference and go through magazines and trade papers for you. He or she can simply clip out the articles you would be interested in. This lessens the need to go through all the magazines and trade papers on your own. It also helps you maintain your concentration by removing sources of other non-essential information.

# ⇨ Sources of information

The basic information needed to maintain your certification will come from Novell in some form. These might include instructor-led courses, videotapes, manuals, bulletins, or seminars. This information is Novell-specific, relating only to Novell, the NetWare products, and your certification.

However, because you should be interested in the complete scope of networking, using Novell as your only source of information will not get you very far. For this reason, other good sources of information include magazines, trade papers, books, online services, and electronic media. Figure 7-2 shows these typical sources of information and provides a little guidance on how to allocate your time.

These other sources of information will help you maintain your Novell certification and will also help you advance to the next level of certification or a better job. Do not fall into the trap of thinking that, now that you have your certification you can stop studying.

# ⇨ Organizing your information

Organization is a major key to retaining a vast amount of knowledge without juggling it in your head all the time. Trying to keep all your knowledge balls in the air at the same time is just plain silly. Put the balls down so you can get some real work done!

The important idea here is to group the information into easily digested chunks, then find a way to access those chunks quickly. Of course, the exact method of organization you use varies by the type of information you want to store. The most flexible media are trade magazines and books. Notes and brochures from seminars are also fairly easy to store. You will find it a lot more difficult to store information from satellite conferences and special training sessions. Information collected at user group meetings might prove to be the most difficult source of all to organize.

Figure 7-2

**Novell
Specific Sources**

Instructor-Led Courses, Seminars,
Product Demonstrations, and
Special Training Groups

Manuals and Bulletins

Video Tapes

Satellite Conferences

**Other
Sources**

Magazines, Trade Papers
and Third Party Books

On-line Services and
Electronic Media

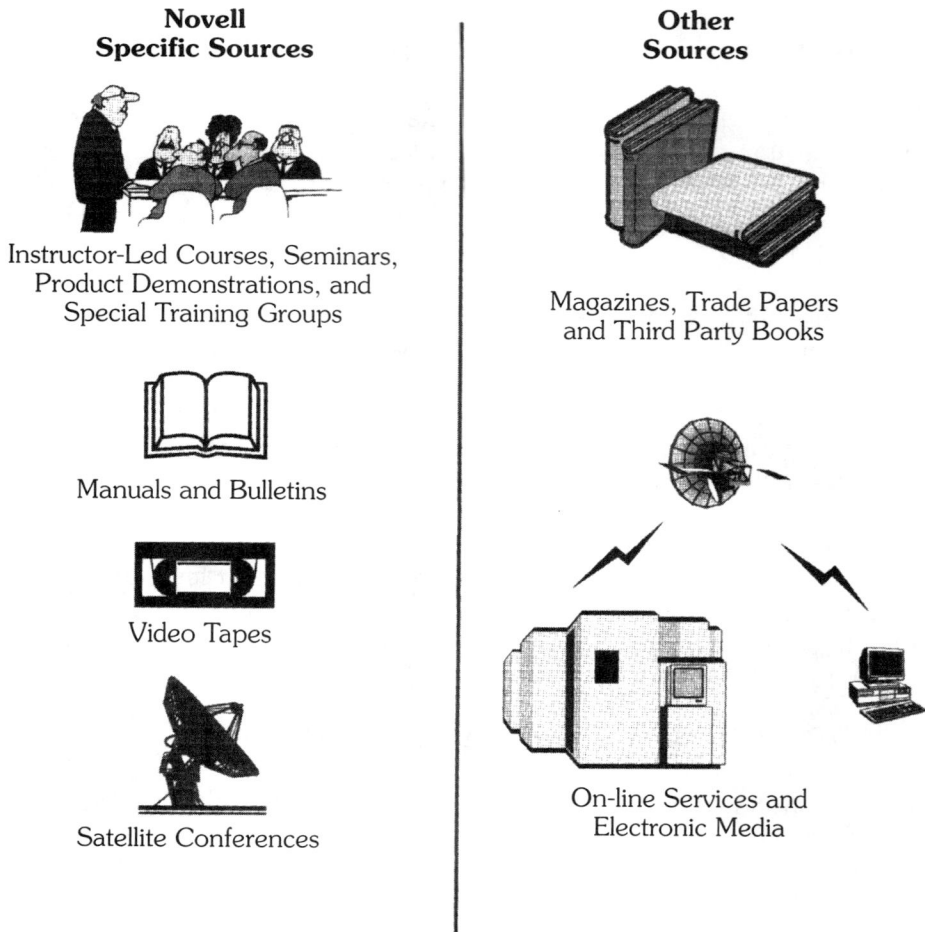

**Follow the 70/30 rule when updating your knowledge base.
30% Novell and 70% Other**

*Sources of continuing education information*

As you wade through the reams of paper and screens of electronic information, you will want to develop a method or style for processing this information. So much is available it's not practical for you to even try to memorize all of it. It's even harder to remember where you saw the information if you can only remember a small part of what you read.

One way is to photocopy the table of contents for books and other materials that provide such aids. Put the photocopies in a notebook. Divide the notebook into sections, such as magazines, trade papers, books, electronic sources, and others. Ordering your magazine and trade paper articles in this manner will allow you to quickly locate what you need. Of course, part of this maintenance involves removing old information as well. For example, you wouldn't want to keep articles that told you about the latest version of the PC—the 8088. Keeping your information up-to-date is part of what's required to reduce information overload.

Another way to reference information is to use a program such as AskSam, DynaText, or Folio Views. The benefit of using AskSam is that you are not restricted by the usual limitations of a standard database. This product is designed to provide storage for data that might or might not fall within a predictable pattern. In fact, it is the perfect database for storing notes and other hard-to-organize information. Folio Views is the same program Novell uses for online help and the *NetWare Buyer's Guide* (which we discuss later in this chapter). Newer versions of NetWare use a different online help viewer, called DynaText, which offers a much better interface than Folio Views. Any of these programs allow you to quickly and easily create an infobase to match your specifications. You can also add paraphrased summaries of articles, books, or other information, to help narrow your search of a particular topic. In fact, you could scan entire articles into the database. While this requires a little more time in creating and maintaining the infobase, you would then be able tc find the information that you are looking for faster.

Other methods of recalling this information might include creating a database using one of the popular database programs, or by converting the data into an electronic format that's retrievable at a later time. Whatever the methods you use to keep track of the important information you find, the key will be to record and document your findings. Do not entrust this information to your memory only.

Ziff Publishing provides a unique method for accessing their articles and reviews. You can order *Computer Library Plus* for a nominal fee. Every month you receive a new CD-ROM disk containing the latest articles and reviews about any topic you can think of. The CD contains the complete text (excluding graphics and advertisements) of more than 170 publications. It also includes 13,000 company profiles and a complete computer glossary. The search engine included as part of the library system allows you to conduct keyword searches throughout the entire database. You can order *Computer Library Plus* by calling 1-800-827-7889. The cost is about $1,000 per subscription. Microsoft provides the same type of library through the *Microsoft Developer Network*. It contains the latest issues of *Microsoft Systems Journal* and many of the Cobb Group newsletters. You can order *Microsoft Developer Network* by calling 1-800-227-4679. The cost is about $195 per subscription.

## ✳ Magazines

Magazines are excellent sources of information. By subscribing to a few good ones you can remain current on most areas of networking. Many publishers produce their magazines on a bi-weekly or a monthly basis. Because you have a couple of weeks to read the magazine, you will be able to study when you have the time. You are also better able to absorb and retain what you read if you're not under pressure or rushed.

Finding the right magazines doesn't present a problem, either. There are many excellent magazines on the shelves at your favorite bookstore. You will also find as many magazines that never make it to the bookstores or magazine racks, not because they are of any less quality; they might just target a different market. Such magazines are usually mailed directly to homes or businesses. You can often find business reply cards for these magazines in the advertising card decks you get in the mail, as part of software packages, or within other magazines. For example, most of the Cobb Group newsletters are advertised in software package. They also send direct mail to those who return registration cards to the software vendors.

Deciding which magazines you will buy is a difficult decision, which you should not rush. Spend the time to research each one, looking for those that concentrate on the topics that concern you. Even if you had the money to buy every one, it would require many hours to read them all.

Many magazines on the newsstands contain too many advertisements, and in some cases the ads get top priority over the articles. This becomes very annoying when some of the articles seem so short the editor had to leave out important information because the ads needed more room. Luckily, as you look at the magazines month after month you will begin to notice which ones are the ad magazines and which ones have good articles with real substance.

You will also begin to see patterns in the type of articles written for the different magazines. Some magazines are into home computing, some are into the latest gadgets, others focus on networking, and others cover every other aspect of computers or electronics. Find the ones that deal with your needs and put them on your required reading list. Make sure you read them each month first; they are your windows into the industry. Afterwards, read the others if you have time.

There are two magazines that you, as a Novell expert, should not miss, *LAN TIMES* and *NetWare Application Notes*.

1 McGraw-Hill publishes *LAN TIMES*, which is basically a Novell-based magazine. This bi-weekly publication covers everything taking place within the PC networking industry. Although it is a Novell-based magazine, it is also one of the most objective magazines available. It doesn't matter who is doing good or bad; *LAN TIMES* will write about it. The magazine includes articles on the latest technologies, internetworking, applications, and network management to name just a few. Also, one article in each issue covers a "hands-on" topic. Usually, this detailed article covers some networking-specific topic directly relating in some way to Novell, giving you theory, uses, and procedures.

2 The second magazine must-read publication, *NetWare Application Notes*, is a Novell-published magazine that goes into great depth on each topic. Each edition usually contains three to five articles, with absolutely no ads. The articles cover such topics as installation, integration, testing, theory, and management. When you become a CNE, Novell will send you one complimentary copy, also referred to as "APP Notes." If you want to continue to receive the magazine after that (and we recommend that you do), you'll find ordering information inside the front cover.

Many other magazines also deal with PC networks. You need to research each one to find those appropriate for you and your needs. Some are free to consultants, administrators and businesses. When you find the ones you like, call or write to the circulation manager and ask about a complimentary subscription; many times, these are available for the asking, even if they only include two or three free issues. This is usually enough time to evaluate them thoroughly. Note that, in many cases, subscriptions for magazines can be tax-deductible as business or education expenses.

Once you finish reading the magazines, remember to document the contents and then store the publication in a safe place. You will only remember a small fraction of the information contained within the articles, but by using some form of documentation you will be able to access it when you need it in the future.

Later, as your experience and knowledge change, so should the magazines, trade papers, and books that you buy. If you find that a particular publication is no longer teaching or informing you, it might be time to drop the subscription. If you keep reading material you already know you are just wasting your time.

## ✳ Trade papers

The weekly trade papers are packed with the latest information about the computer industry. Subscriptions to a few of the more popular ones will keep you up-to-date on what hardware and software vendors are doing. They always have articles about new gadgets, state-of-the-art technology, and trends. Also included are columns about what certain industry people are doing, and what companies they are working for this week.

As with magazines you must find the trade papers that meet your needs, and then put them among your top reading priorities. Some, you will find, are very pro-IBM or pro-UNIX, while others only concern themselves with what Novell or Microsoft is doing. Whenever you see articles of this type within a magazine or trade paper, remember that they only express the opinions of the authors. They do not necessarily represent a right or wrong view of the industry; rather, they give you one person's view. Of course, these people maintain their positions because they are either controversial or correct more often than not. Just make sure they objectively cover the topics that interest you.

The trade papers, when read in addition to books and magazines, will help keep you informed and current with the industry. However, trade papers carry a lot of articles unrelated to what you are doing, and also contain a ton of ads. As with magazines, the publishers will send trade papers directly to your home or place of business, often free of charge. You can also use the same documentation methods to maintain a trade paper section in your private research library.

A few of the trade papers you might want to invest in are *Network World*, *Computer Technology Review*, *Computer Reseller News*, and *PC Week*. By taking some or all of these you will get complete coverage of the industry. Their phone numbers and addresses are in appendix B.

## ✳ Books

Books are also excellent sources of information for continuing education. Plan to build a complete library, and prepare by investing in a good bookcase with plenty of room. By having your books in one place you'll refer to them more often.

Most of the books written about a software product contain the same information that's supplied by the vendor manuals. The difference between third-party books and the vendor manuals is that third-party books often include real-world examples and are written in terms that readers can more easily understand. However, while these books contain a large amount of information they are not for everyone. Most of the material will not be of interest to you if you have much experience with the product. It will be more of a review for you than an education.

However, such books might serve as reference material to give you another point of view on a given subject. One that the network administrator will want to check out is *The Hands On Guide to Networking* by John Mueller and Robert Williams (ISBN 0-8306-4439-3), published by McGraw-Hill. This book provides a lot of tips and techniques for getting your network running smoothly and keeping it that way.

For the dedicated NetWare professional, one book that should be mandatory is the *NetWare Buyer's Guide*. This is published by Novell and is usually updated twice a year. You can get free by calling Novell, it comes in both a paper version and an electronic version. The electronic version has the same appearance and interface as the Novell help utility with NetWare.

Novell divides the *NetWare Buyer's Guide* into four sections:

1 Novell Corporate & Strategic Overview. This section deals with Novell's company background, market leadership, and Novell integrated computing architecture. The role that Novell plays in computer networking is defined. It also tells how Novell works with other computer vendors to ensure that all the products Novell produces will work with third-party products. Also included in this section is the theory of operations for Novell operating systems.

2 Novell Product Overview. This section lists all the products Novell sells and supports. Described here is the history of the Novell products and reasons for using them, but the section does not include explanations of how they actually work. All CNAs, CNEs, ECNEs, CNIs, administrators, consultants, and anyone else who works with Novell operating systems should read this section. Many times, knowing what products are available will give you ideas about making your system work better.

3 Novell Products. Listed in this section are the Novell products, this time by types. The subheadings are operating system, network services, communication services, internetwork, network connectivity, network management, and distributed application development tools. Under each subheading is a listing of every Novell product that relates to the master topic. Here, descriptions of the products include more technical information. This section also explains what makes the products useful, and offers information on implementation, required hardware and software, and any related options. The final part of this section covers specifications and ordering information. This is an excellent section for learning how each product works, and what its hardware and software requirements are.

4 Novell Support and Education. This section deals with the customer support programs offered by Novell, for both resellers and end

users. It features an overview of the Novell services, including technical support, NetWire information, and the reseller authorization program. Also included is an overview of the Novell education and training programs.

The *NetWare Buyer's Guide* will be a real asset to you. Whether you work with the book version or the electronic version, be sure to contact Novell on a regular basis for an upgrade to your *NetWare Buyer's Guide* current.

## ✳ **Online services**

As you would expect, Novell also offers electronic online services so you can use your computer to stay in touch. This section covers Novell's CompuServe forums, a vast array of places you can use to get answers to every conceivable question. These forums also offer download services for free updates of Novell products. Figure 7-3 provides an overview of Novell's CompuServe forums.

As you can see, it's huge! If you feel a little overwhelmed by the number of services that Novell offers, you're not alone. You could spend days just trying to find the right forum for your particular needs.

For that matter, unless you use a product like WinCIM to maneuver through the labyrinth of CompuServe menus, you might never even reach your destination. (Novell does offer a special version of WinCIM that includes all of its forums as standard entries; the problem is that other vendors, such as Microsoft, offer this same service, and you can't combine the various specialty versions of WinCIM into a single program.) Using Fig. 7-3 should make your job a lot easier, and should allow you to use more cost-saving tools such as TapCIS or OzCIS for Windows to find your way on CompuServe. (You can download shareware versions of either product from their CompuServe forums— GO TAPCIS for TapCIS or GO OZCIS for OzCIS for Windows.)

Figure 7-3 is arranged in a hierarchical format, so the upper-level menus appear first. The actual forums appear at the bottom of the hierarchical tree. Notice the GO words in parenthesis beside each menu or forum name. A go word provides a shortcut on CompuServe. If you know the go word you can go directly to the menu or forum that you want to see. Not every menu entry has a go word, but

Figure 7-3

Novell
(NOVELL or
NETWIRE)

Continued on
Page 188

Continued on
Page 188

What's
New
(NOVNEW)

BrainShare
Worldwide
(BSHARE)

Monthly Info
Additions
(NOV585)

NetWire
Usage Tips
(NOV618)

Welcome!
Welcome!
(NOV586)

Press
Releases
(NPRESS)

Upcoming
Online
Conferences
(NOV617)

Events
Calendar
(NOV432)

BrainShare '95

   About BrainShare '95

   Follow-up Files from BrainShare

BrainShare Europe

BrainShare Japan

BrainShare Australia

General Information (NOV733)

Conference Speakers (NOV735)

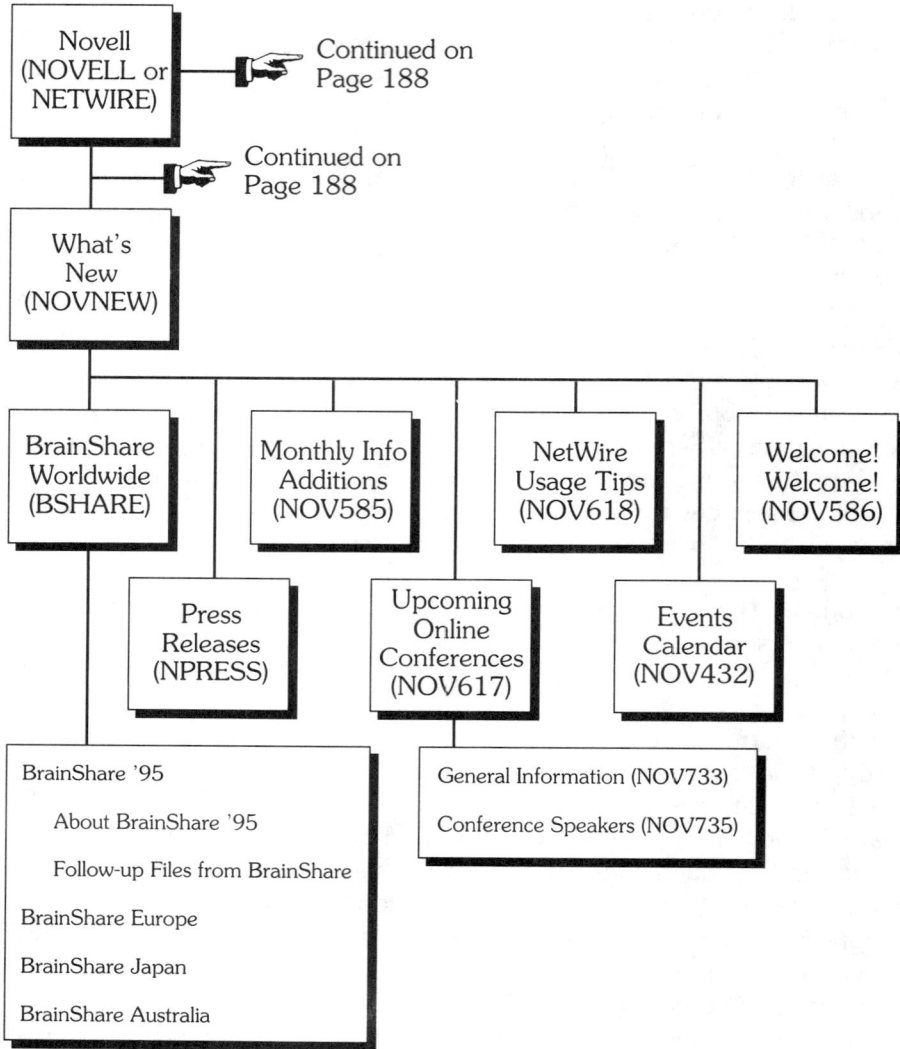

*Novell CompuServe forum structure*

Continued from
Previous Page

Continued on
Next Page

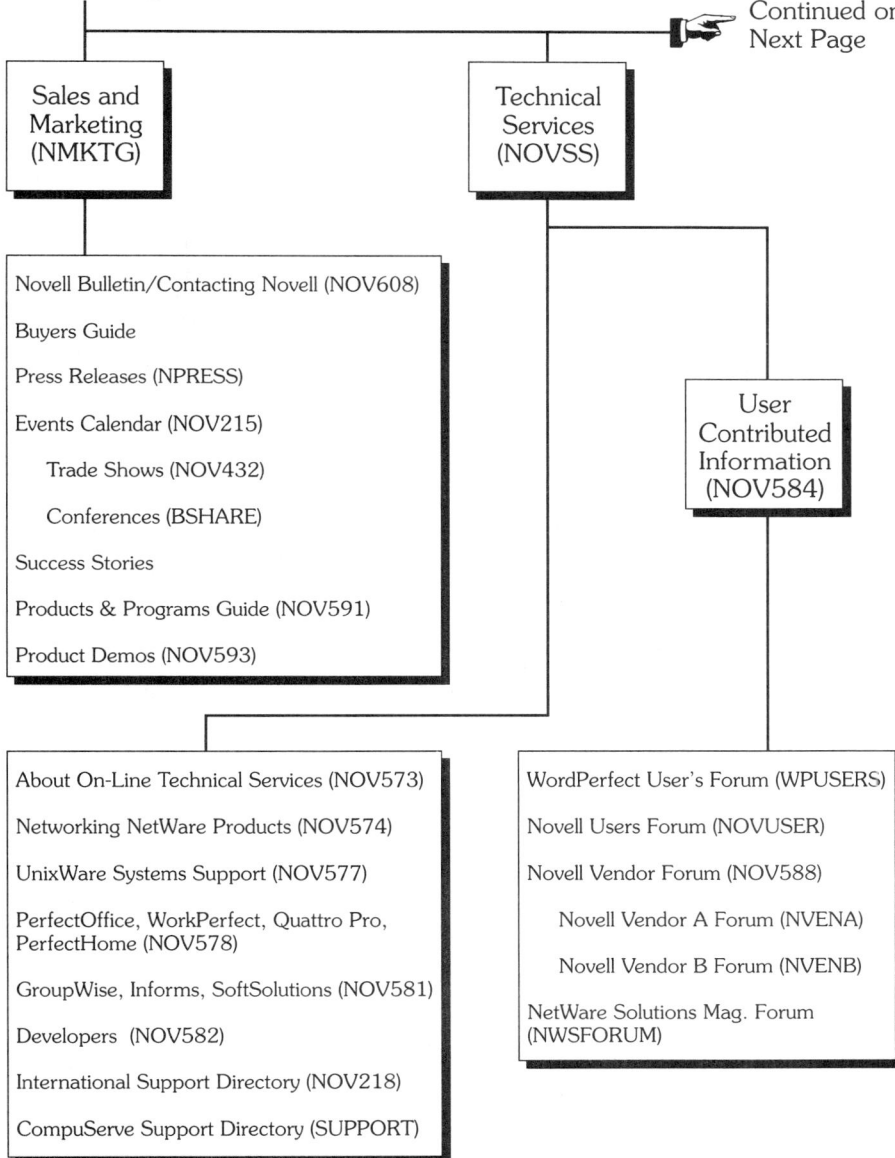

**Sales and Marketing (NMKTG)**

**Technical Services (NOVSS)**

Novell Bulletin/Contacting Novell (NOV608)

Buyers Guide

Press Releases (NPRESS)

Events Calendar (NOV215)

    Trade Shows (NOV432)

    Conferences (BSHARE)

Success Stories

Products & Programs Guide (NOV591)

Product Demos (NOV593)

**User Contributed Information (NOV584)**

About On-Line Technical Services (NOV573)

Networking NetWare Products (NOV574)

UnixWare Systems Support (NOV577)

PerfectOffice, WorkPerfect, Quattro Pro, PerfectHome (NOV578)

GroupWise, Informs, SoftSolutions (NOV581)

Developers (NOV582)

International Support Directory (NOV218)

CompuServe Support Directory (SUPPORT)

WordPerfect User's Forum (WPUSERS)

Novell Users Forum (NOVUSER)

Novell Vendor Forum (NOV588)

    Novell Vendor A Forum (NVENA)

    Novell Vendor B Forum (NVENB)

NetWare Solutions Mag. Forum (NWSFORUM)

*continued*

Figure 7-3

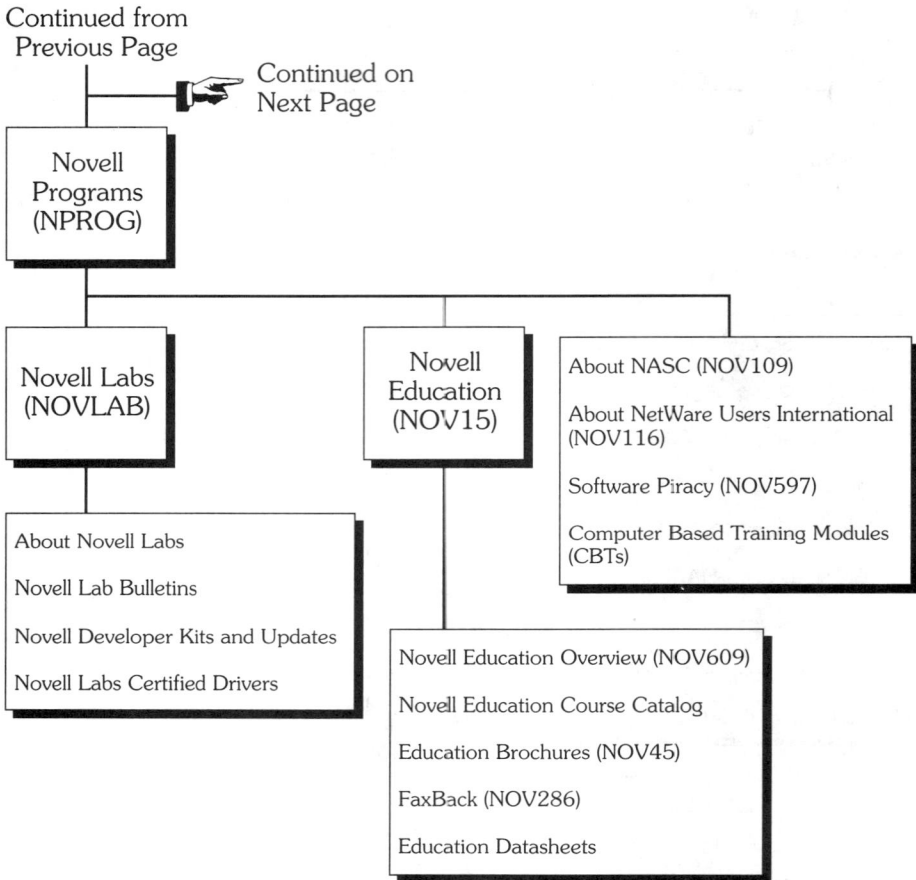

continued

enough are provided in Fig. 7-3 to greatly decrease your search time. Every forum does have a go word, making it easy to get to any forum you want to visit.

The online Novell services fall into two classes: dial-in voice services and computer access services. We just covered the computer access services. The dial-up voice service is Novell's technical information service, update information service, education information and enrollment, and direct product ordering service. It's available seven days a week, 24 hours a day. If you have technical questions about any

Continued from
Previous Page

Continued on
Next Page

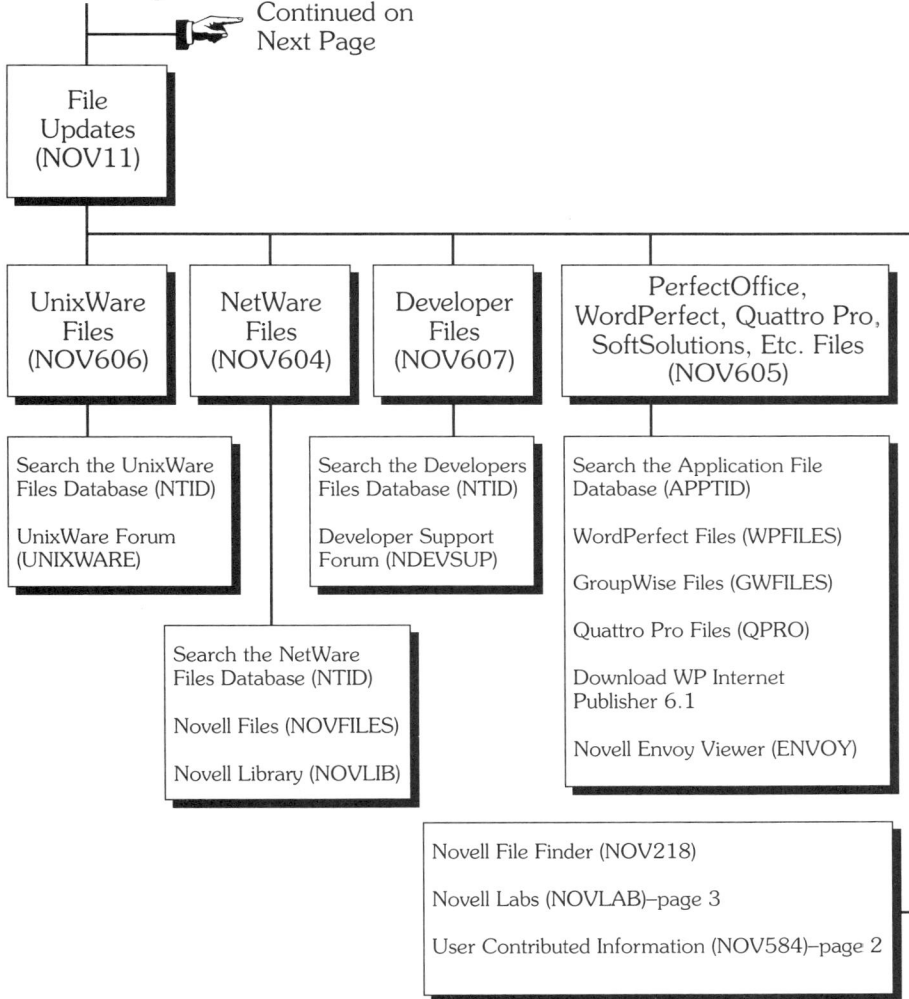

File
Updates
(NOV11)

UnixWare
Files
(NOV606)

NetWare
Files
(NOV604)

Developer
Files
(NOV607)

PerfectOffice,
WordPerfect, Quattro Pro,
SoftSolutions, Etc. Files
(NOV605)

Search the UnixWare
Files Database (NTID)

UnixWare Forum
(UNIXWARE)

Search the Developers
Files Database (NTID)

Developer Support
Forum (NDEVSUP)

Search the Application File
Database (APPTID)

WordPerfect Files (WPFILES)

GroupWise Files (GWFILES)

Quattro Pro Files (QPRO)

Download WP Internet
Publisher 6.1

Novell Envoy Viewer (ENVOY)

Search the NetWare
Files Database (NTID)

Novell Files (NOVFILES)

Novell Library (NOVLIB)

Novell File Finder (NOV218)

Novell Labs (NOVLAB)–page 3

User Contributed Information (NOV584)–page 2

*continued*

Figure 7-3

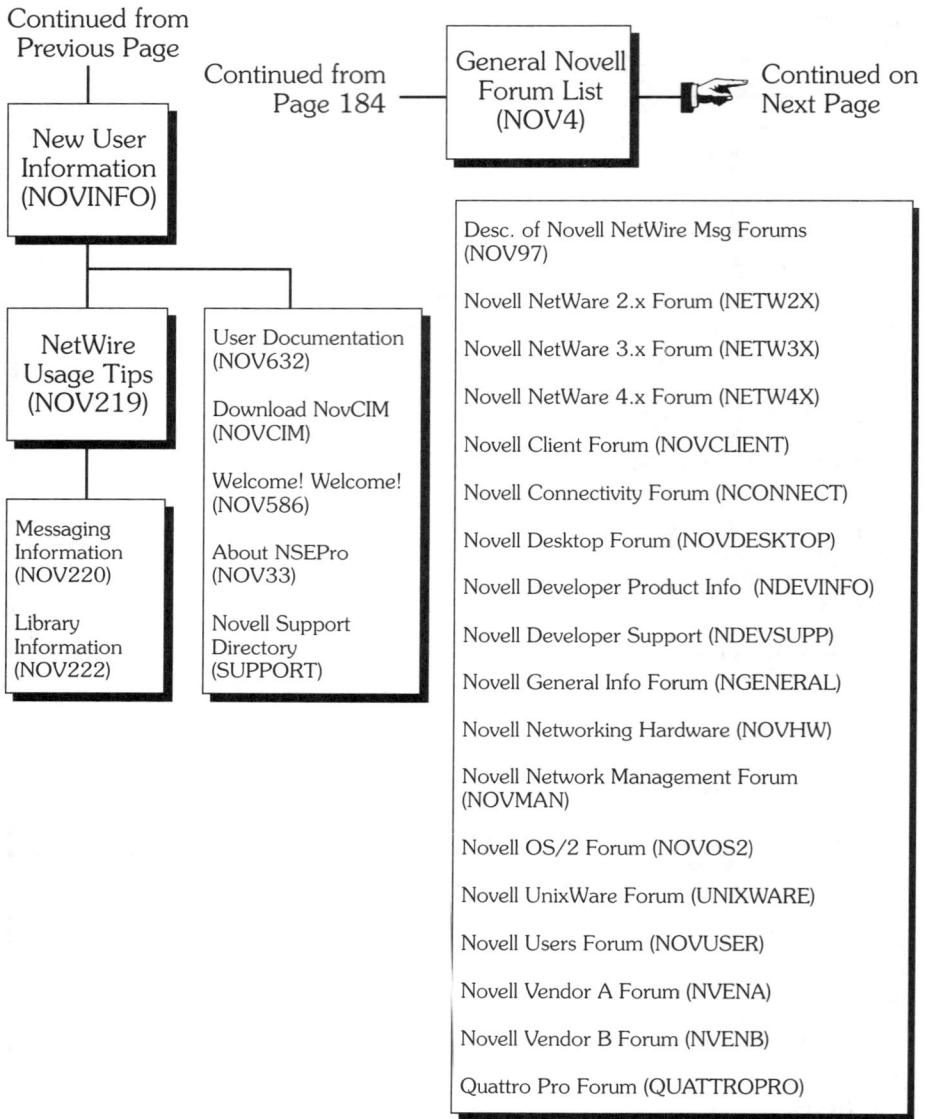

Continued from
Previous Page

Continued from
Page 184

General Novell
Forum List
(NOV4)

Continued on
Next Page

New User
Information
(NOVINFO)

NetWire
Usage Tips
(NOV219)

User Documentation
(NOV632)

Download NovCIM
(NOVCIM)

Welcome! Welcome!
(NOV586)

About NSEPro
(NOV33)

Novell Support
Directory
(SUPPORT)

Messaging
Information
(NOV220)

Library
Information
(NOV222)

Desc. of Novell NetWire Msg Forums
(NOV97)

Novell NetWare 2.x Forum (NETW2X)

Novell NetWare 3.x Forum (NETW3X)

Novell NetWare 4.x Forum (NETW4X)

Novell Client Forum (NOVCLIENT)

Novell Connectivity Forum (NCONNECT)

Novell Desktop Forum (NOVDESKTOP)

Novell Developer Product Info (NDEVINFO)

Novell Developer Support (NDEVSUPP)

Novell General Info Forum (NGENERAL)

Novell Networking Hardware (NOVHW)

Novell Network Management Forum
(NOVMAN)

Novell OS/2 Forum (NOVOS2)

Novell UnixWare Forum (UNIXWARE)

Novell Users Forum (NOVUSER)

Novell Vendor A Forum (NVENA)

Novell Vendor B Forum (NVENB)

Quattro Pro Forum (QUATTROPRO)

*continued*

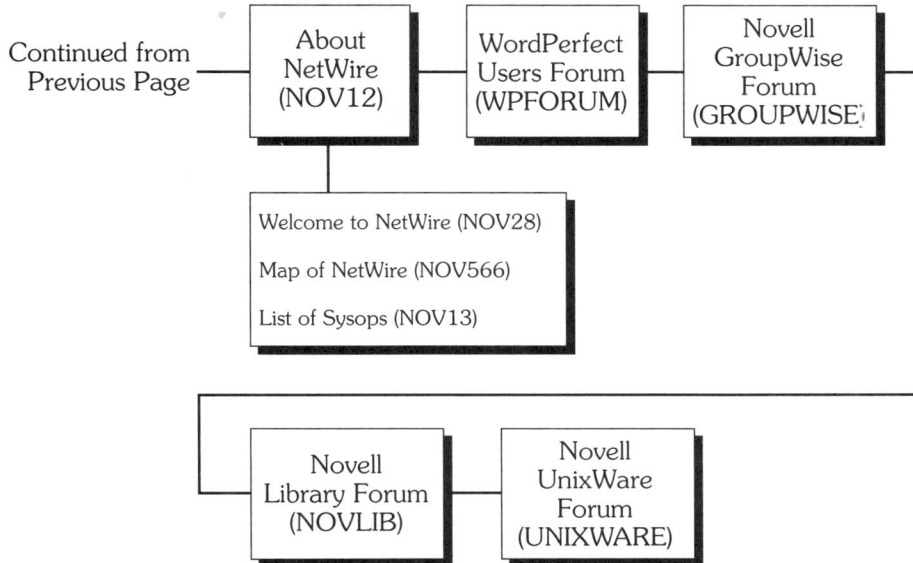

```
                    ┌─────────────┐   ┌─────────────┐   ┌──────────────┐
                    │   About     │   │ WordPerfect │   │    Novell    │
Continued from ─────│  NetWire    │   │ Users Forum │   │  GroupWise   │
Previous Page       │  (NOV12)    │   │  (WPFORUM)  │   │    Forum     │
                    └─────────────┘   └─────────────┘   │ (GROUPWISE)  │
                          │                              └──────────────┘
                    ┌──────────────────────────────────┐
                    │ Welcome to NetWire (NOV28)        │
                    │                                   │
                    │ Map of NetWire (NOV566)           │
                    │                                   │
                    │ List of Sysops (NOV13)            │
                    └──────────────────────────────────┘

          ┌───────────────────────────────────────────────────┐
          │       ┌─────────────┐   ┌─────────────┐            │
          │       │   Novell    │   │   Novell    │
          └───────│Library Forum│───│  UnixWare   │
                  │  (NOVLIB)   │   │   Forum     │
                  └─────────────┘   │ (UNIXWARE)  │
                                    └─────────────┘
```

*continued*

of the Novell products and would like to talk to a Novell technician, you can call the Novell technical support department. Novell entitles you, as a CNE, to two free incident calls during your first year of certification. If, after two calls or the first year of certification, you need more technical support, you may purchase additional support for a reduced rate.

Other services include the opportunity to order many of the Novell products, and updates to your current products. You might also obtain information about the NAEC education centers, and listings of the latest course offerings.

Now that you have a good overview of the online services offered by Novell, let's take a detailed look.

**NetWire** For the latest information about Novell or the NetWare products, Novell offers NetWire. This is a bulletin board service. The NetWire service, referred to as the *Novell forum* or the *NetWire forum*, is available through CompuServe. Once you have access to CompuServe, the NetWire services are then free.

**Sysops** Sysops (short for system operator) perform the maintenance and control the NetWire forum. In the case of NetWire, the sysops are Novell employees and volunteer Novell experts. These men and women monitor the files being uploaded and downloaded on the system. They are also available to answer questions about where to find information, how to use the forums, and any technical concerns relating to the Novell products.

**Questions on the forum** One of the services offered by NetWire is the ability to post questions about NetWare onto the forum, at which point anyone having access can read and answer them. Responses might come from the other users or sysops; in turn, users themselves might be end users, system administrators, CNEs, CNIs, or anyone else with an interest in Novell. Thousands of people use NetWire every day, and there is a very good chance that someone else has had a problem similar to what you might encounter.

**Updates & conferences** Other services offered by NetWire include product update and conferences. Updates typically include the latest patches, fixes, drivers, and enhancements available for the Novell product line. These are downloadable from the service and are free to users of NetWire. Conferences come about when a group of NetWire users has an online discussion about some topic. Some of these discussions are pre-planned and conducted by a Novell sysop or engineer; others will be spur-of-the-moment conferences arising spontaneously among a group of users. The topics range from a problem someone has been having to the theory and implementation of some technology.

For more information about CompuServe and NetWire, please refer to Appendix B of this book.

**FaxBack** The Novell FaxBack service, as mentioned in Chapter 3, provides a good way to locate information without having to contact the CNA/CNE/ECNE division with every individual question you might have. It originates with the Novell education department and allows you to receive, by fax, a listing of the authorized education centers and class information. You can also get general information about the CNA, CNE, ECNE, and CNI certifications, plus training information about the Univel product, general Novell education information, and information about Novell education area managers and Novell self-study products.

**Electronic media** Novell offers a product called the *Network Support Encyclopedia* (NSE). This is an electronic information base containing technical data about Novell networking. The NSE comes in two versions, the standard volume and the professional volume. The standard volume contains Novell's technical notes, hardware and software test information, product documentation, product specifications, NetWire information, Novell press releases, and the *NetWare Buyer's Guide*.

The NSE professional version includes all the information included with the standard version, plus downloadable information. The downloadable information is the same as that available on NetWire; it includes NetWare patches, product fixes, device drivers, product enhancements, troubleshooting charts, the NetWare Application Notes (AppNotes), and additional manuals. The NSE Standard volume is available in both a diskette version and CD-ROM version, while the NSE Professional volume is available only on CD-ROM. Novell updates both versions on a regular basis, the diskette version once a quarter and the CD-ROM version once a month.

Once you become a CNE you will receive one issue of the NSE professional version, in either the diskette or the CD-ROM format. If you want to receive updates for your NSE, on either a quarterly or a monthly schedule, you will have to contact Novell and buy them. While these updates are not mandatory they are well worth the investment.

# CNE continuing education requirements

As a CNE you must update your certification from time to time, to make sure you maintain a certain level of expertise with Novell products. This also supports Novell by ensuring that Novell's customers can receive qualified support for all its products. However, updating is usually necessary only when Novell introduces a new product and feels that all the CNEs should be aware of the update, which happens about once every one or two years. When a certification update is required, Novell will notify you by mail. After that you have 90 days to fulfill the new requirement, which normally involves passing a competency exam. If you do not know the new material, Novell and NAECs will offer classes on the subject.

Even though you have 90 days to meet the certification requirements, don't wait too long. Try to certify as soon as possible, but make sure you give yourself plenty of time to prepare. Remember, the more pressure you are under the higher the odds of failing.

# ECNE continuing education requirements

Continuing education is also a requirement for the ECNE. Any of the certification updates required for the CNE will also be required to maintain your ECNE certification, because you must be a CNE before you can become an ECNE. There might also be recertification requirements that apply only to ECNEs as well. If Novell feels that a product or technology is important and the ECNEs should know about it, they will add it to the continuing education requirement list. Because ECNE certification is more specialized, Novell makes sure they have knowledge of these new products.

# MCNE continuing education requirements

An MCNE's education requirements are about the most extensive of any certification, except for the CNI. In fact, an MCNE will require a broader range of information than a CNI, because an MCNE works with more than just Novell products.

In addition to this broad base of general knowledge, the MCNE will need to stay current on Novell-specific product information. Any of the certification updates required for the CNE will also be required of an MCNE, because you must be a CNE before you can become an MCNE. Novell might also require MCNEs to meet additional education requirements as well. If Novell feels that a product or technology is important and that MCNEs should know about it, they will add knowledge of that product or procedure to the requirements list.

# CNI continuing education requirements

The Novell CNI is a little different from the CNE and ECNE when it comes to recertification. The Novell CNI certification allows its holders to teach either category I, category II, or specialized classes. If Novell releases a new product and will sponsor an instructor-led class that covers the material, then CNIs will have to update their certification in order to teach that class. For example, if for a new operating system a corresponding system administration course is offered, chances are that class will fall in the category I set of classes. If an instructor wants to maintain his category I certification then he must complete any of the new certification requirements. The new certification usually involves attending the course. These classes are taught either by Novell instructors or at an NAEC by instructors already certified. So, after this new completing the course and receiving his or her certificate, the would-be instructor must then pass the CNI version of the proficiency exam. After passing the exam, he must fax a copy of his course certificate to the CNI administration department. When the CNI candidate satisfies these requirements, Novell then permits him (or her) to teach the course.

Another requirement would be for the CNI to attend an instructor evaluation class (IEC) to remain certified. In an IEC, the instructor will conduct lectures on the material that will be part of the course, while being videotaped. The instructor must pass a critique that's based on presentation skills and technical accuracy. Most of the time the instructor will have to attend the IEC only if he wishes to teach the ECNE or specialty classes. Another possible requirement for the CNI would be to attend a seminar-style class. At the seminar, a Novell employed instructor would present information that Novell considers essential for the CNIs to know. The CNI might or might not have an exam on this material.

In summary, the instructors must stay up-to-date on all continuing education requirements, because they are the ones in front of the classroom, teaching the material. If the instructor does not fully comprehend the material, that will make the product seem inferior and will cause problems among the students.

# ⇨ Conclusion

If you desire to maintain a network, you face an ongoing quest for new information. The level and the specifics of the required knowledge might be different for a CNA as opposed to a CNI, but the basic need is still there. But whether you seek information because of your own personal interest in the industry, or to maintain your Novell certification, using magazines, trade papers, and books will help you. Just because you obtain your Novell certification, doesn't mean you can stop studying and learning.

As you find information in the various sources we've suggested, remember to organize the material you archive in a way that will make it retrievable later on. The ideas presented in this chapter, such as photocopying the table of contents from publications and storing them in a binder, can help a lot.

Meeting continuing education requirements is essential to maintaining Novell certifications. The higher the level of customer satisfaction, the better the chances are that Novell will maintain dominance in the market, which always comes back to how certificate holders, such as you, perform. Consistent patterns of high performance will improve the market for CNEs, and will help create more jobs and establish higher income levels. Both the CNE and the ECNE continuing education requirements might seem like wastes of time and money, but they are necessary. Without the extra requirements, many CNEs might get by with an incomplete understanding of Novell and the products they sell and support. When you recertify remember that you are enhancing everyone's marketability in the networking industry, including your own.

# 8

# The consulting approach

**M**ANY consultants make a living by installing and maintaining Novell local area networks (LANs). Installing and maintaining LANs became a very lucrative business when large corporations began to downsize their database applications, from mainframes and minicomputers to PCs. In addition, many small businesses are starting to see the benefit of networking their computers to enhance productivity. Add to this the increasing number of midsize businesses and you have a climate ripe for the entrepreneur. As the business market gets more competitive, the consultant should see an increase in business.

Of course, not every consultant will see an increase in his or her customer base. The difference between a successful consultant and one who simply maintains an installed base is recognition. Unless you get recognition for your achievements as a businessperson, there is little chance that you will increase your client base.

There are other benefits to enhancing your knowledge level, beyond simply working more hours as your client base increases in size. For example, with an increase in capability you can charge higher fees. You might even hire a helper. This could allow you to concentrate on the "fun" jobs and give someone else the headaches. As you can see, the benefits to a Novell certification are many. However, to get the benefits you must first gain recognition.

This chapter specifically targets the networking expert. It provides ideas on how to improve consulting businesses, through proper use of Novell-supplied aids. It also examines some of the ways that the consultant can use his certification to gain and keep new clients. Finally, this chapter examines some thorny issues, such as what to charge clients for network services and how to maintain professional relationships.

# Using the Novell logo

Once you get your certification you need to tell someone about it. Clients usually aren't very eager to hear about your latest achievement, so you need to tell them in an almost subliminal manner.

One of the ways you can do this is to add the Novell logo to all your business correspondence, price lists, and business cards. Here are some of the ways you can use the Novell logo to tell your clients about your capabilities.

# ⇨ Advertisements

There are two elements in advertising, design and distribution. How to effectively design advertising materials is subject to much debate, as the number and variety of advertising packages you get in the mail demonstrates. Distribution is a little easier for the consultant to master; there are only a handful of truly effective ways to distribute your advertisement.

Let's tackle the first problem first, how to design your brochure. Your best source of information on how to solve this problem is the junk mail you receive. What kind of mail attracts your attention? Give the same junk mail to a few people willing to help you out. Ask them to show you what they react to best. Now, throw the rest of it away and go through all the mail you kept, to figure out what works and what doesn't. You might want to perform the same kind of analysis on magazine advertisements and store brochures. Always look at what the competition is doing successfully, then add a few ideas of your own to come up with winning combinations.

Several elements are common to good brochures. First, you need to identify yourself. Unless people know who they're dealing with, you won't get any sales. Second, you need to consider adding a list of services. You can do this in a number of ways. For example, stores usually use graphics to tell people what services they offer—what else do you call a picture of a computer with a price below it? Some businesses use a simple list that looks much like a price list. Still other businesses use descriptive paragraphs to tell people what services they offer. The choice is up to you.

You might want to include price as part of your brochure, but this usually isn't the best idea for consultants. Keeping your price as part of a price list, to be given to the potential client after you make your sales pitch, is usually a better idea. Of course, every form of advertising you create should contain your Novell certification. Have you ever noticed how other vendors use this technique to attract business? Look at other brochures for specific ideas on how to present your certification. Two methods that you should always consider are to include the actual logo as part of your advertisement, and to add some text that says, "Fully Novell-Certified to work on your network."

The second problem you need to deal with is distribution. Some businesses use mass mailings to attract new clients. While this might work fine for your local food store, it usually doesn't work very well for a networking professional. Studies show that most responses from mass mailings now range from one to two percent (frankly, a much lower percentage than it used to be), though some businesses consistently get less than one percent and others consistently get much more. But if your responses are average you'll get only one or two people per one hundred mailings. So how do you get new clients? An advertising brochure is still a good idea, but the method of distribution can make all the difference in the world.

Word of mouth is a very good method for a consultant to gain new clients. Other professionals, such as doctors and lawyers, have relied on it for years. Referrals are another common method—a generalist will refer you to a specialist for particular kinds of work. Both methods work well for professionals certified by Novell. Experience shows that about half a typical consultant's clients came to him or her via word of mouth or referral.

You might also find that local newspapers and computer magazines are good places to advertise, too. Only one percent of the people you reach with a magazine advertisement will respond. Of those who respond, only about less than two percent will actually turn into clients.[1] This means you might have to reach 10,000 people to get a client via this method, but such numbers are not impossible when you consider how large a newspaper or magazine's circulation might be. Check those numbers! However, responses to yellow page advertisements can be much smaller, because the audience is less

---

1 Results obtained from a survey of 50 computer consultants, who relied on all three methods of gaining new clients.

inclined to need computer services. As you can see, the one or two clients you gain using advertisements need to pay off with large work loads and lots of referrals to make the effort worthwhile.

# ⇨ Brochures, business cards, and price lists

There are three documents that do not fall into the advertisement category but can act as subtle reminders of the services you offer. They include brochures, business cards, and price lists. All three of these items should end up in the hands of your clients. If you can get clients to look at these items from time to time, the subtle reminders you include will help them remember what services you offer. They might also prompt them to tell others about you. Remember, referrals are one of your best means of gaining new clients.

Business cards offer very little room for advertising. By the time you add a name, address, and telephone/number, you have little room left over for anything else. However, you can usually add a logo or two, plus a slug line. You normally add your business logo on the same line or directly below the name of your business. The logo identifies your business to people. They might actually look for the logo instead of your name when they look for your business card. Adding your Novell certification logo to the bottom right or left corner of your business card adds a subtle reminder about one of the types of service that you offer. This little graphic says a lot about you and your business.

The slug line usually includes one- or-two word reminders of services you offer, or perhaps says something about your business philosophy. Make sure you add a reference to your Novell certification here, as well. It doesn't have to contain many words. Simply saying "Novell Certified" usually gets your point across to the client.

Price lists are a very important part of your business. Some clients might actually believe that you go out of your way to overcharge them if you don't provide documentation. In addition, some clients view the lack of a price list as an indication that you are willing to negotiate. If you are not willing to make this concession, a price list is the best way

to tell the client. Providing them with a document that spells out what you charge and how you apply those charges is very important in maintaining good client relations.

If you wish to make the price list pay some dividend in increased sales or other tangible benefits, adding something as small and unobtrusive as your Novell logo can provide a big payback. As your client peruses your price list, they also get a reminder of why you charge more than Joe or Sally down the street. Your certification logo reminds them that they are paying for a higher quality of service. It also reminds them to tell their friends about the quality service they receive from you. Even a price list can serve as an advertisement. Make sure you get the full benefit from the investment you make in this document.

The final document is a brochure of some type, which can include everything from pure advertising brochures (containing nothing else) to documents designed to help your client use your services more efficiently. For example, how often has the client asked you about what your certification really represents? It makes good sense to create a brochure that tells clients about your certification and explains why it is important. If your business uses more than one level of certification, your brochure might help clients understand what services they can expect from each of your employees. Make sure you create valuable tools of this type to reduce the time you spend answering client questions. And again, make sure you add your certification logo whenever possible.

# ⇨ Carrying your ID card

The first purpose that comes to many people's minds, with respect to a badge, is identification. It is true that your Novell badge will identify you to your clients. It provides them with a picture, a name, and a certification number they can use for reference. This provides the client with a sense of security; they know who you are and what you represent.

However, if you spend any time going from site to site, you soon realize that clients judge you by your appearance and your demeanor on the first visit. For example, your way of dealing with client questions makes a big impact. A charming idiot will obtain more clients than a surly genius. (Keeping them is another matter; the surly genius who gets the job done usually wins on this count.)

However, we all know the importance of dressing for the job and making sure we present a professional appearance, but this only skims the surface. Use subliminal methods to tell people about you and your business. For example, wearing your Novell badge can lead to a client-initiated conversation about your qualifications. A client who asks about your qualifications is much less likely to think you're boasting about your qualifications, and much more likely to think you provide complete and reasonable answers to his questions.

Your badge says a lot. Wearing it helps people see that your qualification means a lot to you. It also shows that you have the knowledge required to keep their network running or to get it installed, and that you take pride in your abilities. People tend to remember first impressions; that's why it's so difficult for a consultant to overcome a negative one. Make sure you make the right first impression by helping people see you as a true professional.

# ⇨ Determining what services to offer

To determine what services you want to offer, begin by inventorying your skills. You also need to consider what prospective clients in your area need the most, and what they view as the most valuable. The first part is fairly easy; simply create a list of your skills then rank them from 1 to 10. Figure 3-1 provided you an opportunity to survey your networking skills. Figure 8-1 provides the same opportunity but involves more of your skills.

Notice that there are four sections in this survey. The first section asks you about your hardware experience. The second and third sections ask about your software and training experience respectively. These are the three major areas of participation for a consultant, but there are other areas as well. For example, the fourth section contains a

Figure 8-1

Hardware

| Skills | Level | | | | | | | | | |
|---|---|---|---|---|---|---|---|---|---|---|
| | High | | | | | | | | | Low |
| | 10 | 9 | 8 | 7 | 6 | 5 | 4 | 3 | 2 | 1 |
| Cable Installation | | | | | | | | | | |
| Computer System Building | | | | | | | | | | |
| Computer System Installation | | | | | | | | | | |
| Computer System Repair/Maintenance | | | | | | | | | | |
| Routers/Bridges/Hubs/etc. | | | | | | | | | | |
| Mini and Mainframe Connections | | | | | | | | | | |
| Scientific/Specialty Installations | | | | | | | | | | |
| Others: | | | | | | | | | | |
| | | | | | | | | | | |
| | | | | | | | | | | |
| | | | | | | | | | | |
| | | | | | | | | | | |
| | | | | | | | | | | |

*Network consultant skills survey*

listing for the lucrative area of technical writing. How does each of these areas relate to your Novell certification? As you gain knowledge and experience with networks, your hardware experience will grow. In addition, companies will call on your networking experience when they try to get their software to work. This knowledge is always a

Software

| Skills | Level | | | | | | | | | |
|---|---|---|---|---|---|---|---|---|---|---|
| | High | | | | | | | | | Low |
| | 10 | 9 | 8 | 7 | 6 | 5 | 4 | 3 | 2 | 1 |
| Programming | | | | | | | | | | |
| Installation/Upgrades | | | | | | | | | | |
| Configuration Management (the software configuration for each machine) | | | | | | | | | | |
| License Management | | | | | | | | | | |
| Fault Resolution (making the hardware and software work together) | | | | | | | | | | |
| Others: | | | | | | | | | | |
| | | | | | | | | | | |
| | | | | | | | | | | |
| | | | | | | | | | | |
| | | | | | | | | | | |
| | | | | | | | | | | |
| | | | | | | | | | | |

Networking

*continued*

marketable skill. And how many times have you walked into a situation in which the client had little or no documentation for his network? The need for technical writers becomes obvious when you look at this need. You can enhance each of these skills when you get your Novell certification.

Figure 8-1

Training

| Skills | Level | | | | | | | | | |
|---|---|---|---|---|---|---|---|---|---|---|
| | High | | | | | | | | | Low |
| | 10 | 9 | 8 | 7 | 6 | 5 | 4 | 3 | 2 | 1 |
| Database | | | | | | | | | | |
| Spreadsheet | | | | | | | | | | |
| Word Processing | | | | | | | | | | |
| Graphics Software | | | | | | | | | | |
| Custom Software | | | | | | | | | | |
| Network Maintenance/Administration | | | | | | | | | | |
| Hardware Maintenance/Repair | | | | | | | | | | |
| Technical Support Technician | | | | | | | | | | |
| Peripheral Device Support (print server support) | | | | | | | | | | |
| Others: | | | | | | | | | | |
| | | | | | | | | | | |
| | | | | | | | | | | |
| | | | | | | | | | | |
| | | | | | | | | | | |
| | | | | | | | | | | |

*continued*

Other

| Skills | Level | | | | | | | | | |
| | High | | | | | | | | Low | |
| | 10 | 9 | 8 | 7 | 6 | 5 | 4 | 3 | 2 | 1 |
| Technical Writing (network documemtation and user manuals) | | | | | | | | | | |
| | | | | | | | | | | |
| Others: | | | | | | | | | | |
| | | | | | | | | | | |
| | | | | | | | | | | |
| | | | | | | | | | | |
| | | | | | | | | | | |
| | | | | | | | | | | |

*continued*

You can answer the second part of the new services equation in two ways. First, you can simply ask your clients what they need. You might want to ask them leading questions that produce more than yes or no answers. Make sure you look at their business for opportunities. You might find that various clients have not considered certain service items in the past. Don't be surprised if the client turns down some of your ideas. They might not see a need to pursue them, and any arguments on your part might serve to alienate the client. Figure 8-2 provides you with a simple survey you can ask the client to fill out, or simply use as a reference document when you ask the questions in person.

The sample survey shows you how to phrase an open-ended question. Notice that we didn't ask the client if they planned to expand the number of products they produced, but what new products they already have in mind. This assumes that the client's business is in good shape and that they plan to grow—you really wouldn't want to assume anything else. You might also want to explore the outer reaches of networking with your questions. For example, we ask clients about their mainframe databases. Many clients do not even think of downsizing their current applications until you ask them about it. Make the client see your visions as their own ideas. Asking questions like the ones shown in Fig. 8-2 will make it appear that the client had the idea, not you.

Figure 8-2

1. In what ways do you see your need for customized software support growing in the future? How far into the future?

2. What types of new products are you planning to build in the future? How will this affect your network.

3. When do you plan to downsize your current mainframe database to a PC LAN?

4. How can we improve the reliability of your network? What types of hardware and software purchases are you willing to support to make these changes?

5. Are there tasks that you would like the network to perform but that you can't get it to do?

6. Have you considered any contingency plans if the network fails? If so, have you actually tested them?

7. Which methods do you find most effective for protecting your software investment?

8. Are there any other ways you could use my business help in making your's grow?

*Sample customer survey*

The second way you can identify the services your clients need is to look in your local newspaper and read case studies in the magazines or trade papers. These sources of information can provide ideas you can add to your survey. You might even want to simply offer a given service and see how many clients respond. Often, a client will say he is not interested in a service if you indicate it might be brand new, but the same client might respond favorably if the service were already in place.

# ⇨ Showing clients what your certification means

Your clients might not even know what your certification means—your clients are probably less informed than you. Yet this is one area they really do need to know about.

As a Novell-certified professional you can usually charge a little more than your noncertified competition for the same service. The reason is simple; you have demonstrated that you possess a set of fully developed skills, while the competition hasn't. However, your client will not see the value of this demonstration until you tell him or her about it. Until they do understand the significance of certification, client reactions to the higher rates you charge will range from accusations of overcharging to threats to retain someone else. But many of these objections go away once you make them aware of the advantages of certification.

The approach you take to the education process depends on the techniques you use to run your business. A hard-sell consultant might want to schedule a meeting with each client, to talk about his new certification and to make a proposal based on what it represents. A soft-sell consultant might simply print a brochure that fully explains what certification means, and might then provide it to his clients during scheduled visits. Other consultants might use a combination of both approaches, including mentioning it during regular meetings. Your management style will determine which techniques feel the most comfortable to you. However, the question of informing the client is clear. If you don't tell your clients why your certification is important they will never know.

There are specific advantages to each technique we describe for keeping your client informed. For example, brochures can double as advertisements. If a client passes your brochure on to a friend, you might find yourself with a new client. On the other hand, the special-meeting approach might yield a new networking job. A mention during a regular meeting might also improve the relationship between you and your client. Your client might feel that you're letting him in on something special. This often translates into greater customer loyalty and support.

You need to consider the temperament of your client when approaching him with news of your certification. Some clients like to talk with a consultant who lets them think about whatever the consultant has to say. They like to take time to think about what the new certification could mean to their business. For example, many educational and professional organizations, such as those run by doctors and lawyers, fall into this category. Other clients might appreciate the hard sell. They take it as a sign that you are an aggressive businessperson when you present your certification quickly, then add a proposal on how they could use the certification within their business.

# ⇨ Determining what to charge

Figuring out what to charge is always a difficult question. Charging too much can kill your business, yet charging too little might give you more business but too little profit. You need to find the middle ground. Unfortunately, this is like one of those psychology tests that we all hate. There are no right answers; just right answers for *you*. No matter how little you charge, someone who really wants a lower price can probably find it. The same holds true for higher prices. Of course, the people who determine the extremes are your competitors. Your competitors are the ones who will steal your clients and put you out of business, if possible. The bottom line is this. If a client sees an opportunity to get the same level of support that you provide from someone else, you can be sure they will use it.

So, how do you determine what the middle ground might be? You can start by doing a little research. Simply call the competition to see what they charge. There is no reason for them to withhold an answer from you if you call as someone looking for information rather than as a competitor. Another place to look is your local computer magazine or newspaper. Vendors often publish their rates for installations of specific types.

Sometimes, these methods don't produce any results. When this happens, try an alternative. For example, if you have a large client base with fairly new LANs, you can always ask your clients what they paid in the past for service. Also, federal, state, and local governments keep statistics on what businesses charge for certain services. You might find what you need to know from these sources as well, though you'll probably have to interpolate at some point.

There are other resources you should consider using. For example, CompuServe and other online services host a wide variety of consultant-based forums. You can usually determine the current rate for a given service by polling such groups of people. One word of caution here; many of the consultants that frequent these online services are at the upper end of the pay scale. You might not get a true reading on what the true average rate of pay is for a specific service.

As you can see, the only limits on the sources of information you use are the resources you want to tap. Deciding what you want to charge doesn't stop here. You also need to resolve such issues as what to charge for parts. Some consultants don't charge anything at all, beyond their own cost. They make it up by charging higher hourly rates. Other consultants tack 10 to 15 percent onto the price of the parts they sell, and charge a lower hourly rate. Both approaches are equally useful. You need to decide which approach your clients will appreciate more.

There is also the issue of when to apply different rates. Some consultants offer more than one service. You need to decide if you want to charge the same rate for software installation as you do for network maintenance. If you do decide to charge one all-inclusive rate, you might find that some customers balk when you present a bill for training that costs the same as their network installation.

If you want to use different pay scales for different services you need to decide when one pay scale ends and the other begins. Here, consultants can run into trouble. Some clients will try to cheat the consultant by saying that the service they performed should have been at a lower rate than the service the consultant actually performed. For example, what happens if the client constantly interrupts you with questions during a network installation. Do you charge them the network installation rate or the lower training rate? The client might choose the training rate. They might not feel you deserve the full networking rate because you spent so much time training them. The best course of action is to tell the client what rate you are charging for the work you are performing. Make sure you inform them when the rate changes, because the task you perform changes, too.

Rate setting is not the easiest part of consulting. You need to provide your clients with written rates and the criteria you use for charging them. You also need to make them aware of when rates change, and why. If possible, always make sure you write down the rules for rate changes, and get the customer's signature. Many consultants refuse to work without a signed contract; it's very easy to see why.

# ⇨ Professionalism

Respect is not given, it's earned. Many of us have heard that saying as we've advanced along our career paths. Yet how many really know what it means? Professionalism in the way you perform your job is what earns the respect of your clients. Professionalism means that you are proud of your abilities and the work you do. It also means that you set certain standards for yourself and stand by your work. Some people call this type of behavior old-fashioned or out-of-date, but most clients appreciate a professional when they see one.

Where do you stand on this issue? How do you know when you achieve professional status? Some people set up a stiff set of rules and call it professionalism. Nothing could be further from true professionalism than a set of stiff rules. Even crooks and thieves set up rules for themselves, then they misuse the rules to skirt their real responsibilities, and neglect to fulfill their promises. Professionalism is more of a mindset than many people realize. Figure 8-3 provides you with a checklist that you can use to measure your professionaliam rating.

As you can see, in many situations you might need to think about the consequences of your actions before you actually do them. For example, when does a client deserve warranty service? Is it always cut-and-dried? Sometimes the gray areas make this a hard question to answer. For example, imagine that a client calls you in for warranty

Figure 8-3

☐ Use high-quality parts whenever possible. High quality does not necessarily mean high cost. Look for product reviews in trade magazines and newspapers. It also helps to look for opinions from other network professionals on CompuServe or other on-line media.

☐ Try to reduce costs whenever it will not affect the quality or usefulness of a product the client needs. If a product breaks the first time you use it or the part does not perform the task the client requires, then buying it at discount does not solve any problems. In fact, it actually creates more problems. However, buying a high-priced product simply to get the name value discredits your ability to help the client make prudent buying decisions.

☐ Always consider the cost of losing a client versus the cost of losing the money from one job. Losing a client always costs you more money than you'll lose from one job. If the client feels you mistreated him/her, find out what it will take to restore confidence. Often this means that you'll lose the profit from a job to save the client's trust.

☐ Never break the law to meet the demands of an unyielding client. For example, some clients will insist that you install pirated software on their network even though they know such an act is illegal. It is always better to lose a client than to knowingly break the law. Otherwise the client will expect you to break the law as often as they see fit. In addition, you will share in the client's guilt if you get caught performing the illegal act.

☐ Try to honor your warranty whenever possible. Many clients will try to convince you to honor unreasonable interpretations of the warranty you offer as part of your services. It often helps to honor the unreasonable request to maintain the client. Of course, this can backfire if the client starts expecting you to perform this service every time there is a dispute. The most reasonable course of action is to make sure the client understands that you are honoring the unreasonable request in the hope of maintaining a good relationship.

☐ Use the clearest wording possible in any written documentation you provide the client. This includes contracts and warranties. Make sure you go through the contract or warranty with the client and explain anything they don't understand. Using this technique helps reduce confusion later. It might also prevent you from losing a valued client by reducing the chances of misunderstandings.

*Professional network consultant's business guide*

Figure 8-3

☐ Always perform the work to the best of your ability. Even if the client does not possess the level of technical competence that you do, they do know what task the network should perform when you finish. Make sure that both hardware and software are up to par. Alert the user to potential problems with equipment that you did not install. Help the client understand why there are specific limitations to the installation you create for them.

☐ Never be afraid to admit that you can't perform a specific task. The client can respect you if you simply say that you can't perform a specific task they need help with. Trying to perform the task when you lack the skills will make the customer less likely to hire you again in the future.

*continued*

service on a drive that broke during use. If it appears that the client broke the part through negligence, you might feel they should pay for it. On the other hand, the client might feel he used the part in the manner prescribed by the vendor. Or, the vendor might make it so poorly there is no way to use the part without breaking it. What if this is a very expensive part and the vendor has a reputation for not honoring his warranties? (This happens more often than you might think with inexpensive parts.) If you perform the warranty service you will lose money. On the other hand, if you don't provide warranty service you will lose a valuable client.

Perhaps the most difficult part of being a professional is figuring out when actions on your part could prevent a negative situation from occurring at all. For example, in our previous illustration you might choose to use a higher quality part during installation. The higher quality part might last longer, so you might never need to figure out whether to honor your warranty. Also, because you used a higher quality part, both you and the client might be happier with the results. Setting such a standard for yourself might lose you a few jobs because you couldn't compete on cost, but it might prevent you from losing money later when the inexpensive parts break down. Every job has potential risks and rewards. The professional weighs the cost of each action and chooses the course that produces the best long-term results.

Professionalism is important for another reason. When people see you as a technician certified by Novell to maintain their network, they expect a higher standard of service. You are supposed to represent the best that the client can get in quality workmanship. Your certification proves that you care more about how people perceive your services than the person who does not choose to get certified. When you are on the job you represent not only yourself, but also every other certified individual who follows you.

As you can see, professionalism is not a mere word. There are many "experts" performing network installations today, but few professionals. You need to maintain a professional mindset as your career progresses, especially if you expect people to consider you something more than a hammer mechanic. Maintaining a high standard is hard work, but it pays many dividends.

Finally, even if professionalism is old-fashioned, people still respect it and look for it whenever possible. They want to know someone who takes the time to get the job done right the first time. Any other course of action is a waste of time and materials, and it reduces the value of your certification. Remember, you worked hard to become certified by Novell to do the work you do. Maintain your professionalism.

# Conclusion

We designed this chapter to meet the needs of the networking professional. It provides all the tools you need to efficiently market your new skills to both current and prospective clients.

The first section looked at the guerrilla warfare aspect of marketing your certification. How do you get the client to recognize your new skill without boring him or her to death? Many consultants find that this is one of the more difficult aspects of selling their certification.

The second section talks about the benefits of carrying your identification card. Pride in your work and your appearance are two things a client looks for in a consultant. Carrying your badge in a conspicuous place not only tells the client that you are a professional, it also helps sell your certification. Remember, networking jobs can help you raise the bottom line. Working at a higher rate of pay is always a desirable goal for the networking professional.

The third section of this chapter talks about what you need to do once you get the client interested. This includes everything from deciding what services to offer to telling the client what your certification means. Once you get the client's interest it's up to you to sell him on the benefits of your certification.

The final section helped you determine what certification means from a business perspective. For example, what do you charge for the new services you want to offer your clients? Trying to charge too much might cost you clients, both current and future. A higher rate of pay also means that you need to address some professionalism concerns. If you are charging your clients more, they deserve some side benefits in addition to the main service you provide. Where do you draw the line? What level of professionalism do you need to maintain to keep your current clients, gain a few new ones, and still get that pay increase we're all looking for?

# A

# Important
# phone numbers

Novell Main Office: 1-800-453-1267

Novell Education Department fax: 1-801-429-2500

Novell FaxBack: 1-800-233-3382 or 1-801-429-5363

Drake/Sylvan Testing Registration: 1-800-RED-EXAM

Novell Technical Support: 1-800-NET-WARE

Novell Users International (NUI): 1-800-873-3976 or 1-214-419-7882

Novell Education: 1-800-233-EDUC or 1-801-429-5508

Novell After-market Products: 1-800-346-7177 or 1-801-429-7000

Novell Education Materials Order: 1-800-346-6855

Novell Education Area Manager, Western U.S.: 1-408-747-4339

Novell Education Area Manager, West Central U.S.: 1-214-387-7900

Novell Education Area Manager, East Central U.S.: 1-708-228-7676

Novell Education Area Manager, Northeast U.S.: 1-215-647-0664

Novell Education Area Manager, Southeast U.S.: 1-404-698-8350

Novell Education Area Manager, Canada: 1-416-940-2670

CompuServe Registration: See your startup kit for instructions.

# B

# Sources of additional information

*Computer Technology Review*
924 Westwood Blvd., Suite 650
Los Angeles, CA 90024-2910
310-208-1335

*Data Communications*
1221 Avenue of the Americas
New York, NY 10020
1-800-525-5003

*Data Based Advisor*
Data Based Solutions, Inc.
4010 Morena Blvd., Suite 200
San Diego, CA 92117
619-483-6400
Fax: 619-483-9851

*Hands-On Guide to Network Management*
McGraw-Hill
Blue Ridge Summit, PA 17294-0850
1-800-233-1128
ISBN #0-8306-4440-7

*LAN Computing*
Professional Press, Inc.
101 Witmer Rd.
Horsham, PA 19044
215-957-4269

*LAN Technology*
P.O. Box 52315
Boulder, CO 80321-2315
1-800-456-1654

*LAN Times*
Publication Office
1900 O'Farrell St., Suite 200
San Mateo, CA 94403
1-800-525-5003

*NetWare Application Notes*
Novell
122 E. 1700 S.
Provo, UT 84606
1-800-377-4136
303-297-2725

*NetWare Buyers Guide*
Novell
122 E. 1700 S.
Provo, UT 84606-6194
1-800-873-2831

*NetWare Solutions*
DB Media Publications, Inc.
10711 Burnet Rd., Suite 305
Austin, TX 78758
512-873-7761
Fax: 512-873-7782

*Network Computing*
CMP Publications
600 Community Dr.
Manhasset, NY 11030
1-516-562-5071

*Network News*
CNE Professional Association
Mail Stop E-31-1
122 E. 1700 S.
Provo, UT 84606-6194
1-800-926-3776

*Network World*
161 Worcester Rd.
Framingham, MA 01701-9172
1-508-820-7444

*PC Magazine*
Ziff-Davis Publishing Co.
One Park Avenue
New York, NY 10016
212-503-5255

*PC Novice*
Reed Corporation
120 West Harvest Dr.
P.O. Box 85380
Lincoln, NE 68501
1-800-544-1264

*Systems Integration*
Cahners Publishing Associates/
Reed Publishing (USA), Inc.
275 Washington St.
Newton, MA 02158
617-964-3030
Fax: 617-558-4506

# C

# Course descriptions

## DOS for NetWare Users

The DOS for NetWare users course is a self-paced, workbook-based tutorial that you can use to learn about the Novell way of looking at DOS. If you have used DOS on a fairly consistent basis you won't need this course, because you will probably have the required knowledge. This course is for the person who has no prior DOS experience. Anyone who intends to learn about networking using NetWare should learn about DOS before they attempt any of the other courses in this book. Even though this course is no longer required for CNE certification under the new plan, you can still use it as part of the old certification program. CNAs will also benefit from the material in it. Topics in this course include:

➤ Introduction to DOS

➤ DOS Command Execution

➤ Disk Drive Operations

➤ File Maintenance

➤ Directory Maintenance

➢ Batch Files

➢ Configuration of DOS Systems

This course is a workbook-only tutorial. There are no instructor-led courses associated with it. You will need to order workbook number 883-001304-003. There are no prerequisites for this course. Once you complete this workbook, order the Microcomputer Concepts for NetWare Users course described in the following paragraph. It will help you study for the second part of the exam associated with this course.

Course length:      Approximately 6 hours
Course number:      1100
Test number:        50-15
Number of credits:  2

# Microcomputer Concepts for NetWare Users

The Microcomputer Concepts for NetWare Users course is a self-paced, workbook-based tutorial that you can use to learn about the Novell way of looking at your hardware. Most people who have worked with the hardware installed in their machine won't need this course, because they will have the required knowledge. This course is for the person who has no prior hardware-related experience. Anyone who intends to learn about networking, using NetWare, should learn about their machine before they attempt any of the other courses in this book. Even though this course is no longer required for CNE certification under the new plan, you can still use it as part of the old certification program. CNAs will also benefit from the material in this course. Topics in this course include:

➢ Introduction to Microcomputer Hardware

➢ Introduction to Microprocessors

➢ Data Bus

➢ Memory

> Disks and Disk Drives

> Video Displays

> Serial and Parallel Ports

> Computer System Configurations

This course is a workbook-only tutorial. There is no instructor-led courses associated with it. You will need to order workbook number 883-001305-002. There are no prerequisites for this course. Once you complete this workbook, order the Microcomputer Concepts for NetWare Users course described in the following paragraph. It will help you study for the second part of the exam associated with this course.

Course length:     Approximately 6 hours
Course number:    1101
Test number:       50-15 or 50-107 or 50-207
Number of credits:  2

# ⇨ NetWare 2.2 System Manager

The NetWare 2.2 System Manager Course teaches you the fundamentals of managing and maintaining a Novell v2.2 network. This course is for the person who is a system administrator, backup system administrator, or a beginner who wants to learn more about the workings of NetWare. Topics in this class include:

> NetWare hardware and software basics

> NetWare directory structures

> Drive mappings

> NetWare Security

> NetWare Console and command line utilities

> NetWare Menu Utilities

> Basic Printing

- ➤ Creating and Using Login Scripts
- ➤ Creating Novell Menus
- ➤ Loading Applications

This course includes instructor-led lectures and hands-on exercises. The hands-on exercises follow the same steps and procedures used in setting up and maintaining networks for real companies.

Prerequisites for this class include a basic working knowledge of DOS and knowing what a LAN is. The student's understanding of DOS must include directory hierarchy and how to create directories, plus how to create ASCII files, copy files, delete files, and change directories.

Course length:      3 days
Course number:      501
Test number:        50-20
Number of credits:  3

# NetWare 2.2 Advanced System Manager

The NetWare 2.2 Advanced System Manager course covers the advance management features of Novell NetWare version 2.2. The target audience for this course is the person who manages an existing NetWare 2.2 network, or a consultant needing advanced information about the NetWare 2.2 operating system. Topics in this course include:

- ➤ NetWare 2.2 Installation Overview
- ➤ NetWare Accounting
- ➤ Advanced Printing
- ➤ Advanced Menu Utilities
- ➤ Performance Management
- ➤ Troubleshooting Network Problems
- ➤ Memory Management

This course includes instructor-led lectures and structured, hands-on lab exercises. The lectures and lab exercises will enhance the student's understanding of the tasks and duties performed daily by system administrators and consultants working in the field of networking.

Prerequisites for this class include a working knowledge of DOS and NetWare. In addition, you must attend the 2.2 System Manager course before attending this course. The pace of the course is quite fast, making prior knowledge of NetWare a necessity.

Course length:     2 days
Course number:     502
Test number:       50-44
Number of credits: 2

# NetWare 3.x System Manager

The NetWare 3.x System Manager course centers on the basic tasks and duties for the administrator who is using the Novell NetWare 3.x operating system. The intended audience for this course includes network managers and networking consultants. This course will teach you the basics of using, managing, and maintaining a network running 3.x NetWare. Topics covered in the course include:

➢ NetWare 3.x Basics

➢ Setting up Directory Structures

➢ Working with NetWare Drive Mappings

➢ Understanding and Implementing NetWare Security

➢ Menu Utilities for Administrators

➢ File Server Administration Utilities

➢ Network Printing

➢ Customizing Users Access and Use to the Network

➢ Managing Network Applications

➢ Using Novell's Backup Utility

This course includes instructor-led lectures and hands-on exercises. The hands-on exercises follow the same steps and procedures used in setting up and maintaining networks for real companies.

Prerequisites for this class include a basic working knowledge of DOS and understanding basic LAN concepts. The student's understanding of DOS must include the directory hierarchy, how to create and manage directories, create ASCII files, copy files, and delete files.

Course length:        3 days
Course number:        505
Test number:          50-91
Number of credits:    3

# NetWare 3.x Advanced System Manager

The Novell NetWare 3.x Advanced System Manager course is an extension of the 3.x System Manager course. The lectures and lab exercises will enhance the student's understanding of the tasks and duties performed daily by system administrators and consultants working in the field of networking. The intended audience for this course includes system administrators and consultants. These advanced features include printing and the art of fine-tuning the network. Other topics covered in the course include:

➤ Advanced Command Line and Menu Utilities

➤ Concepts and Procedures of Performance Management

➤ Advanced Setup and Troubleshooting of Network Printing

➤ NetWare's Remote Management Utilities

➤ Concepts and Procedures of Open Protocol Support

➤ NetWare's Prevention and Maintenance Utilities

This course includes instructor-led lectures and structured, hands-on lab exercises. The lectures and lab exercises will enhance the actual tasks and duties performed by system administrators and consultants working in the field of networking.

Prerequisites for this class include having a working knowledge of DOS and NetWare. In addition, you must attend the 3.x System Manager course before attending this course. The pace of the course is quite fast, making prior knowledge of NetWare a necessity.

Course length:      2
days
Course number:      515
Test number:        50-82
Number of credits:  2

# NetWare 3.x Installation and Configuration Workshop

The NetWare 3.x Installation and Configuration Workshop teaches the student how to plan and install the NetWare 3.x operating system and client workstations. This course is for the person who has prior NetWare experience, and whose duties include managing or maintaining the network. This includes system managers and consultants. Combining this course with the NetWare 3.x Administration and NetWare 3.x Advanced Administration courses provides a complete understanding of NetWare 3.x. Topics in this course include:

➢ Installing the NetWare 3.11 Server

➢ Upgrading a NetWare 3.11 Server to NetWare 3.12

➢ Installing a NetWare 3.12 Server

➢ Installing the Client-DOS Requester

➢ Configuring the NetWare 3.x Server

➢ Managing the NetWare 3.x Server

➢ Strategies for Working in the NetWare 3.x Environment

➢ Performing NetWare Case Studies

This course includes instructor-led lectures and hands-on exercises. It concentrates on hands-on exercises using case studies that simulate typical network setups. The hands-on exercises follow the same steps and procedures used in setting up and maintaining NetWare 3.x for real companies.

Prerequisites for this class include a basic working knowledge of the NetWare 3.x operating system. You must complete the NetWare 3.x Administration (course 508) and NetWare 3.x Advanced Administration (course 518) courses or have equivalent experience before you take this class.

Course length:        2 days
Course number:        802
Test number:          50-132 or 50-232
Number of credits:    2

# NetWare 4.x Administration

The NetWare 4.x Administration course teaches you the fundamental knowledge and skills to manage and administer a Novell NetWare 4.x network. This course is for the person who currently manages or plans to manage a network running NetWare 4.x, or a consultant planning to support the operating system. Topics in this course include:

➤ Introduction of NetWare 4.x

➤ Connecting to and Using NetWare 4.x Resources

➤ The NetWare Directory Services (NDS)

➤ NetWare 4.x File System

➤ File System Security

➤ Directory Services Security

➤ NetWare 4.x File Server Management

➤ Introduction to Printing

➤ Setting Up the Users Network Environment

This course includes instructor-led lectures and hands-on exercises. The hands-on exercises follow the same steps and procedures used in setting up and maintaining networks for real companies.

Prerequisites for this class include a basic working knowledge of DOS and understanding basic LAN concepts. The student's understanding of DOS must include the directory hierarchy, how to create and manage directories, and how to create ASCII files, copy files, and delete files. The student should also have a working understanding of Windows 3.0 or above.

Course length:        4 days
Course number:        520
Test number:          50-122
Number of credits:    3

# NetWare 4.x Advanced Administration

The NetWare 4.x Advanced Administration course continues where the 4.x administration course stops. This course is for the manager or consultant working with a complex network installation. The course will teach you about planning, implementing, fine-tuning, and overseeing a complex network using NetWare 4.x. Topics in this course include:

➤ An Introduction to Complex Novell Networks

➤ Planning and Managing the NetWare Directory Services (NDS)

➤ Advanced Security Features

➤ Resource Auditing Features

➤ Advanced Printing

➤ Managing Client and Network Features and Services

➤ Fine-tuning NetWare 4.x for Optimum Performance

This course includes instructor-led lectures and hands-on exercises. The hands-on exercises follow the same steps and procedures used in setting up and maintaining networks for real companies.

Prerequisites for this class include having a working knowledge of DOS and NetWare. In addition, you must attend the 4.x administration course before attending this course. The pace of the course is quite fast, making prior knowledge of NetWare a necessity. The student's understanding of DOS must include the directory hierarchy, how to create and manage directories, and how to create ASCII files, copy files, and delete files. The student should also have a working understanding of Windows 3.0 or above.

Course length:        3 days
Course number:        525
Test number:          50-123
Number of credits:    2

# NetWare 3.x to 4.x Update

The NetWare 3.x to 4.x Update course identifies the new and enhanced features of the NetWare 4.x operating system over the 3.x operating system. The course is for the person who has experience working with networks, especially Novell NetWare 3.x. This includes system administrators and consultants. Combining this course with the NetWare Installation and Configuration Workshop course offers a complete overview of NetWare 4.x. Topics in this course include:

➢ NetWare 4.x Overview

➢ NetWare Directory Services (NDS) Concepts and Implementation

➢ NetWare 4.x Security for NDS and the File System

➢ Client and Utility Changes

➢ NetWare 4.x Print Services

➢ Resource Auditing Services

➢ Storage Management Features and Services

This course includes instructor-led lectures and hands-on exercises. The hands-on exercises follow the same steps and procedures used in setting up and maintaining networks for real companies.

Prerequisites for this class include prior NetWare experience (preferably with NetWare 3.x). Also required is a basic working knowledge of DOS and an understanding of basic LAN concepts. The student's understanding of DOS must include the directory hierarchy, how to create and manage directories, and how to create ASCII files, copy files, and delete files. The student should also have a working understanding of Windows 3.0 or above.

Course length:        3 days
Course number:        526
Test number:          50-124
Number of credits:    2

# NetWare 4.x Installation and Configuration Workshop

The NetWare 4.x Installation and Configuration Workshop teaches the student how to plan and install the NetWare 4.x operating system and client workstations. This course is for the person who has prior NetWare experience, and whose duties include managing or maintaining the network. This includes system managers and consultants. Combining this course with the NetWare 3.x to 4.x Update course provides a complete understanding of NetWare 4.x. Topics in this course include:

➤ Installing the 4.x Operating System

➤ Installing the DOS and Windows Workstation Client

➤ Migrating from NetWare 3.x to NetWare 4.x

➤ Managing the NetWare Directory Services (NDS)

➤ Setting up NetWare Printing Services

➤ Backing up and Restoring Data Using Netware Utilities

➤ Managing the File Server Using New NetWare Utilities

This course includes some instructor-led lectures, with most of the course consisting of hands-on exercises. The hands-on exercises follow the same steps and procedures used in setting up and maintaining networks for real companies.

Prerequisites for this class include prior NetWare experience (preferably with NetWare 3.x). Also required is a basic working knowledge of DOS and an understanding of basic LAN concepts. The student's understanding of DOS must include the directory hierarchy, how to create and manage directories, and how to create ASCII files, copy files, and delete files. The student should also have a working understanding of Windows 3.0 or above.

Course length:        2 days
Course number:        804
Test number:          50-126
Number of credits:    2

# ⇨ NetWare Service and Support

The NetWare Service and Support course will teach the student various hardware topics related to installing and maintaining the NetWare operating system. During this course you will install and configure network interface cards and disk subsystems, connect cables, and install both NetWare 2.x and 3.x. Other topics that the course will cover include:

➣ NetWare 2.x Architecture

➣ NetWare 3.x Architecture

➣ Multiserver Networks

➣ Internetworks

➣ Network Addressing

➣ Network Board Configurations

➣ Network Cabling

➣ Disk Storage

➣ Workstation Installation

- NetWare 2.x and 3.x Installation
- NetWare Router Installation
- NetWare Upgrading Procedures
- Troubleshooting Techniques and Tools
- Novell Diagnostics Utilities
- Common Network Problems

This course is instructor-led, with the students performing many hands-on exercises. The information and exercises in this course are the same tasks that technicians perform on a daily basis.

Prerequisites for this class include a working knowledge of the Intel-based personal computer. Other beneficial prerequisites would include knowledge of LAN and DOS basics.

| | |
|---|---|
| Course length: | 5 days |
| Course number: | 701 |
| Test number: | 50-46 |
| Number of credits: | 5 |

# Networking Technologies

The Networking Technologies course provides in-depth instruction that covers the theory and protocols of networking. Discussed in this class are the seven layers of the OSI model, the applications of each layer, and how they relate to networking. The course also contains information about the communication protocols of Novell's IPX/SPX and the TCP/IP protocol used by UNIX. Other topics of this course include:

- Understanding the History of Networking
- The Standards Setting Committees
- Data Encoding Schemes
- Data Transmission Modes
- Signal Multiplexing and Signal Conversion
- Network Topologies

➤ Circuit, Message and Packet-Switching Techniques

➤ The PSTN Network

➤ Functions of the IEEE 802.3, 802.4 and 802.5 Standards

➤ LocalTalk and AppleTalk Technology

➤ The SDLC and HDLC Protocols Used by Mainframe Networks

➤ NetWare Protocols of IPX/SPX

➤ Internet Protocols of TCP, UDP and IP

➤ SNA and DNA Network Architectures

This course is lecture-only with no hands-on computer exercises. However, the manuals provide written exercises at the end of every one of the twenty-nine chapters. The course covers many subjects related to networking, in just three days. By comparison to this intensive training, a college course usually covers less material in a whole year.

Prerequisites for this class are a basic understanding of LANs and a strong desire to learn more about the theories of networking. Because this course covers so much material, from the general to the specific, there is no other Novell-offered course that would provide so much assistance.

| | |
|---|---|
| Course length: | 3 days |
| Course number: | 200 |
| Test number: | 50-80 |
| Number of credits: | 3 |

# ⇨ GroupWise 4.x Administration

The GroupWise 4.x Administration course teaches you the fundamental knowledge and skills required to manage and administer a Novell GroupWise network. This course is for the person who currently manages or plans to manage a network running GroupWise, or a consultant planning to support GroupWise as part of their business. Topics in this course include:

> ➤ GroupWise Messaging System Structure

> ➤ Responsibilities of the GroupWise Administrator

> ➤ Single Post Office Administration

> ➤ Client Administration

> ➤ Multiple Post Office Administration

> ➤ Multiple Domain Systems

This course includes instructor-led lectures and hands-on exercises. The hands-on exercises follow the same steps and procedures used in setting up and maintaining networks for real companies.

Prerequisites for this class include a basic working knowledge of DOS, microcomputer concepts, Windows 3.x, and an understanding of basic LAN concepts. The student's understanding of DOS and microcomputer concepts must include all of the topics included in the DOS for NetWare Users (1100) and Microcomputer Concepts for NetWare Users (1101) courses described in this appendix. Successful completion of the NetWare 3.x Administration (508) or NetWare 4.x Administration (520) courses, or equivalent knowledge, are also required. The student should also have a working knowledge of the GroupWise user tools, but this isn't a requirement to begin the course.

Course length:       3 days
Course number:       325
Test number:         50-395, 50-154, or 50-254
Number of credits:   3

# ⇨ GroupWise 4.x Advanced Administration

The GroupWise 4.x Advanced Administration course continues where the GroupWise 4.x Administration course stops. This course is for the manager or consultant working with a complex network installation. The course will teach you about planning, implementing, fine-tuning, and overseeing a complex network using GroupWise. Topics in this course include:

This course includes instructor-led lectures and hands-on exercises. The hands-on exercises follow the same steps and procedures used in setting up and maintaining networks for real companies.

Prerequisites for this class include having a working knowledge of DOS, microcomputer hardware, and NetWare 3.x or 4.x Administration. In addition, you must attend the GroupWise Administration course (325) before attending this course. (You may also start the course by demonstrating the requisite experiential knowledge.) The pace of the course is quite fast, making prior knowledge of GroupWise a necessity. The student's understanding of DOS and microcomputer concepts must include all of the topics included in the DOS for NetWare Users (1100) and Microcomputer Concepts for NetWare Users (1101) courses described in this appendix.

| | |
|---|---|
| Course length: | 3 days |
| Course number: | 328 |
| Test number: | 50-604 |
| Number of credits: | 2 |

# GroupWise 4.x Asynchronous Gateways and Remote Client Support

The GroupWise 4.x Asynchronous Gateways and Remote Client Support course teaches you how to add and configure an asynchronous gateway to an exiting GroupWise installation. It also shows how to provide support for a remote client. This course is for the manager or consultant working with a complex network installation. The course will teach you about planning, implementing, fine-tuning and overseeing a complex network using UnixWare. Topics in this course include:

- ➤ GroupWise Asynchronous Gateway Overview

- ➤ DOS and OS/2 Asynchronous Gateways

- ➤ Microsoft Windows Remote Client

- ➤ Monitoring and Troubleshooting Asynchronous Gateways and Remote Clients

This course includes instructor-led lectures and hands-on exercises. The hands-on exercises follow the same steps and procedures used in setting up and maintaining networks for real companies.

Prerequisites for this class include having a working knowledge of DOS, Windows, microcomputer hardware, and NetWare 3.x or 4.x Administration. In addition, you must attend the GroupWise Administration course (325) before attending this course. (You may also start the course by demonstrating the requisite experiential knowledge.) An overall knowledge of OS/2 is also good, but not required to complete the course. The pace of the course is quite fast, making prior knowledge of GroupWise a necessity. The student's understanding of DOS and microcomputer concepts must include all of the topics included in the DOS for NetWare Users (1100) and Microcomputer Concepts for NetWare Users (1101) courses described in this appendix.

| | |
|---|---|
| Course length: | 2 days |
| Course number: | 326 |
| Test number: | 50-155 or 50-255 |
| Number of credits: | 1 |

# D

# Sample
# test questions

Throughout this book we give you many tips and provide insights on how to prepare for the certification exams. The chapters also include in-depth information about the course outlines, how to study for the courses, and detailed information about which courses are necessary to help you obtain your certification. To fully prepare for the exams, you should also know what the questions will look like.

This appendix introduces you to the types of questions you will see when you take the test to become Novell-certified. These questions are meant to help you prepare by showing you what the questions will look like. It is not our intent to create questions exactly the same as the ones that are on the tests, although some of them could be similar.

Each section of this appendix starts with a brief paragraph containing some test-taking tips to help you pass the exams. Also contained in the opening paragraphs are some of the traps to watch for that Novell has put into the test questions. After each tips and traps paragraph is a series of questions written about the core exams. As you take each of the tests, read the questions carefully. You will find the correct answers to each set of test questions at the end of this appendix.

If you want more sample test questions, Novell offers a computer-based program containing sample test questions from many of the CNE, ECNE and CNI exams. To receive a copy of this program, contact the Novell education department for a diskette or download the program from the NetWire forum on CompuServe.

When taking the test, read the test questions and answers thoroughly. Many times the word "not" is used to create a reverse-logic question; there will be a correct answer listed for reading the question both with and without the word "not". Another problem with the test questions is that they are poorly worded or phrased, or just very ambiguous. When you find these types of questions, reason out the answer by applying each answer to the question and finding the one that feels right. Similarly, for some questions, every answer seems to be correct. In these cases, put on your Novell glasses and choose the one that Novell itself recommends in the student manuals.

Finally, remember that sometimes more than one answer really *is* correct. The old tests always had one correct answer, but the new tests allow more than one correct answer. The rule of thumb? If you see two similar answers, pick the one that is most correct. If you see two equally correct but different answers, then select both.

# ⇨ DOS/Micro-Hardware

The DOS/Micro-Hardware exam covers the basic and intermediate concepts pertaining to DOS commands and hardware knowledge. Things to watch for in the DOS section include understanding the configuration files and what commands go in each one, DOS external command syntax, DOS internal command syntax, and knowing how DOS interfaces with input, output and storage devices. The hardware section of the test covers topics such as the history of computers, processors, memory, storage devices, input and output devices, video, and a general knowledge of the Apple Macintosh and Intel-based computers.

# ⇨ Sample DOS/Micro-Hardware test questions

1. Which microprocessor was developed first?
   A. 8088
   B. 80286
   C. 80386
   D. 80486

2. To warm boot a computer you must
   A. turn the machine off then back on while it is still warm.
   B. press the reset button.
   C. press the Ctrl, Alt and Del keys all at the same time.
   D. use the setup disk.

3. Personal computers work with data in which format?
   A. ASCII          C. English
   B. Binary         D. Hexadecimal

4. The second set of 128 ASCII characters is known as
   A. ASCII-II.       C. UNIX.
   B. EBCDIC.         D. Extended character set.

5. To set the time on a personal computer you can
   A. use the DOS time command.
   B. use the set time command.
   C. power the computer off.
   D. It cannot be done.

6. The last drive statement is placed in the _____ file.
   A. Autoexec.bat    C. Command.com
   B. Config.sys      D. Either A or B

7. The DOS path command is used to
   A. tell DOS where to look for files.
   B. instruct DOS how to run programs.
   C. instruct DOS which circuit paths to use.
   D. All of the above.

8. One of the purposes for creating directories is
   A. it's fun.
   B. it's mandatory.
   C. the only way to run programs.
   D. to help organize your files.

9. Legal DOS wild card characters consist of _____ and _____.
   A. *, ?            C. ?, &
   B. *, !            D. ., :

10. The maximum length of a DOS file name is
    A. 7       C. 11
    B. 9       D. 13

11. One of the new features that DOS 7.0 adds is
    A. larger hard drive capability.
    B. a new file system.
    C. long filenames.
    D. more extended memory.

12. Types of NICs include
    A. Ethernet.        C. ArcNet.
    B. Internet.        D. Token Ring.

13. Config.sys does not contain
    A. the DOSKEY command.
    B. the FILES setting.
    C. any configuration information.
    D. memory-resident programs.

14. The parallel port communicates data 8 bits at a time.
    A. True        B. False

15. The DOSSHELL command does the following:
    A. Displays the status of Command.com.
    B. Allows you to multitask DOS applications.
    C. Prevents you from running Windows.
    D. Allows you to task switch DOS applications.

16. The two pin configurations for a serial port are
    A. 15-pin and 9-pin.
    B. 25-pin and 9-pin.
    C. 15-pin and 25-pin.
    D. There aren't two configurations.

17. Your machine normally _____ during the boot process.
    A. Executes the instructions in Config.sys, then Autoexec.bat
    B. Executes the instructions in Autoexec.bat, then Config.sys
    C. Loads the command processor
    D. Tests memory

18. The VER command
    A. Displays the version of the software you're currently using.
    B. Creates a new version of your boot files.
    C. Displays the current DOS version.
    D. Eliminates version information from the DOS environment.

19. The acronym SVGA stands for
    A. Some Video Graphics Adapter.
    B. System Virtual Graphics Access.
    C. Super Virtual Graphics Adapter.
    D. Super Virtual Graphics Array.

20. EMM386 performs what function(s) under DOS?
    A. Extended memory support
    B. Expanded memory support
    C. Memory configuration services
    D. It doesn't perform any service.

21. What are the current forms of extended memory support under DOS?
    A. DPMI              C. EMM
    B. LIM EMS 4.0       D. VCPI

22. WIN.INI contains
    A. Information that helps you win when using DOS.
    B. Windows configuration information.
    C. Windows system file entries.
    D. Windows setup program information.

23. You can optimize your DOS memory setup using
    A. the MEM command.          C. the RAMDRIVE utility.
    B. the MEMMAKER utility.      D. the EMM386 driver.

24. The 80386 processor can directly access
    A. 4 MB of RAM.       C. 4 GB of RAM.
    B. 16 MB of RAM.      D. 16 GB of RAM.

25. Jumpers perform what function?
    A. They allow you to configure peripheral devices.
    B. They allow you to short out specific settings on a card.
    C. They allow you to select a specific IRQ.
    D. They allow you to select a specific port address.

# ⇨ NetWare v2.2 Systems Manager

The NetWare v2.2 System Manager exams normally contain many questions about the security structure and how it works. Because this is one of the most important parts of NetWare, it makes sense that Novell would spend much time and ask many questions in this area. Other areas of focus include questions about drive pointers, login scripts, menu utilities and printing.

When taking the v2.2 and v3.11 System Manager exams, keep in mind which operating system you are taking the test for. Many of the questions are generic so that Novell can use them for either the v2.2 or v3.x11 operating system. The set of answers for each question will also be correct for both operating systems. The correct answer is the one that has to do with the test you are taking.

# Sample NetWare v2.2 System Manager test questions

1. A NetWare v2.2 dedicated file server can utilize a maximum of _____ of RAM.
   A. 8 MB      C. 16 MB
   B. 12 MB    D. 255 MB

2. The NetWare operating system resides at the _____ and controls the _____ devices.
   A. File server, Shared      C. File server, Workstation
   B. Workstation, Local       D. Both A and B

3. Which is not a system-created directory?
   A. The ETC directory        C. The Public directory
   B. The System directory     D. The Login directory

4. Which of the following is the correct MAP syntax?
   A. MAP S2:=FS1/SYS:PUBLIC/DOS
   B. MAP S3:FS1\VOL1/APPS\DB
   C. MAP G:=FS1\SYS;USERS\BOB
   D. MAP S2:=SYS:VOL1:PUBLIC\DOS

5. The NetWare security feature has _____ type(s) of security that is implemented at _____ levels.
   A. 4, 3      C. 1, 4
   B. 1, 3      D. None of the above

6. Which of the following access rights are not assigned to a user?
   A. Normal      C. Erase
   B. Read        D. Access control

7. The file attribute SRO is the abbreviation for
   A. System Read/Open.
   B. Shareable Read/Open.
   C. Shareable Read/Only.
   D. System Read/Only.

8. In NetWare you have the capability to create 3 types of operators; they are _____, _____, and _____.
   A. Console, Print Queue, Print Server
   B. Print Queue, Print Server, System
   C. System, Print Services, Back-up
   D. Print Queue, Print Server, Back-up

9. To print to a printer that is attached directly to the file server, you must
   A. Load the Pserver NLM at the file server.
   B. Load the Pserver EXE file at the file server.
   C. Link the core printing services during the install of the operating system.
   D. None of the above.

10. What are the three types of login scripts in order of execution?
   A. User, System, Network
   B. Default, System, User
   C. System, User, Default
   D. User, System, Default

# ⇨ NetWare v2.2 Advanced System Manager

The NetWare v2.2 Advanced System Manager exam focuses mainly in the areas of printing, troubleshooting, managing the network, and utilities that will help streamline the setup of the network. Topics that require the most attention and study by most people are printing and the meaning of the statistics in FConsole. Both of these areas are very important topics, pertaining to networking in the real world. Without proper understanding of how to properly use and work with them, you will find yourself in a real quandary.

You will find that many of the test questions relate to real-world situations. The more trouble people have with a particular topic on their network, the more Novell wants to be sure that anyone they certify knows how to handle these problems. Keeping this in mind, you can better prepare yourself for the exams by studying the most difficult areas of networking.

# Sample NetWare v2.2 Advanced System Manager test questions

1. The minimum and maximum amounts of RAM a nondedicated file server can effectively address are
   A. 2.5 MB and 8 MB.
   C. 2 MB and no limit.
   B. 2.5 MB and 12 MB.
   D. 2.5 MB and 16 MB.

2. What is not an option on the NetWare installation menu?
   A. Basic installation
   B. Advanced installation
   C. Maintain existing system
   D. Transfer from another server

3. What is not a valid type of workstation shell file?
   A. Netx.com
   C. XMSnetx.exe
   B. EMSnetx.exe
   D. LIMnetx.exe

4. What is the NetWare utility that is used to create the interface between the workstation and the network interface card, and what is the file name that is created?
   A. Shgen, Netx.com
   C. Shgen, IPX.com
   B. WSgen, Netx.com
   D. WSgen, IPX.com

5. A NetWare router will not work in which of the following modes?
   A. Dedicated protected mode
   B. Dedicated real mode
   C. Nondedicated protected mode
   D. None of the above

6. The NetWare accounting utility stores all of its entries in which file?
   A. NET$REC.DAT
   C. ACCOUNT$.DAT
   B. NET$ACCT.DAT
   D. Both A and B

7. The makeuser program is an alternative to which NetWare utility?
   A. SYSCON
   C. USER
   B. FILER
   D. CREATE

8. The D group memory segment is the most important part of the file server memory block. Adding more RAM to the file server increases the amount of this D group memory space.
   A. True
   B. False

9. The Fconsole utility can be used by all users of the network.
   A. True
   B. False

10. The Fconsole utility is also known as NetWare's _____ utility.
    A. Virtual console        C. D-bug
    B. Friendly               D. All of the above

11. The _____ memory pools of NetWare v2.2 can be viewed in the _____ screen of Fconsole.
    A. 4, Statistic Summary    C. 3, Memory Summary
    B. 3, Statistic Summary    D. 4, Memory Usage

12. By caching data into file server memory you can increase data access speeds by as much as _____ times.
    A. 10        C. 50
    B. 30        D. 100

13. The NetWare print services program can be loaded onto a
    A. File server.        C. Router.
    B. Workstation.        D. All of the above.

14. Print services are automatically setup during installation of the operating system.
    A. True        B. False

15. Which NetWare utility is used to set up basic network printing?
    A. PRINTDEF        C. PRINTCON
    B. PCONSOLE        D. PSC

# NetWare 3.x Installation and Configuration Workshop

The goal of this test is to determine your ability to install and configure NetWare 3.x, you will see questions on both hardware and software installation. It also means that you will need to be familiar with some, but not all, of the material related to setting up NetWare directories. Because this exam covers such a broad range of topics, you will need to spend a lot more time studying for it. Make certain that you understand the differences between various types of hardware, and what you need to do to configure them. Try performing several different types of NetWare 3.x installation as well. For example, there are some differences between a floppy disk and a server installation that you will need to know about.

## ⇨ Sample NetWare 3.x Installation and Configuration Workshop test questions

1. You must set aside _____ MB of hard disk space for a DOS partition prior to installing NetWare.
   A. 1  C. 5
   B. 2  D. 10

2. What command must you use to install a network adapter?
   A. Load <LAN Filename>
   B. Load <Protocol>
   C. Bind <Protocol> To <Adapter>
   D. None of the Above

3. Where are the NetWare server files usually located on the file server?
   A. \SERVER        C. \HOST
   B. \NETWARE.312   D. \SERVER.312

4. What disk must you put in the A drive during initial server software installation?
   A. SYSTEM_1   C. SYSTEM
   B. SERVER     D. LICENSE

5. The _____ directory on the installation CD-ROM contains the Install program used to start the installation process.
   A. \NETWARE\INSTALL
   B. \NETWARE.312\INSTALL
   C. \NETWARE\ENGLISH
   D. \NETWARE.312\ENGLISH

6. NetWare version 3.12 uses the _____ viewer to allow you to access the online documentation.
   A. Folio Views    C. Windows Help
   B. DynaText       D. DocView

7. File server names can have the following characteristics:
   A. The name can be from 2 to 47 characters.
   B. Valid characters include alphanumeric characters, hyphens, and underscores.
   C. You must use a number or letter for the first character in the name.
   D. The name cannot contain a period (.).
   E. Spaces are not allowed.

8. NetWare allows you to use any internal IPX number except _____
   and _____.
   A. 1, 2
   B. 0, FFFFFFh
   C. 0, FFFFFFFFh
   D. 0 through 9, F0000000h through FFFFFFFFh

9. The two components required to implement Burst Mode are the
   _____ file for the server and the _____ shell for the client.
   A. PBURST.NLM, BNETX.EXE
   B. BURST.NLM, NETX.EXE
   C. PBURST.NLM, NETX.EXE
   D. PBURST.NLM, VLM.EXE

10. The acronym NCP stands for
    A. Novell Circuit Protection.      C. Novell Core Protocol.
    B. NetWare Core Protocol.          D. NLM Cancellation Protocol.

11. The _____ login script command would allow user JOHNM to
    request access to file server FS1.
    A. ATTACH JOHNM/FS1
    B. ATTACH FS1/JOHNM
    C. LOGIN JOHNM/FS1
    D. LOGIN FS1/JOHNM

12. You would use the DISPLAY login script command to
    A. Change the settings for the user's display.
    B. Switch to another display in a dual display system.
    C. Show the current user configuration settings.
    D. Output a text file to the screen.

13. Which of the following is not a login script command?
    A. FIRE PHASERS        D. FDISPLAY
    B. EXIT                E. None of the above.
    C. PCCOMPATIBLE

14. The SYSCOM utility allows you to set up users and groups.
    A. True        B. False

15. The INSTALL utility creates these four directories as a default.
    A. LOGIN, SYSTEM, MAIL, and SUPER
    B. LOGIN, MAIL, PUBLIC, and PRIVATE
    C. LOGIN, MAIL, SYSTEM, and PUBLIC
    D. SUPER, LOGIN, SYSTEM, AND PUBLIC

16. Your file server must have a minimum of _____ of RAM to run NetWare 3.12.
    A. 2 MB        C. 8 MB
    B. 4 MB        D. 16 MB

17. Communication buffers and directory cache buffers use the _____ memory pool.
    A. Semi-permanent        C. Cache nonmovable
    B. Cache movable         D. Permanent

18. The default packet receive buffer size for a NetWare v3.12 server is _____.
    A. 1 KB        C. 4 KB
    B. 2 KB        D. 8 KB

19. The acronym SAP stands for _____.
    A. Special Access Protocol.        C. Service Access Protocol.
    B. Serial Access Protocol.         D. Service Advertising Protocol.

20. When upgrading a 2.x server to a 3.12 server, you need the _____ on the _____ disk.
    A. UPGRADE.NLM, SYSTEM_1
    B. UPGRADE.NLM, SYSTEM_2
    C. 2XUPGRDE.NLM, SYSTEM_1
    D. 2XUPGRDE.NLM, SYSTEM_2

21. To upgrade a 3.x server to a 3.12 server, you must have _____ of free space on volume SYS.
    A. 15 MB        C. 25 MB
    B. 20 MB        D. 30 MB

22. You would add the MOUNT ALL command to the _____ file.
    A. Autoexec.bat        C. Startup.ncf
    B. Autoexec.ncf        D. Config.ncf

23. The two migration methods provided by NetWare include
    A. in place and across the wire.
    B. same server and remote.
    C. same server and across the wire.
    D. in place and remote.

24. Before starting the migration process, you must ensure that Config.sys contains a _____ entry and that Net.cfg contains a _____ entry.

A. FILES=20, IPX RETRY COUNT = 60
B. FILES=40, IPX RETRY COUNT = 40
C. FILES=100, IPX RETRY COUNT = 100
D. FILES=60, IPX RETRY COUNT = 60

25. The SYS:PRIVATE directory contains
    A. operating system files and supervisor-specific utilities.
    B. special user-oriented utility files.
    C. programs needed to log in.
    D. There is no SYS:PRIVATE directory in the default setup.

# ⇨ NetWare 3.x11 System Manager

The NetWare v3.x11 System Manager exam is very similar to the v2.2 System Manager exam. You will also notice similarities to the NetWare 4.x System Administration exam; in some situations the same questions appear on both the 3.x and 4.x exams, but different answers will apply because of the differences between operating systems. Subjects that demand extra study time include the concepts of NetWare, security, menu utilities, drive mappings, the proper mapping command syntax, and automating the login process with the use of login scripts. Of these topics, security is the one to pay the most attention to. Make sure that you know how the trustee rights, directory rights, and file rights affect each other, and how to implement them. You also need a comprehensive understanding of the concepts of attributes, at both the file and directory level, and how to assign them.

The same type of questions will appear on the test; possibly, the same questions from the other 2.2 System Manager or 4.x System Administration tests. Remember that the only difference between the v2.2 or 4.x answers and the v3.x11 answers is the test that you are taking. In other words, the question will not specify the operating system and the answer will have the correct answer for both NetWare v2.2, 4.x, and v3.x11. Because you are now taking the test for v3.x11, the correct answer will be the one that deals with the v3.x11 operating system.

You might also note that some questions are poorly worded or seem a little confusing. As in any real-life situation, you have to think about what the question is asking before you answer it. One of the big things to remember is to put on your Novell "red" glasses before you enter the testing area, because there is only one right answer—the one that Novell expects you to provide as a certified individual.

# Sample NetWare v3.x11 System Manager test questions

1. NetWare v3.x11 does not support which one of the following operating systems?
   A. DOS
   B. UNIX
   C. MACINTOSH
   D. WINDOWS
   E. None of the above

2. The NetWare operating system supports _____ of RAM and _____ of disk storage.
   A. 4 GB, 32 TB
   B. 12 MB, 2 GB
   C. 16 MB, 2 GB
   D. 255 MB, 4 GB

3. There are _____ letters available for assignment as network regular drive pointers.
   A. 5
   B. 16
   C. 21
   D. 26
   E. No limit

4. Each NetWare user can have _____ search drive assignments.
   A. 5
   B. 16
   C. 21
   D. 26
   E. No limit

5. NetWare v3.x11 has _____ levels of security.
   A. 2
   B. 3
   C. 4
   D. None of the above

6. Which of the following is not a NetWare bindery file?
   A. NET$OBJ.SYS
   B. NET$PROP.SYS
   C. NET$BIND.SYS
   D. NET$VAL.SYS

7. Which of the following are not allowed to create user accounts on the network?
   A. Workgroup managers
   B. User account managers
   C. Supervisor
   D. Supervisor equivalent

8. The modify security right allows a user to change a file's
   A. contents.          C. attributes.
   B. security rights.    D. All of the above.

9. If a user is explicitly granted the RF rights to a directory, but the directory has had the R and W rights removed, what are the user's effective rights for that directory?
   A. RW          C. F
   B. RF          D. No rights

10. NetWare attribute security can be assigned to
    A. files only.              C. files and users.
    B. files and directories.    D. All of the above.

11. When using the NetWare menu utilities, the F3 key will _____ an entry.
    A. Modify        C. Mark or toggle
    B. Delete        D. Insert

12. The SYSCON utility can be used to
    A. create a new user account.    D. both A and B.
    B. create a new group account.   E. All of the above.
    C. change file attributes.

13. NetWare console commands are divided into the four categories of
    A. screen, configuration, maintenance and installation.
    B. installation, maintenance, load and bind.
    C. down, load, bind and monitor.
    D. configuration, maintenance, installation and monitor.

14. The user login script runs from the _____ file, which is located in the _____ directory.
    A. Login.exe, user's mail    C. Personal, user's home
    B. User$log, mail            D. Login, user's mail

15. When creating a NetWare menu, the script file must have a _____ extension.
    A. .SPT        C. .EXE
    B. .MNU        D. .DAT

16. The NetWare utility to backup and restore DOS and MACINTOSH files on a v2.x and v3.x file server, you would use the _____ utility.
    A. SBackup      C. NBackup
    B. Narchive     D. None of the above

17. A Macintosh must have _____ of installed memory to use NetWare
    Tools when running System 7.0 or above.
    A. 640 KB          C. 3 MB
    B. 2.5 MB          D. 4 MB

18. Apple scrambled passwords are supported on NetWare servers.
    A. True          B. False

19. The NetWare backup utility log contains which of the following
    entries.
    A. Session date and time
    B. Description of the backup session
    C. Target
    D. Media set ID
    E. Data backup list and file name-space type

20. A _____ backs up all data modified since the last full backup.
    A. Full                C. Differential
    B. Incremental         D. Custom

21. Which utility allows you to close the files left open by a
    workstation that crashed?
    A. CLEAR STATION          C. CLOSE STATION
    B. DISABLE LOGIN          D. CLEAR USER

22. The acronym TTS stands for
    A. transition tracking system.
    B. testing and tasking software.
    C. transport transition simulation.
    D. transaction tracking system.

23. The ACONSOLE utility allows you to
    A. connect to a remote workstation using a modem.
    B. connect to a remote file server using a modem.
    C. create an archive of any console commands you execute.
    D. display the active console commands.

24. You would use the _____ utility to upgrade a workstation running
    IPX drivers to ODI drivers.
    A. WSUPGRD          C. INSTALL
    B. WSUPDATE         D. SETUP

25. You can increase password security by requiring which of the
    following?

A. A minimum password length
B. A numeric password
C. A periodic change in the password
D. A unique password

# NetWare v3.x11 Advanced System Manager

The advanced system manager exam for NetWare v3.x11 deals quite a bit with the management strategies and performance management of the operating system. Many of the questions on the test deal with how to set up the workstation files, such as the standard IPX and NETX interface, as well as the ODI shells, the shell enhancement configuration files of NET.CFG and SHELL.CFG, and the commands that go into them. You will also find that the performance management and advanced printing sections of the student manual receive heavy emphasis during the exam. Remember that these are the areas that give the most grief to network administrators, so Novell will want to make sure that you fully comprehend the concepts and uses of each area. Other areas that generate quite a few questions are the prevention and maintenance sections. These areas have some very good information about general maintenance and prevention strategies for your networks, and about the SBACKUP utility. You can count on having a question or two about SBACKUP.

# Sample NetWare v3.x11 Advanced System Manager test questions

1. The NetWare command line utility that can list all the files and the location of each file for a specific user is
   A. DIR.
   B. LISTDIR.
   C. FILEFIND.
   D. NDIR.

2. At the workstation, a user can modify the shell files by using a _____ file.
   A. Config.sys
   B. Net.cfg
   C. Net.sys
   D. Shell.sys

3. The shell.cfg and net.cfg file will modify
   A. Ipx.com.        C. Command.com.
   B. Netx.com.       D. Both A and B.

4. To automatically start the file server monitor utility during the
   server startup, you would place the appropriate command into the
   _____ file.
   A. Config.sys      C. Autoexec.bat
   B. Startup.ncf     D. Autoexec.ncf

5. The secure console command would prevent anyone from doing
   the following:
   A. Loading NLMs from the C drive.
   B. Entering the operating system debugger.
   C. Loading DOS after the file server has been downed.
   D. All of the above.

6. NetWare uses which tables to locate files on the hard disk?
   A. File Allocation     C. File location
   B. Directory entry     D. Both A and B

7. On a file server with multiple volumes, the DET is located
   A. only on volume SYS.
   B. on the C drive.
   C. on any volume the installer specifies.
   D. each volume.

8. The Directory entry table holds information about
   A. files.           C. file trustees.
   B. directories.     D. All of the above.

9. Disk allocation blocks can be divided into _____ block size for each
   volume.
   A. 4k       C. 64k
   B. 32k      D. All of the above

10. If the disk allocation blocks are set to 4k on one volume and 16k
    on another volume, then the file cache buffers should be set to
    _____ in size.
    A. 4k              D. 16k
    B. 8k              C. 12k
    E. Any of the above

11. File server memory that is not used by the operating system, or
    DOS, is given to the _____ pool.

A. File cache buffer     C. Allocate memory
B. Permanent memory     D. System reserve memory

12. If total cache buffers fall to _____ percent or below, you should add more RAM immediately to the file server.
   A. 10     C. 50
   B. 20     D. 80

13. NetWare printing performance is affected by
   A. the number of print jobs.     C. the number of printers.
   B. the size of print jobs.     D. All of the above.

14. If changes are made to an existing print server setup, the changes will take effect
   A. immediately.
   B. the next day.
   C. after the file server is downed.
   D. the next time the print server is brought up.

15. The NetWare remote management feature allows the system manager to allow a workstation to act as the file server console.
   A. True     B. False

16. The NetWare name space allows non-DOS operating systems to
   A. store files in native format.
   B. retain file names longer than 11 characters.
   C. retain file attributes.
   D. All of the above.
   E. None of the above.

17. The NetWare SBackup utility will
   A. backup 2.x and 3.x file servers.
   B. be run from a workstation with a tape unit attached to it.
   C. be used from the file server only.
   D. back up UNIX files only.

18. The SBackup utility creates temporary files in the _____ directory during the backup process.
   A. Public     C. Mail
   B. System     D. ETC

19. Before running the VRepair utility, you must first
   A. Get written permission from Novell.
   B. Log every user out of the network.
   C. Dismount the volume.
   D. Down the file server.

20. At the file server, the track on command is used to
    A. turn on the router tracking screen.
    B. track what each user does on the network.
    C. track disk usage.
    D. None of the above.

21. _____ rights are the rights a user can exercise in a given directory or file.
    A. Trustee        C. IRM
    B. Directory      D. Effective

22. The _____ right overrides the Inherited Rights Mask and can be revoked only from the directory where it was granted.
    A. Supervisory    C. Super user
    B. Modify         D. Access control

23. You would use the _____ utility to set up the print server and print queues, control network printing, and view network printing information.
    A. PRINTDEF       C. PCONSOLE
    B. PRINTCON       D. FCONSOLE

24. Novell provides the CAPTURE utility to provide the following services:
    A. Print screen displays.
    B. Print to a network printer from an application not designed to do so.
    C. Print text files from the command line.
    D. Print data to a network file.

25. You would use the _____ utility to allow NetWare to store non-DOS files (like those from the Macintosh) on a NetWare volume.
    A. ALLOW          C. CAPTURE
    B. ADD NAME SPACE D. FILER

# ⇨ NetWare 3.x to NetWare 4.x Update

There are several goals in this test. The main goal is to determine your ability to install and configure NetWare 4.x. This means that you will see questions on both hardware and software installation. It also means that you will need to know some, but not all, of the material related to setting up NetWare directories. The test will also test your knowledge of the differences between the NetWare 3.x and NetWare 4.x operating systems. You will need to demonstrate some knowledge of both, but obviously you won't get tested in a detailed manner. Finally, this test looks at your ability to handle any difficulties you will encounter when moving from one operating system to the other. You should expect to see at least a few questions that test your ability to diagnose and fix hardware- and software-related problems.

Because this exam covers such a broad range of topics, you will need to spend a lot more time studying for it. Make certain that you understand the differences between various types of hardware and what you need to do to configure them. Try performing several different types of NetWare 4.x installations as well (the various migration methods are especially important in this exam). For example, there are some differences between a floppy disk and a server installation that you will need to know about.

NetWare Directory Services (NDS) will be a major part of the NetWare 4.x specific information that this test will cover, because this is one item that a CNE doesn't work with as part of the NetWare 3.x operating system. You will want to spend some time working with objects and need to know how NDS makes NetWare 4.x different.

# Sample NetWare 3.x to NetWare 4.x Update test questions

1. NetWare v3.0 is not supported by the In-Place Upgrade.
   A. True      B. False

2. Which of the following resources must a server have before you can upgrade from NetWare 3.x to NetWare 4.x?
   A. Minimum 8 MB of RAM on the server.
   B. An 80486 processor.
   C. Minimum of 50 MB free space on volume SYS:.
   D. A VGA or above display adapter.
   E. None of the above.

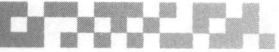

3. You will find a 3.x SERVER.EXE file on the _____ diskette.
   A. SETUP_1      C. UTILITY
   B. SETUP_2      D. UPDATE

4. NetWare 4.x installation requires a minimum of _____ of RAM when performing the in-place upgrade from 3.0 to 4.x.
   A. 4 MB       C. 12 MB
   B. 8 MB       D. 16 MB

5. NetWare requires the following information if you plan to upgrade a 3.1x server into an existing Directory tree:
   A. Tree name.             C. Administrator's name.
   B. Server context.        D. Administrator's password.

6. NetWare 4.x requires _____ of RAM for each user connection.
   A. 1 KB       C. 4 KB
   B. 2 KB       D. 8 KB

7. There is no change in directory and file rights from NetWare 3.12 to 4.x.
   A. True       B. False

8. The NetWare 4.x _____ right is the same as the NetWare 2.15 Delete right.
   A. Erase         C. Access control
   B. Delete        D. Parental

9. You no longer need the Open right because it is included with the _____ right(s).
   A. Read       C. Create
   B. Write      D. Erase

10. Novell recommends that you use electrical outlets with standard _____ wire grounded outlets, with the ground wire connected to a(n) _____ ground.
    A. two-, earth        C. two-, neutral
    B. three-, neutral    D. three-, earth

11. NetWare for OS/2 does not provide device drivers that allow the NetWare 4.x server software to run on an OS/2 computer.
    A. True       B. False

12. NetWare for OS/2 supports most NetWare 4.x drivers and NLMs except
    A. MONITOR.      C. DOMAIN.
    B. CDROM.        D. MATHLIB.

13. NetWare allows you to carry out any of these tasks on your print jobs if you have Queue User status:
    A. Place a job on hold.
    B. Release a job from hold.
    C. Determine the date and time a job will print.
    D. Delete a job.

14. To run the NetWare Tools application on a Macintosh running System 6.0.5 or later, you must have a minimum of _____ of RAM installed.
    A. 2 MB      C. 3 MB
    B. 2.5 MB     D. 3.5 MB

15. If a Macintosh user can see other AppleTalk services, but not the NetWare server (yet other Macintosh users can see the NetWare server), then the most likely cause is
    A. a faulty AppleTalk installation on the server.
    B. a bad NIC.
    C. that the server is not properly setup for that workstation.
    D. a faulty cable or router.

16. The /N parameter of the NetWare 4.x TSA_SMS utility allows you to specify
    A. an NDS name for the workstation.
    B. an NDS name for the file server.
    C. the name of the person performing the backup.
    D. the next workstation that you want to back up.

17. NetWare 4.x requires _____ of RAM for file compression enabled on any server volume.
    A. 75 KB      C. 250 KB
    B. 125 KB     D. 500 KB

18. The NAME CONTEXT = entry in NET.CFG allows you to set your current position in the directory tree structure.
    A. True      B. False

19. The Browser displays the NetWare Directory Services (NDS) objects in your
    A. current tree.      C. all contexts.
    B. all trees.        D. current context.

20. The File Scan right is assigned automatically when any of the NetWare rights is assigned.
    A. True      B. False

21. The NDS related _____ and _____ rights are new to NetWare 4.x.
    - A. parental, object
    - B. process, context
    - C. object, property
    - D. context, property

22. NetWare provides a set of default mappings between filename extensions and Macintosh information, about the application that created the file, if you enable extension mapping on a NetWare 4.x server.
    - A. True
    - B. False

23. Which of the following NDS objects are used to help manage print services and appear in the Directory tree in the Browser window?
    - A. Print User
    - B. Print Server
    - C. Print Context
    - D. Print Queue

24. The NetAdmin utility allows you to manage
    - A. Objects.
    - B. Properties.
    - C. Object Rights.
    - D. File System Rights.

25. The Access Control right no longer assigns the right to _____ or _____ subdirectories.
    - A. Delete, rename
    - B. Scan, rename
    - C. Create, rename
    - D. Create, delete

# ⇨ NetWare 4.x Installation and Configuration

The goal of this test is to determine your ability to install and configure NetWare 4.x. This means that you will see questions on both hardware and software installation. It also means that you will need to know some, but not all, of the material related to setting up NetWare directories. You will also need to know something about setting up NetWare users. It is likely that you will see some NDS-specific questions in this exam as well. However, the other exams look at this subject in depth, so the number of NDS-specific questions will be few. Because this exam covers such a broad range of topics, you will need to spend a lot more time studying for it than you would for an administration exam. Make certain that you understand the differences between various types of hardware, and what you need to do to configure them. Try performing several different types of NetWare 4.x installations as well. For example, there are some differences between a floppy disk and a server installation that you will need to know about.

# Sample NetWare 4.x Installation and Configuration test questions

1. One of the new features in NetWare 4.x is a global, distributed, replicated database that maintains information about *every* resource on the network called
   A. The Internet.
   B. NDS.
   C. SAP.
   D. The bindery.

2. An NDS object consists of categories of information, called _____, and the data they contain.
   A. Events
   B. Elements
   C. Properties
   D. Qualities

3. The minimum hard drive space required to install a new NetWare 4.x server is _____, but Novell recommends you have a minimum of _____.
   A. 2 MB, 5 MB.
   B. 5 MB, 10 MB.
   C. 5 MB, 7 MB.
   D. 2 MB, 10 MB.

4. You must run the _____ utility before installing your NetWare server if you are using a DCB disk driver for a disk subsystem.
   A. DISKSET.EXE
   B. DBCSET.EXE
   C. DISKSET.NLM
   D. DBCSET.NLM

5. The acronym NDS stands for
   A. Novell Directory System.
   B. NetWare Directory System.
   C. Novell Directory Services.
   D. NetWare Directory Services.

6. The new file compression capability provided by NetWare 4.x will allow you to reduce file size by up to
   A. 25%.
   B. 33%.
   C. 63%.
   D. 65%.

7. For NetWare for OS/2, the minimum hard disk size is
   A. 50 MB.
   B. 120 MB.
   C. 60 MB.
   D. 100 MB.

8. A User object includes which of the following properties?
   A. Workstation IPX address      C. e-mail address
   B. Login name                    D. Password restrictions

9. When installing an NIC on an EISA or an MCA bus machine, you should install the board then run the computer's Setup or Reference program.
   A. True        B. False

10. The _____ directory on the installation CD-ROM contains the Install program used to start the installation process.
    A. \NETWARE\ENGLISH
    B. \NETWARE.4xx\ENGLISH
    C. \NETWARE\INSTALL
    D. \NETWARE.4xx\INSTALL

11. The INSTALL.NLM helps automate the installation process by performing which of the following tasks?
    A. Loading disk drivers
    B. Copying NetWare system files
    C. Loading LAN drivers
    D. Installing NetWare Directory Services
    E. Letting you edit the STARTUP.NCF and AUTOEXEC.NCF files

12. The Packet Burst protocol is designed to transmit multipacket messages efficiently over the internetwork.
    A. True        B. False

13. The acronym LIP stands for
    A. Level Internetworking Protocol.
    B. Large Internet Packets.
    C. Low-level Internet Protocol.
    D. Large Internet Protocol.

14. The ACL property contains the trustee assignments and the Inherited Rights Filter (IRF).
    A. True        B. False

15. When using an IDE drive you should load the _____ disk driver at the server.
    A. ISADISK.NLM        C. ISADISK.DSK
    B. IDE.NLM            D. IDE.DSK

16. A volume SYS: is _____; its minimum size is _____.
    A. optional, 50 MB        C. mandatory, 50 MB
    B. optional, 60 MB        D. mandatory, 60 MB

17. NetWare 4.x print server enhancements include which of the following?
    A. Ability of one print server to now service up to 256 printers
    B. Support for third-party print job configurations
    C. Support for configuring print queue polling time
    D. Support for Macintosh and NFS clients
    E. An unlimited number of print job configurations.

18. Object rights control the object as a single piece in the Directory tree and allow access to information stored within that object.
    A. True    B. False

19. Novell suggests that, if performance is most important, you should span one NetWare volume over many hard disks with one segment of the volume on each hard disk.
    A. True    B. False

20. The NetWare 4.x online documentation requires _____ of hard disk space.
    A. 15 MB    C. 60 MB
    B. 30 MB    D. 120 MB

21. The default volume block size if you have a 500 MB hard disk is
    A. 4 KB.    C. 16 KB.
    B. 8 KB.    D. 32 KB.

22. Block suballocation saves server disk space by storing files in blocks of _____ bytes, in addition to the volume's configured block size (4, 8, 16, 32, or 64 KB)
    A. 128    C. 512
    B. 256    D. 1024

23. The four types of rights in NetWare 4.x include
    A. Object, Property, Directory, and File.
    B. Object, Context, Directory, and File.
    C. Event, Property, Directory, and File.
    D. Context, Object, Property, and User.

24. NetWare 4.x supports a maximum of _____ of RAM, and a maximum disk storage space of _____.
    A. 16 MB, 4 GB    C. 4 GB, 32 TB
    B. 4 GB, 32 GB    D. 16 GB, 32 TB

25. What types of objects make up the Directory tree?
    A. Root objects       C. Property objects
    B. Container objects   D. Leaf objects

# ⇨ NetWare 4.x Administration

The NetWare 4.x System Administration exam is very similar to the 3.x System Administration exam; in some situations the same questions appear on both the 3.x and 4.x exams, but different answers will apply because of the differences between operating systems. Subjects that demand extra study time include the concepts of NetWare, security, menu utilities, drive mappings, the proper mapping command syntax, and automating the login process with the use of login scripts. Of these topics, security is the one to pay the most attention to. Make sure that you know how the trustee rights, directory rights, and file rights affect each other, and how to implement them. You also need a comprehensive understanding of the concepts of attributes, at both the file and the directory level, and how to assign them. NDS also plays a very important part in NetWare 4.x, so make sure you take time to study that topic in detail.

As previously stated, the same type of questions will appear on this test as you saw on other system administration tests, possibly the same questions from the 3.x System Administration test. Remember that the only difference between the 3.x answers and the 4.x answers is the test that you are taking. In other words, the question will not specify the operating system and the suggested answers will include the correct answers for both NetWare 3.x and 4.x. (In some situations, Novell throws in the correct 2.x answer as well, for good measure.) Because you are now taking the test for 4.x, the correct answer will be the one that deals with the 4.x operating system.

You might also note that some questions are poorly worded or seem a little confusing. As in any real-life situation, you have to think about what the question is asking before you answer it. One of the big things to remember is to put on your Novell "red" glasses before you enter the testing area because there is only one right answer (or answers, if more than one is correct)—the one that Novell expects you to provide as a certified individual.

# ⇨ Sample NetWare 4.x Administration test questions

1. The Change Context command in the NetAdmin utility allows you to change where you are in the directory tree structure.
   A. True          B. False

2. The acronym MAC means
   A. Micro Address Central.
   B. Median Access Control.
   C. Media Access Control.
   D. Massive Address Control.

3. The layers of the OSI model are
   A. Application, Process, Session, Transport, Network Data Link, Interface, and Physical.
   B. Application, Presentation, Session, Transport, Network, Data Link, and Physical.
   C. Operating System, Process, Session, Transport, Network, Data Link, and Physical.
   D. Application, Process, Sequence, Transport, Network, Data Link, and Physical.

4. You can use login scripts to
   A. Map drives and search drives to directories.
   B. Display messages.
   C. Set environment variables.
   D. Execute programs or menus.

5. The UIMPORT workstation utility allows you to
   A. Distribute your NDS database by placing replicas of database partitions on different servers.
   B. Check and repair the database.
   C. Create one Directory tree from two separate trees by merging them at the root.
   D. Import information from an existing database to the NDS database.

6. A network printer, which includes _____, can print jobs sent from any network workstation.
   A. a DOS or OS/2 workstation with NPRINTER.EXE loaded
   B. a printer containing the NPRINTER software
   C. a NetWare server with PSERVER.NLM loaded
   D. a NetWare server with NPRINTER.NLM loaded

7. It is possible to remove NDS from a server using the
   A. Remove Directory Services from this Server option of the INSTALL.NLM.
   B. Remove Directory Services from this Server option of the DOS INSTALL utility.
   C. Remove Directory Services from this Server option of the UNINSTALL.NLM.
   D. It is impossible to remove NDS once you still it.

8. There are many differences in the way that login scripts work for DOS, Windows, and OS/2 workstations.
   A. True          B. False

9. The _____ object allows you to assign printer objects to print servers.
   A. Printer          C. Print Queue
   B. Print Server     D. Organization

10. The REGISTER MEMORY console command allows
    A. The use of older disk adapter boards, which use 16- or 24-bit DMA or Bus-Master DMA.
    B. You to exclude a range of memory from operating system use.
    C. You to load a special NetWare memory manager.
    D. The operating system to recognize installed memory above 16 MB.

11. You configure TCP/IP software on a NetWare v4.0 server using the _____ utility
    A. TCPCON.          C. INETCFG.
    B. INSTALL.         D. CONFIG.

12. Even if your application supports NetWare print services, you still need CAPTURE, NPRINT, and print job configurations to send network print jobs.
    A. True          B. False

13. You can create additional partitions and replicas using the
    A. NetWare Administrator graphical utility.
    B. CONFIG server utility.
    C. FILER text utility.
    D. PARTMGR text utility.

14. The three types of login script are _____, _____, and _____.

A. System, configuration, user     C. System, user, profile
B. Standard, special, hidden       D. Supervisor, user, private

15. Users running virtual DOS sessions under OS/2 should not use
    the COMSPEC command in the login script.
    A. True       B. False

16. The acronym TCP/IP stands for
    A. Transmission Control Process/Internet Process.
    B. Transmission Central Protocol/Internet Protocol.
    C. Transmission Control Protocol/Interprocess Protocol.
    D. Transmission Control Protocol/Internet Protocol.

17. The _____ console module allows you to maintain and repair the
    NetWare Directory Services (NDS) database.
    A. CONFIG       C. DSREPAIR
    B. DSMERGE     D. VOLUMES

18. NetWare token-ring networks can use the following frame types
    A. Token-Ring 802.2.       C. Token-Ring SNAP.
    B. Token-Ring 802.3.       D. IEEE Standard 802.2.

19. In order to provide network printing services via the AppleTalk
    Printer Access Protocol, you need to have both _____ and
    installed _____ on your NetWare 4.0 server.
    A. ATALK.NLM, PSERVER.NLM
    B. PSERVER.NLM, NPRINTER.NLM
    C. ATXNP.NLM, NPRINTER.NLM
    D. ATXNP.NLM, ATALK.NLM

20. The login script FULL_NAME identifier variable is used to display
    A. The user's full name in the Directory context.
    B. The user's complete name in the Directory context.
    C. The user's full name in bindery-based NetWare.
    D. The user's complete name in bindery-based NetWare.

21. _____ lets a user access protocol-specific services, such as
    NetWare and Telnet, simultaneously.
    A. IPX       C. TCP/IP
    B. ODI       D. OSI

22. The Packet Burst protocol code requires about _____ of memory.
    A. 2 KB       C. 6 KB
    B. 4 KB       D. 8 KB

23. You can use the SWAP login script command to
    A. Restart LOGIN after executing a # command.
    B. Move the # command out of conventional memory into higher memory.
    C. Change the screen display from a menu to a DOS prompt.
    D. Move LOGIN out of conventional memory into higher memory.

24. If your application can only print to a local port, you can use the _____ utility to send print jobs.
    A. NPRINTER     C. NETUSER
    B. CAPTURE     D. NPRINT

25. If you must delete Server objects which provide NDS database services, you must use
    A. NETADMIN.
    B. NetWare Administrator.
    C. One of the Partition Manager tools.
    D. DSREPAIR.

# ⇨ NetWare 4.x Advanced Administration

The advanced system manager exam for NetWare 4.x deals quite a bit with the management strategies and performance management of the operating system. Many of the questions on the test deal with how to set up the workstation files, such as the standard IPX and VLM interface, as well as the ODI shells, the shell enhancement configuration file, NET.CFG, and the commands that go into it. You will also find that the performance management and advanced printing section of the student manual receive heavy emphasis during the exam. Remember that these are the areas that give the most grief to network administrators, so Novell will want to make sure you fully understand them. Other areas that generate quite a few questions are the prevention and maintenance sections. These areas include some very good information about general maintenance and prevention strategies for your networks, and also cover the SBACKUP utility. You can count on having a question or two about SBACKUP. NDS also plays a very important part in NetWare 4.x, so make sure you study that topic in detail. The NDS questions you see on this exam will be a lot more detailed than the ones you saw on the NetWare 4.x Administration exam.

# ⇨ Sample NetWare 4.x Advanced Administration test questions

1. The DSREPAIR console utility
   A. Distributes your NDS database by placing replicas of database partitions on different servers.
   B. Checks and repairs the database.
   C. Creates one Directory tree from two separate trees, by merging them at the root.
   D. Imports information from an existing database to the NDS database.

2. You can specify SHELL.CFG options in the NET.CFG file.
   A. True     B. False

3. NetWare 4.x currently supports ____ tape size(s).
   A. ¼"        C. 8 mm
   B. 4 mm     D. None of the above

4. The SMDR ( Storage Management Data Requester) passes commands and information between
   A. Target Service Agents (TSAs) and Storage Device Interface.
   B. Storage Device Interface and SBACKUP.
   C. Workstation Manager and Storage Device Interface.
   D. SBACKUP and Target Service Agents (TSAs).

5. A socket is the part of an IPX internetwork address, within a network node, that represents the destination of an IPX packet.
   A. True     B. False

6. Always use a NET.CFG file whenever you
   A. Change the default hardware settings on the network board.
   B. Are using multiple protocols.
   C. Are using Novell's LAN Workplace.
   D. Need to map new network drives to the current workstation.

7. A new partition is created by default when you install or upgrade a NetWare v4.0 server into a new context.
   A. True     B. False

8. You must have a minimum of _____ of memory available on the workstation to create an NDS partition using Network Administrator.
   A. 2 MB      C. 6 MB
   B. 4 MB      D. 8 MB

9. Controls on the Windows 3.1 "Network" dialog box allow you to specify
   A. Whether messages are enabled at start-up.
   B. Whether drive mappings affect all sessions.
   C. The maximum number of print jobs shown in the Print Manager.
   D. The maximum print buffer size.
   E. How often the Print Manager updates its list of print jobs.

10. One of the reasons to use ODI drivers in place of dedicated IPX drivers is that ODI drivers are easier to configure; you do not have to link a new driver when you change the NIC's interrupt or I/O address.
    A. True      B. False

11. If an SCSI controller and its device driver are ASPI compatible, you can use _____ to run a tape device connected to the controller.
    A. DCB.DSK      C. TAPEDAI.DSK
    B. ASPITRAN.DSK      D. MNSDAT.DSK

12. The Windows 3.1 _____ driver performs virtualization among sessions for the NetWare shell. It is only used with 386 Enhanced Mode.
    A. NETWARE.DRV      C. VIPX.386
    B. VNETWARE.386      D. VODI.386

13. To install NCP packet signature on a DOS or Windows workstation, add the following parameter, under the _____ heading, to the NET.CFG file of each workstation
    A. "Link Driver", SIGNATURE LEVEL=<number>
    B. "NetWare DOS Requester", SIGNATURE LEVEL=<number>
    C. "Link Driver", NCP PACKET LEVEL=<number>
    D. "NetWare DOS Requester", NCP PACKET LEVEL=<number>

14. NetWare for Macintosh contains built-in support for Macintosh-standard Hierarchical File System (HFS) CD-ROM discs.
    A. True      B. False

15. Your workstation must meet which of the following requirements before you can use PARTMGR to create a new NDS partition?
    A. Running DOS 3.30 or later
    B. A minimum of 6 MB of RAM
    C. A minimum of 512 KB of RAM
    D. The Supervisor object right to the container object you are partitioning

16. The default number of SBACKUP buffers is
    A. 2.      C. 6.
    B. 4.      D. 8.

17. To configure a server to use the IP Tunnel, you must first load and bind _____ to the interfaces you plan to use.
    A. ODI      C. CSMA/CD
    B. IPX      D. TCP/IP

18. The AppleTalk Print Services Console (ATPSCON) utility allows you to perform which of the following tasks?
    A. Configure printer servers.
    B. Configure print spoolers.
    C. Define a printer type for ATPS use.
    D. View printer and system logs, but not the level of detail that they contain.
    E. Specify a directory on the file server for the ATPS files and queues.

19. Once you create a new NDS partition, the new partition appears on screen. The name of the partition is the same as the container name. The object class is listed as
    A. "Copy".      C. "Partition".
    B. "New".      D. There is no object class.

20. The NP MAX MACHINE NAMES = number entry in NET.CFG specifies
    A. The maximum number of Named Pipes that can be open at once.
    B. The maximum number of communication buffers the extender can use to communicate with the named pipes server.
    C. The required number of named pipes that you need open.
    D. How many named pipe servers you want cached on the DOS machine.

21. There are five bindery object properties, including
    A. Group, queue, server, user, and volume.
    B. Group, supervisor, server, user, and volume.
    C. Printer, queue, server, user, and volume.
    D. Group, queue, printer, server, and volume.

22. The acronym SMS stands for
    A. Sub-Multiplexing Source.
    B. Storage Monitoring Services.
    C. Storage Management Services.
    D. Standard Multiplexed Signal.

23. To fix the entire NDS database, you must run the utility on
    A. A single server that contains any part of the database.
    B. Any server on the network.
    C. The server where the master replica resides.
    D. Each server which contains a part of the database.

24. You normally need to increase the NetBIOS Broadcast Count
    value in NET.CFG if
    A. You cannot attach to a gateway.
    B. You cannot attach to a router.
    C. The packet loss rate is high.
    D. You are running on more than one network or LAN segment.

25. Partitions contain NDS database information, along with file and
    directory data or information.
    A. True          B. False

# ⇨ NetWare 4.x Directory Services Design

The NetWare 4.x Directory Services (NDS) Design exam is an in-depth
look at NDS. Not only will you need to define the terms used within
NDS, but you will need to know how these various items work as well.
The exam will test your ability to use NDS to set up various types of
networking environments. The two special areas of consideration are
the department and the organization. It is extremely important that

you spend some hands-on time with NDS before you take this exam. For example, you will need to know how to create multiple contexts, and the methods for replicating the NDS on other NetWare 4.x servers. The exam looks at partitioning as well. Finally, this exam takes another look at migrating a NetWare 2.x and NetWare 3.x server to a NetWare 4.x server. You will need to know the procedures for both prior to taking the exam. This exam also takes a look at the implications of making the move. For example, it looks at the results of using the IEEE 802.2 frame type.

# ⇨ Sample NetWare 4.x Design and Implementation test questions

1. Which of the following reasons show why it is important to plan your Directory tree?
   A. It provides fault-tolerance for the Directory database.
   B. It decreases traffic on the network.
   C. It makes it easy for users to look up information.
   D. It makes it easy for network supervisors to administer the network.

2. A _____ document details how to name objects (Users, Printers, Servers, etc.) as well as object property values, such as telephone numbers.
   A. NetWare Directory Services Details
   B. NetWare Directory Services Outline
   C. NetWare Directory Services Standards
   D. NetWare Directory Services Design

3. If you plan to have decentralized management of the NDS directory tree, you can use up to _____ levels.
   A. Three      C. Five
   B. Four       D. Six

4. One of the reasons for loading the 802.3 frame type on your NetWare 4.x server is that some routers might not support the Ethernet 802.2 frame type.
   A. True       B. False

5. An across-the-wire migration consists of
   A. Installing the NetWare 4.x files from another server on the same network.
   B. Changing your older NetWare server or LAN Server to a NetWare 4.x server.
   C. Transferring your network information from an older NetWare server or LAN Server to an existing NetWare 4.x server that is on the same network.
   D. None of the above.

6. You must manually set the object and property rights; once migration from NetWare 3.x to NetWare 4.x is complete, the Install utility does not perform this task automatically.
   A. True          B. False

7. A typical default partition includes which of the following objects?
   A. Root                    D. Server
   B. Organization            E. Other Leaf Objects
   C. Organizational unit

8. You can use the _____ utility to migrate login scripts from bindery-based NetWare to NetWare 4.x Directory Services (NDS).
   A. WSUPDATE        C. UIMPORT
   B. WSUPGRD         D. NWXTRACT

9. The Root object can be modified or deleted by its trustees.
   A. True          B. False

10. Which of the following methods allow you to control access to objects within the NDS Directory tree?
   A. Grant trustee assignments to any object for any other object.
   B. Create Group objects to give groups of users limited or unlimited access to particular objects in the tree.
   C. Create an Inherited Rights Filter for an object to limit access to that object.
   D. Make a User object the security equivalent to any other objects to allow access.

11. There is no change in directory and file rights when moving from NetWare _____ to 4.x.
   A. 2.15 and above      C. 3.0 and above
   B. 2.2 and above       D. 3.11 and above

12. To enable time synchronization in INSTALL, you need to specify
    A. The time zone, Daylight Savings Time rules, and server location.
    B. The current time, the time zone, and server location.
    C. The time server type, the time zone, and Daylight Savings Time rules.
    D. The time server type, the time zone, and the current time.

13. The Country and Organizational Unit objects are _____; you must include at least _____ Organization object(s) in your Directory tree.
    A. Optional, one        C. Optional, two
    B. Mandatory, one       D. Mandatory, two

14. Object rights include
    A. Supervisor, Compare, Read, Write, Add.
    B. Supervisor, Compare, Read, Write, Delete.
    C. Supervisor, Browse, Create, Delete, Access Control.
    D. Supervisor, Browse, Create, Delete, Rename.

15. The "Upgrade PRINTCON Database" option of the PUPGRADE utility allows you to convert NetWare 3.x
    A. Print definitions for use with NDS.
    B. Print jobs for use with NDS.
    C. Print forms for use with NDS.
    D. Print servers and printers to NDS objects.

16. A user has BCDR rights at the Organizational level. The IRF for the SALES Organizational Unit level are SBC. What are his effective rights?
    A. SBCDR        C. SBC
    B. BCDR         D. BC

17. If you chose to assign random passwords during migration, you will find the new assignments in the _____ file. (Users should change their passwords immediately.)
    A. PASSWORD.TXT        C. PASSWORD.NEW
    B. RANDOM.PWD          D. NEW.PWD

18. You must convert a NetWare 2.15 file server to a NetWare _____ server before you can perform the NetWare 4.x in-place upgrade.
    A. 2.2        C. 3.11
    B. 3.0        D. 4.0

19. You must have at least _____ replicas of every Directory partition; otherwise, you could permanently lose access to a part of your tree.
    A. One  C. Three
    B. Two  D. Four

20. Using the _____ frame type allows other pre-NetWare 4.0 servers and routers to see the NetWare 4.x server.
    A. 802.1  C. 802.3
    B. 802.2  D. 802.4

21. The six categories of security features are
    A. Login security, trustees, groups, rights, inheritance, effective rights
    B. Login security, trustees, rights, inheritance, attributes, and effective rights
    C. Login security, trustees, file and directory, object, groups, property
    D. Login security, trustees, rights, inheritance, attributes, and property

22. Which of the following server types are time source servers?
    A. Primary  C. Reference
    B. Secondary  D. Single Reference

23. One of the methods for providing faster access to the NDS directory information through a WAN is by placing a replica of the necessary partition on a local server.
    A. True  B. False

24. NetWare 3.x uses the _____ ethernet frame type, while NetWare 4.x defaults to using the _____ frame type even though you can still load the older specification.
    A. 802.2, 802.3  C. Raw, IEEE
    B. 802.3, 802.2  D. None of the above

25. Default leaf objects for a typical NetWare 4.x installation include
    A. NetWare Server object, Volume object SYS, User object SUPERVISOR, and User object GUEST.
    B. NetWare Server object, Volume object SYS, User object ADMIN, and User object GUEST.
    C. NetWare Server object, Volume object SYS, User object ADMIN, and User object EVERYONE.
    D. NetWare Server object, Volume object SYS, User object ADMIN, and User object SUPERVISOR.

# ⇨ NetWare Service and Support

The service and support exam questions are fairly straightforward. This is a hands on-class that deals with physically installing the network from the cable to the operating system, and troubleshooting problems on the network. Study the sections on multiserver networks and internetworks. Know the specifications for each of the cable types listed in the book (yes, they might ask you the minimum allowable amount of cable between nodes in a 10base2 network, with the answer in either feet or meters). Also, memorize the options that are on the installation screens for NetWare v2.15, v2.2, and v3.x,11 and 4.x. You must also know the minimum hardware requirements for each of the operating systems, as well as for the workstations. This is one exam for which it really helps if you install the operating systems many times before taking the exam. You will find that this course and manual also cover the NetWare repair utilities. If you take the course you should use them at least once; chances are high that there will be questions about their use and functions.

# ⇨ Sample NetWare Service and Support test questions

1. If a single network has more than one file server on the same physical cabling system, it is known as a(n)
   A. Multiserver network.   C. One cable network.
   B. Internetwork.   D. Both A and B.

2. The network address has a maximum length of _____ digits.
   A. 6   C. 12
   B. 8   D. 16

3. Each workstation on the network must be assigned a(n) _____ address.
   A. I/O   C. Node
   B. Office   D. Video

4. When using thin net ethernet cabling, each trunk segment must not exceed
   A. 3035 feet.   C. 185 meters.
   B. 925 meters.   D. 2000 feet.

5. NetWare's hot fix feature is used to
   A. Remove NICs from the computer while it is running.
   B. Physically repair hard disk drives.
   C. Watch for bad data blocks during writes.
   D. Repair NetWare volumes.

6. WSgen is used to create what file?
   A. Netx.com
   B. Net.cfg
   C. IPXODI.com
   D. IPX.com

7. During the install process of NetWare v2.2, the ztest utility will
   A. Erase all data on the disk.
   B. Not affect data on the disk.
   C. Test the network adapter.
   D. Test the entire disk for bad blocks.

8. To create an internal router in NetWare v2.2 you must
   A. Select more than one network adapter during the operating
      system generation.
   B. Use the BRgen software.
   C. Use the Routegen software.
   D. Use the Introute software.

9. To install NetWare v2.15 you would use the _____ utility.
   A. Install.exe
   B. Server.exe
   C. Netgen.exe
   D. Sysgen.exe

10. To upgrade a file server from NetWare v2.x to v3.x, using the
    transfer method, you must have
    A. Two file servers.
    B. Two networks.
    C. Two supervisors.
    D. A tape drive.

11. The first step in network troubleshooting is to
    A. Take corrective action.
    B. Bill the customer.
    C. Complete the pre-site planning checklist.
    D. Test every assembly on the network.

12. When talking to a person who is giving you information about a
    network problem, you should
    A. Buy them lunch.
    B. Ask general questions, so as not to intimidate them.
    C. Talk to their supervisor.
    D. Ask isolating questions.

13. To repair the NetWare bindery files, you would use the _____ utility.
    A. Vrepair      C. Dconfig
    B. Syscon      D. Bindfix

14. NetWire is Novell's technical BBS.
    A. True      B. False

15. When using the Dconfig utility, it is possible to add another LAN driver to the operating system.
    A. True      B. False

16. An NE1000 is a(n)
    A. 8-bit token ring NIC.      C. 8-bit ethernet NIC.
    B. 16-bit token ring NIC.      D. 16-bit ethernet NIC.

17. _____ is the most common access method used by linear bus topologies.
    A. CSMA/CD      C. Polling
    B. Token bus      D. Token ring

18. The maximum distance from a network node to an active hub on an ArcNET network is
    A. 100 feet.      C. 607 feet.
    B. 164 feet.      D. 2000 feet.

19. Advantages of using fiber optic cable include which of the following?
    A. It does not emanate electrical or magnetic signals.
    B. It is less expensive than twisted pair cable.
    C. It is immune to interference, cross-talk, lightning, and corrosion.
    D. It is useful in high-speed applications.

20. The /T option of the NetWare 4.x NWXTRACT utility allows you to specify the type of file to extract. Valid file types include
    A. MAC.      D. WIN.
    B. OS2.      E. UNX.
    C. SER.

21. The NetWare 4.x PSC utility performs the same tasks as the NetWare 3.x _____ utility.
    A. PRINTCON      C. PRINTDEF
    B. PCONSOLE      D. All of the above

22. NetWare 4.x Property rights include
    A. Supervisor, Compare, Read, Write, Add/Delete Self.
    B. Supervisor, Compare, Read, Write, Delete.
    C. Supervisor, Browse, Create, Delete, Access Control.
    D. Supervisor, Browse, Create, Delete, Rename.

23. The acronym ATM stands for
    A. Asynchronous Traffic Movement.
    B. Automated Teller Machine.
    C. Asynchronous Transfer Mode.
    D. Automated Transfer Mode.

24. The maximum stations on one trunk when using thick ethernet is
    A. 30.   C. 100.
    B. 96.   D. 120.

25. You may connect a passive hub to another passive hub on an ArcNET network.
    A. True   B. False

# Networking Technologies

This is the most difficult exam that you will take. The course covers twenty-nine chapters in just three days. The information from this course is not Novell-specific, so those who have years of NetWare experience should plan to burn the midnight oil in preparation for this exam. The best advice for helping you to pass this exam is to memorize the student manual and to learn as many of the acronyms as possible. The course and manual are so in-depth that there is not any one single section or topic that is more important than any other. Take the test immediately after you study the manuals so you have less time to forget anything you have just read. If you fail the exam the first time do not get discouraged; almost everyone does. Use this as a learning tool for the next time, and write down all the questions that you can remember immediately after the test. Use these questions as a study guide for the next time. Chances are you won't have the same test questions, but you will get the feel of what Novell expects on the test.

# Sample Networking Technologies test questions

1. At layer five of the OSI reference model is the _____ layer, which is located between the layers of _____ and _____.
   A. Session, application, presentation
   B. Session, Transport, presentation
   C. Network, transport, session
   D. Network, data-link, session

2. All vendors are OSI compliant.
   A. True       B. False

3. The U.S. representative to the ISO is
   A. ANSI.       C. IBM.
   B. IEEE.       D. Novell.

4. In an analog signal the _____ is the measurement from the reference line to the top of the wave.
   A. Frequency       C. Curl
   B. Phase           D. Amplitude

5. In a TTY interface or PC that is TTY compatible, the encoding scheme that is typically used is
   A. Return to zero.     C. Biphase.
   B. Unipolar.           D. Manchester.

6. Base band transmission systems use
   A. Digital signals.     C. TV signals.
   B. Analog Signals.      D. Both A and B.

7. An example of a DTE is a
   A. Modem.       C. Codec.
   B. PC.          D. Telephone.

8. Asynchronous transmission uses start and stop bits to synchronize the signal. This clocking only needs to be accurate for _____ to _____ ticks.
   A. 1, 2       C. 8, 14
   B. 2, 5       D. 18, 24

9. Two of the most common token passing LAN standards are
   A. IEEE 802.4 and 802.5.       C. Arcnet and Ethernet.
   B. 10baseT and Token ring.     D. Ethernet and Token ring.

10. Repeaters operate at the _____ layer of the OSI reference model.
    A. Physical
    B. Data-link
    C. Network
    D. Transport

11. Gateways use which layers of the OSI reference model?
    A. Application
    B. Transport
    C. Session
    D. All of the above

12. HDLC, SDLC and LAPB are all examples of protocols that operate at the _____ layer of the OSI model.
    A. Application
    B. Transport
    C. Data-link
    D. Session

13. The IEEE project 802 is mainly concerned with what two layers of the OSI model?
    A. Application and presentation
    B. Network and transport
    C. Network and data-link
    D. Data-link and physical

14. If you wanted to get information on broad band technology, which IEEE committee would you talk to?
    A. 802.1
    B. 802.6
    C. 802.7
    D. 802.8

15. In an 802.5 environment, how many bytes does the token consist of?
    A. 1
    B. 2
    C. 3
    D. 4

16. Arcnet uses a _____ protocol.
    A. Character-oriented.
    B. Byte-oriented.
    C. Hybrid.
    D. Contention-oriented.

17. In a local talk frame, the FCS is calculated on all fields except
    A. The flags.
    B. The abort sequence.
    C. Both A and B.
    D. None of the above.

18. The Internet protocol provides _____, _____ delivery of packets.
    A. Connectionless, non-guaranteed
    B. Connectionless, guaranteed
    C. Connected, non-guaranteed
    D. Connected, guaranteed

19. The SNA reference model includes _____ layers.
    A. 4      C. 7
    B. 5      D. 9

20. Above the _____ layer of the OSI reference model, DNA permits two access modes.
    A. Transport      C. Network
    B. Session        D. Data-link

21. The acronym SNMP stands for
    A. Single Network Maintenance Protocol.
    B. Single Network Management Protocol.
    C. Simple Network Maintenance Protocol.
    D. Simple Network Management Protocol.

22. The EIA provides which of the following standards?
    A. X.25       C. 802.2
    B. RS-232C    D. OSI Model

23. Data communications consist of
    A. Sender.      C. Medium.
    B. Receiver.    D. Message.

24. Full duplex transmissions allow
    A. Information flow in only one direction.
    B. Information in two directions, but only one direction at a time.
    C. Information flow in both directions at once.
    D. None of the above.

25. The Function Management Services layer of SNA corresponds to the _____ layer of OSI.
    A. Application    C. Session
    B. Presentation   D. Transport

# ⇨ Sample test question answers

Listed below are the answers to the sample test questions. There is room next to each answer for you to write notes about each question, or to list the page number on which you found the answers.

## ⇨ DOS/Micro-Hardware

| | | | | |
|---|---|---|---|---|
| 1. A | 6. B | 11. C | 16. B | 21. A, D |
| 2. C | 7. A | 12. A, C, D | 17. A, C, D | 22. B |
| 3. B | 8. D | 13. A | 18. C | 23. A, B, C, D |
| 4. D | 9. A | 14. A | 19. D | 24. C |
| 5. A | 10. C | 15. D | 20. B | 25. A |

## ⇨ NetWare v2.2 System Manager

| | | | | |
|---|---|---|---|---|
| 1. B | 3. A | 5. A | 7. C | 9. C |
| 2. A | 4. A | 6. A | 8. A | 10. C |

## ⇨ NetWare v2.2 Advanced System Manager

| | | | | |
|---|---|---|---|---|
| 1. A | 4. D | 7. A | 10. A | 13. D |
| 2. D | 5. D | 8. B | 11. A | 14. B |
| 3. D | 6. A | 9. A | 12. D | 15. B |

## ⇨ NetWare 3.x Installation and Configuration Workshop

| | | | | |
|---|---|---|---|---|
| 1. C | 6. B | 11. B | 16. B | 21. C |
| 2. A, B, C | 7. A, B, C, D, E | 12. D | 17. D | 22. B |
| 3. D | 8. C | 13. E | 18. A | 23. C |
| 4. A | 9. A | 14. A | 19. D | 24. A |
| 5. D | 10. B | 15. C | 20. C | 25. D |

## ⇨ NetWare v3.x11 System Manager

| | | | | |
|---|---|---|---|---|
| 1. E | 3. D | 5. C | 7. B | 9. B |
| 2. A | 4. B | 6. C | 8. C | 10. B |

| 11. A | 14. D | 17. D | | 20. C | 23. B |
|---|---|---|---|---|---|
| 12. D | 15. B | 18. B | | 21. A | 24. A |
| 13. A | 16. C | 19. A, B, C, D, E | | 22. D | 25. A, C, D |

# NetWare v3.x11 Advanced System Manager

| 1. D | 6. D | 11. A | 16. D | 21. D |
|---|---|---|---|---|
| 2. B | 7. D | 12. B | 17. C | 22. A |
| 3. D | 8. D | 13. D | 18. B | 23. C |
| 4. D | 9. D | 14. D | 19. C | 24. A, B, D |
| 5. D | 10. A | 15. A | 20. A | 25. B |

# NetWare 3.x to NetWare 4.x Update

| 1. A | 8. A | 14. B | 20. A |
|---|---|---|---|
| 2. A, C | 9. A, B, C | 15. D | 21. C |
| 3. D | 10. D | 16. A | 22. A |
| 4. C | 11. B | 17. C | 23. B, D |
| 5. A, B, C, D | 12. C | 18. A | 24. A, B, C, D |
| 6. B | 13. A, B, C, D | 19. D | 25. C |
| 7. A | | | |

# NetWare 4.x Installation and Configuration

| 1. B | 7. B | 13. B | 19. A | 25. A, B, D |
|---|---|---|---|---|
| 2. C | 8. B, C, D | 14. A | 20. C | |
| 3. A | 9. A | 15. D | 21. D | |
| 4. A | 10. B | 16. C | 22. C | |
| 5. D | 11. A, B, C, D, E | 17. A, B, C, D, E | 23. A | |
| 6. C | 12. A | 18. B | 24. C | |

## NetWare 4.x Administration

| | | | | |
|---|---|---|---|---|
| 1. A | 6. A, B, D | 11. C | 16. D | 21. B |
| 2. C | 7. A | 12. B | 17. C | 22. C |
| 3. B | 8. B | 13. A, D | 18. A, C | 23. D |
| 4. A, B, C, D | 9. B | 14. C | 19. D | 24. B, C, D |
| 5. D | 10. D | 15. A | 20. B,C | 25. C |

## NetWare 4.x Advanced Administration

| | | | | |
|---|---|---|---|---|
| 1. B | 6. A, B, C | 11. C | 16. B | 21. A |
| 2. A | 7. A | 12. B | 17. D | 22. C |
| 3. A, B, C | 8. C | 13. B | 18. A, B, C, E | 23. D |
| 4. D | 9. A, B, C, D, E | 14. A | 19. C | 24. A |
| 5. A | 10. A | 15. A,C,D | 20. D | 25. B |

## NetWare 4.x Design and Implementation

| | | | | |
|---|---|---|---|---|
| 1. A, B, C, D | 6. A | 11. D | 16. D | 21. B |
| 2. C | 7. A, B, C, D, E | 12. C | 17. D | 22. A, C, D |
| 3. D | 8. C | 13. A | 18. C | 23. A |
| 4. A | 9. B | 14. D | 19. B | 24. B |
| 5. C | 10. A, B, C, D | 15. B | 20. C | 25. D |

## NetWare Service and Support

| | | | | |
|---|---|---|---|---|
| 1. A | 4. C | 7. A | 10. A | 13. D |
| 2. B | 5. C | 8. A | 11. C | 14. A |
| 3. C | 6. D | 9. C | 12. D | 15. B |

| | | | | |
|---|---|---|---|---|
| 16. C | 18. D | 20. A, B, C, D, E | 22. A | 24. C |
| 17. A | 19. A, C, D | 21. B | 23. C | 25. B |

# ⇨ Networking Technologies

| | | | | |
|---|---|---|---|---|
| 1. B | 6. A | 11. D | 16. A | 21. D |
| 2. B | 7. B | 12. C | 17. C | 22. B |
| 3. A | 8. C | 13. D | 18. A | 23. A, B, C, D |
| 4. D | 9. A | 14. C | 19. C | 24. C |
| 5. B | 10. A | 15. C | 20. A | 25. B |

# Glossary

**ACS**  *See* asynchronous communications server.

**ad hoc solution**  A technique for an event or problem that requires an immediate solution. It usually refers to something that is not planned, but implemented without consideration of any side effects. For example, an ad hoc report solves the need to present information in a specific manner without programming that report into the application that prepares it.

**ASCII (American Standard Code for Information Interchange)**  A standard method of presenting the numeric representations available in a computer in human-readable form. For example, the number 32 represents a space. There are 128 characters (7 bits) in the standard ASCII code. The extended ASCII code uses 8 bits for 256 characters. Display adapters from the same machine type usually use the same upper 128 characters. Printers, however, might reserve these upper 128 characters for nonstandard characters. For example, many Epson printers use them for italic representations of the lower 128 characters.

**asynchronous communications server (ACS)**  A special network node containing one or more modems. The ACS allows users on the LAN to communicate with other LANs, BBS, and online services. An ACS also allows off-site employees to dial into the LAN to upload/download files, use application programs, or read e-mail.

**bindery** The set of files used to store network-specific configuration information on a NetWare network. These files contain user data, security information, and other network configuration data. You cannot start the file server without this information. Corruption of any of these files might prevent the network from starting properly as well.

**cache buffers** A term that refers to the smallest storage elements in a cache (an area of RAM devoted to storing commonly used pieces of information normally stored on the hard drive). Think of each buffer as a box that can store a single piece of information. The more buffers (boxes) you have, the greater the storage capacity of the cache.

**CBT** *See* computer-based-training

**CD-ROM (Compact Disk Read-Only Memory)** A device used to store up to 650 MB of permanent data. You cannot use a CD-ROM as you would a hard or floppy disk drive, because you cannot write to it. The disk looks much like an audio CDs, but requires a special drive to interface it with a computer.

**central configuration** The files required to tell an application, operating system, or application environment how to configure itself to interact with the user's workstation. This file might also contain user preferences, such as screen colors or macros. Usually these files appear on the local hard drive of each user's workstation. However, in a central configuration the files appear in one place on the file server's hard drive.

**certification** A quantified method of measuring the expertise of a network or other professional. This measure is usually a combination of written exams and practical evaluations. In most cases, a certification represents the knowledge level of a participant rather than his or her ability to actually perform the required work in every circumstance. Certification assures nonskilled or semiskilled managers that a person has a specific level of knowledge required to perform the work that the certification tests for.

**Certified NetWare Administrator (CNA)** The Certified NetWare Administrator (CNA) is Novell's entry-level certification. It is for the person who needs to administer the network on a day-to-day basis. Usually these people work for one company and perform the administrator tasks in concert with their other duties.

**Certified NetWare Engineer (CNE)** The Certified NetWare Engineer (CNE) is Novell's intermediate level certification. This certification is for people who require a higher level of expertise than a system administrator. Many people who obtain the CNE certification are consultants, system integrators, or an employee of a company that needs a person with more skill and knowledge to help maintain the overall network.

**Certified NetWare Instructor (CNI)** The Certified NetWare Instructor (CNI) is Novell's advanced level certification. This certification is for the individual who wants to teach certified NetWare courses. These courses are taught at Novell Authorized Education Centers (NAEC) and use the Novell courseware.

**channel service unit (CSU)** A device used to terminate a dataphone digital service (DDS) communications line. Terminating the line reduces noise and signal variances that could interfere with communications. A CSU is used for T-1 communications.

**Character Mode Interface** A menu or other application selection system that uses ASCII characters to display information. The menuing system keeps the workstation's video adapter in character mode rather than using the display adapter's graphics mode. All line drawing characters are part of the extended ASCII character set.

**common user access (CUA)** A technique for creating application menus so that applications that require similar functions use similar menus. For example, the File menu on every application will contain a Quit option. It also determines the order in which entries appear. For example, the File menu is always the first menu on the left side of the menu bar while Help is the last menu on the right side of the menu bar.

**computer-based training (CBT)** An alternative means of receiving Novell training. This method uses a combination of manuals, on-screen lessons, and simulated tests to help the candidate prepare for certification exams.

**CNA** *See* Certified NetWare Administrator.

**CNE** *See* Certified NetWare Engineer.

**CNI** *See* Certified NetWare Instructor.

**CRC** *See* cyclic redundancy code.

**CSU** *See* channel service unit.

**CUA** *See* common user access.

**cyclic redundancy code (CRC)** A technique used to ensure the reliability of information stored on hard drives, transported across network cabling, or sent from one place to another. It uses a cyclic calculation to create a numeric check number. The computer performs the same calculation when it retrieves the data and compares it to the CRC. If the two match there is no data error. Otherwise, the sending machine must either resend the data or the receiving computer must reconstruct it.

**DAT drive** Digital audio tape. A tape drive that uses a cassette to store data. The cassette and drive use the same technology as the audio version of the DAT drive. However, the internal circuitry of the drive formats the tape for use with a computer system. DAT tapes allow you to store large amounts of information in a relatively small amount of space. Typical drive capacities range from 1.2 GB to 8 GB.

**data grade line** A specially constructed telephone line that uses higher quality media and less multiplexing to reduce overall line noise and increase reliability. Data grade lines usually use fiber optic connections to ensure a minimum of disruption from external signal sources.

**data service unit (DSU)** A device, similar to a modem, which connects a PC or terminal to a dataphone digital service (DDS) communications line. One end of the DSU connects to the terminal through a standard serial port. The other end of the DSU connects through the CSU to the four wire DDS line. A DSU is used for T-1 communications.

**DDE** *See* dynamic data exchange.

**dial-in/dial-out connectivity** A service that allows employees to call the company network from a remote location and use the network's services. For example, someone who needed to use the company e-mail system to check his or her incoming mail, or to create messages for other people in the company, could use this service. This service also allows satellite offices to update or download information from the company database. The dial-out portion of the service allows people within the company to send faxes or to call online services using the company modem. There are a number of other uses for dial-in/dial-out connectivity.

**dirty power** Electricity that contains impure elements, such as power spikes or noise. These impure elements might damage computer equipment by momentarily driving the component beyond its specified limits. Spikes usually occur as the result of motor starts and stops. Switches and other devices that change the flow of electricity might also cause spikes. Noise usually comes from electric lighting, transformers, or other devices that produce radio frequency signals.

**disk cache** A technique that increases the apparent speed of a hard disk drive, by storing some of the data in RAM. There are many methods that the disk cache software uses to determine which data remains in RAM. The caching technique determines how much of a speed increase you see from the disk cache.

**DOS (disk operating system)** The underlying software used by many PCs to provide basic system services and to allow the user to run application software. The operating system performs many low level tasks through the BIOS. The specifics of the services that it offers are defined by the current revision number of the software; check your user manual for details. Replacement operating systems include Windows NT and OS/2.

**downsizing** The process of moving applications from a large, centralized mainframe or minicomputer environment to a decentralized PC LAN environment. Downsizing might involve using the mainframe or minicomputer as a database host or as a storage device. All user interface, security, print, and e-mail functions reside on the local PC LAN. Many large businesses use downsizing as a means for reducing operating costs. A typical PC LAN requires less resources to install and maintain than a mainframe or minicomputer with similar capacity.

**Drake Testing Center** The only company authorized by Novell to administer your certification examinations. This company specializes in providing quiet and comfortable test centers that cater to a wide range of specialties, including CPAs and Registered Nurses.

**DSU** *See* data service unit.

**dynamic data exchange (DDE)** The ability to cut data found in one application and paste it into another application; for example, cutting a graphic image created by a paint program and pasting it into a word processing application as part of a word processing document. Once pasted, the data does not reflect changes made to it by the originating application.

**ECC** *See* error checking and correcting.

**ECNE** *See* enterprise certified NetWare engineer.

**emoticon** A figure created with the symbols on a keyboard. To read an emoticon, tilt your head to the left and visualize the person's expression. Emoticons convey the intent behind a humorous or tongue-in-cheek comment.

**enhanced mode**  A Windows operating mode that supports the capabilities of the 80386 and above processors. This means that Windows will use any extended memory found in the workstation by using the processor's protected mode. This mode also fully supports the virtual memory capabilities of the 80386, which means the size of the hard disk's swap file plus the amount of physical RAM determines the amount of memory available for applications. You also receive the full multitasking capabilities of the 80386 using this mode.

**Enterprise Certified NetWare Engineer (ECNE)**  The Enterprise Certified NetWare Engineer (ECNE) is Novell's advanced intermediate level certification. This certification is a continuation of the CNE program. A person who becomes an ECNE usually has some special requirements or interests in the advanced or specialized areas of networking. For example, a consultant or a network administrator might need to connect NetWare, using TCP/IP and NFS, or might need to create a wide area network using Novell's dial-in/dial-out products.

**error checking and correcting (ECC)**  This term originally referred to a self-diagnostic technique used to correct errors in RAM. The term now includes the same type of diagnostics provided with tapes, hard disks, and floppy disk drives. In all cases, the device uses some type of microcode contained in a peripheral chip to detect and correct soft errors in the data stream.

**extended attribute (EA) file**  An OS/2 system file that stores the icon and other descriptive information about a particular data file or application. Extended attributes include long file names and positions within the Workplace Shell, as well. Damage to the EA file usually results in a lack of descriptive information, but no loss in application functionality.

**FAT**  *See* file allocation table disk format.

**file allocation table (FAT) disk format** The method of formatting a hard disk drive used by DOS and other operating systems. This technique is one of the oldest formatting methods available.

**file server** The centralized storage area for files and applications. Special features of the network operating system enable the file server to control access to these files and applications. This allows several people to share the same file(s) and/or application(s) without damage to the data. A file server usually contains larger hard drives and more memory than a standard workstation. It also provides access to one or more printers. The user-perceived capabilities of a file server depend on a combination of available hardware and NOS capabilities.

**file statistic** A fact about one or more files on the network. These statistics can include the creation and last update dates, who created the file, who owns the file, when someone last accessed the file, who has access to it, and which user last updated it. Other statistics might include the number of file accesses, any security restrictions, or other pertinent file information.

**filter condition** A Boolean (logical) statement that allows some part of the whole to pass. Think of a filter; for example, a coffee filter allows the brewed coffee to pass but retains the coffee grounds.

**graphical user interface (GUI)** A system of icons and graphic images that replace the character mode menu system used by many machines. The GUI can ride on top of another operating system (such as DOS), or it can reside as part of the operating system itself (as with OS/2). Advantages of a GUI are ease-of-use and high-resolution graphics. Disadvantages consist of higher workstation hardware requirements and lower performance over a similar system using a character mode interface.

**graphics workstation** A PC specifically designed for graphics-oriented work. Many workstations of this type use operation system, although they might use OS/2 or Windows as alternatives. Tektronics and many other companies make high performance workstations for graphic artists or draftsmen.

**GUI** *See* graphical user interface.

**HDLC** *See* high-level data link control.

**high-level data link control (HDLC)** A standard communication line protocol developed by the International Standards Organization (ISO). The protocol defines how two devices talk to each other. Think of the protocol as a type of language used by the two devices.

**high performance file system (HPFS)** The method of formatting a hard disk drive used by OS/2. While it provides significant speed advantages over other formatting techniques, only the OS/2 operating system and applications designed to work with that operating system, can access a drive formatted using this technique.

**HPFS** *See* high-performance file system.

**icon** A symbol used to graphically represent the purpose and/or function of an application or a file. For example, a text file might appear as a sheet of paper with the name of the file below the icon. Applications designed for the environment or operating system usually appear with a special icon depicting the vendor's or product's logo. Icons normally appear as part of a GUI environment or operating system such as Windows or OS/2.

**instructor performance evaluation (IPE)** The practical examination required by Novell to certify that an instructor can convey information to a student. The examination includes course preparation and other instructor related tasks. A typical IPE lasts two days. On the first day, the candidate is tested on his ability to prepare to teach a class. On the second day, he is tested on his actual teaching ability.

**IPE** *See* instructor performance evaluation.

**IPX (Internet packet exchange)** This is NetWare's peer-to-peer communication protocol. It describes a set of rules that allows two nodes to talk to each other. Think of this as the language used on the network. If everyone speaks the same language, then all the nodes can understand each other. Messages are exchanged in the form of packets. Think of a packet as one sheet of a letter. There is a letterhead saying who sent the letter, an introduction saying who the letter is for, and a message that tells the receiving party what the sending party wants to say.

**LAN** *See* local area network.

**local area network (LAN)** Two or more devices connected together using a combination of hardware and software. The devices, normally computers and peripheral equipment such as printers, are called nodes. A NIC (network interface card) provides the hardware communication among nodes through an appropriate medium (cable or microwave transmission). There are two common LANs (also called networks). Peer-to-peer networks allow each node to connect to any other node on the network with shareable resources. This is a distributed method of sharing files and peripheral devices. A client-server network uses one or more servers to share resources. This is a centralized method of sharing files and peripheral devices. A server provides resources to clients (usually workstations). The most common server is the file server which provides file sharing resources. Other server types include print servers and communication servers.

**logic analyzer** A device that receives clock or other internal computer signals and interprets them. The resulting output is a display of the line logic. In many cases, an analysis of the logic between two components will show whether the circuitry is operating correctly. A technician might also use this data to interpret the content of the information the chips transmit between themselves.

**logo** A graphic representation of a company name or other identifier. It usually appears in iconic form on personal computers. For example, Microsoft FoxPro uses a picture of a fox as its logo.

**loopback plug** A device used to transfer signals from the output side of a computer port to the input side. A loopback plug allows the network administrator to test an entire serial or parallel port.

Without a loopback plug, the administrator might only test the port internal circuitry. There are also loopback plugs for various NICs and other interface devices.

**Master Certified NetWare Engineer (MCNE)** The Master Certified NetWare Engineer (MCNE) is Novell's advanced network professional level certification. This certification is a continuation of the CNE program. A person who becomes an MCNE usually has some special requirements or interest in the advanced or specialized areas of networking. For example, a consultant or a network administrator might need to connect NetWare and a mainframe or create a wide area network in an enterprise network. Most MCNEs are either managers in companies with large networks, or independent consultants who specialize in working with large companies.

**MCNE** *See* Master Certified NetWare Engineer.

**memory footprint** The amount of memory used by an application once it loads and initializes itself. In some cases, an application requires more memory to load than to reside in memory; for example, most TSRs. This is especially true when loading a TSR into high memory.

**multiprotocol router** A device used to connect two LANs together. The router moves signals from one LAN to the other. The difference between a standard router and a multiprotocol router is that the multiprotocol router can move signals between dissimilar LANS. For example, a multiprotocol LAN can move data between a token ring LAN and an ethernet LAN.

**multitasking** The ability of some processor and operating environment/system combinations to perform more than one task at a time. The applications appear to run simultaneously. For example, you could download messages from an online service, print from a word processor, and recalculate a spreadsheet at the same time. Each application receives a slice of time before the processor moves on to the next application. Since the time slices are small, it appears to the user as if these actions were occurring simultaneously.

**multithreading** This is an operating-system-specific technique for breaking one or more application tasks into multiple threads of execution. Using this technique allows the operating system to devote more resources to higher priority tasks, increasing perceived system performance. The programmer must write the application to take advantage of this operating system feature when it is available.

**NAEC** *See* Novell Authorized Education Center.

**NEAP** *See* Novell Education Academic Partner.

**NetWare loadable module (NLM)** An executable file that loads on a NetWare 3.x/4.x file server. An NLM usually adds some capability that the entire network shares. Examples of NLMs include tape backup software, virus protection, UPS detection/management, and database servers. The NLM replaces the VAP provided in NetWare 2.x. Unlike a VAP, an NLM can be loaded or unloaded while the file server is active.

***Network Support Encyclopedia, Professional Edition (NSEPro)*** *The Network Support Encyclopedia, Professional Edition* contains a complete set of Novell manuals, along with articles and other information that the certified individual requires. The professional version of this product also contains a wide variety of product patches. Most of this additional material is available on the NetWire forum of CompuServe.

**network** *See* local area network (LAN).

**network administrator** The person most responsible for installing, maintaining, and upgrading the network used by a corporation. This includes managing system security and user needs, as well as equipment needs.

**network configuration plan** A plan that states current equipment status, network problem areas and fixes for those problems, and future upgrades. This plan can appear in either tabular or outline format and should fully answer the questions users might have about network equipment status. The plan normally includes a map as well.

**NetWork File System (NFS)** A distributed file system developed by Sun Microsystems. NFS allows users of different operating systems, network architectures, protocols, or processor types to share data. More than one hundred software vendors have licensed NFS from Sun Microsystems for use with their products. Novell offers NFS products to allow sharing of data from a Novell NetWare 3.x and 4.x to a UNIX host with NFS operational.

**network interface card (NIC)** The device responsible for allowing a workstation to communicate with the file server and other workstations. It provides the physical means for creating the connection. The card plugs into an expansion slot in the computer. A cable that attaches to the back of the card completes the communication path.

**network loadable module (NLM)** An executable file that loads on a NetWare 3.x/4.x file server. An NLM usually adds some capability that the entire network shares. Examples of NLMs include tape backup software, virus protection, UPS detection/management, and database servers. The NLM replaces the VAP provided in NetWare 2.x. Unlike a VAP, an NLM can be loaded or unloaded while the file server is active.

**network operating system (NOS)** The operating system that runs on the file server or other centralized file/print sharing device. This operating system normally provides multiuser access capability and user accounting software in addition to other network specific utilities.

**NFS** *See* network file system.

**NIC** *See* network interface card.

**NLM** *See* netware loadable module.

**Node** A single element in a network. In most cases the term node refers to a single workstation connected to the network. It might also refer to a bridge, router, or file server. It does not refer to cabling, or passive or active elements that do not directly interface with the network at the logical level.

**NOS** *See* network operating system.

**Novell Authorized Education Center (NAEC)** A training facility authorized by Novell to train CNA, CNE, ECNE, MCNE, and CNI candidates in the latest network operating system technology. An NAEC always uses Certified NetWare Instructors (CNIs) as instructors. It is the only place (besides NEAPs) where you can receive training guaranteed to help you pass your Novell certification examinations.

**Novell Education Academic Partner (NEAP)** A college or university authorized by Novell to train CNA, CNE, ECNE, MCNE, and CNI candidates in the latest network operating system technology. An NEAP usually provides less variety in the way of courses than an NAEC. However, it provides more in the way of structured curriculum because the training is part of the courses that it offers. An NEAP always uses Certified NetWare Instructors (CNIs) as instructors. It is the only place (beside NAECs) where you can receive training guaranteed to help you pass your Novell certification examinations.

**NSEPro** *See Network Support Encyclopedia, Professional Edition.*

**object linking and embedding (OLE)** The process of packaging a file name, application name, and any required parameters into an object, then pasting this object into the file created by another application. For example, you could place a graphic object within a word processing document or spreadsheet. When you look at the object it appears as if you simply pasted the data from the originating application into the current application (similar to DDE). The data provided by the object automatically changes as you change the data in the original object. Often you can start the originating application and automatically load the required data by double clicking on the object.

**OJT** *See* on-the-job training.

**OLE** *See* object linking and embedding.

**on-the-job training (OJT)** A method of training in which you learn by doing the tasks you want to perform. Each mistake you make and correct helps you understand another area of the job. Often, this form of training is supplemented with advice from other people who know how to perform the work. This method works well for simple tasks. It does not work well for learning the principles of network operating systems. However, it is an important part of the post-training learning process.

**operating system (OS)** The software that forms the computer interface between the user and the hardware. The operating system normally provides some type of command processor, along with low-level functions used by applications. The user sees these low-level services as the ability to send data to the printer or receive information about a file on the hard drive. The operating system also schedules tasks, maintains the file system, and provides many vital security features.

**OS** *See* operating system.

**password protection** An operating-system-enforced technique for restricting access to a network or data. The user must enter characters, numbers and/or special symbols in the correct sequence before the operating system will allow access.

**policies and procedures document** A set of written guidelines that the network user can refer to in an emergency. This document also outlines the network rules and regulations. In addition, it contains the procedures for performing specific network related tasks.

**print queue** The network version of a print spooler. It spools all print jobs for a particular printer to a network drive or the drive of a print server. Local workstation performance is not affected by a print queue. The print queue uses file or print server CPU cycles to perform its work.

**print spooler** A special program that intercepts data going to the printer and places it in RAM or on disk. Once the application sending the data completes its work, the print spooler looks for clock cycles during which the computer is not performing useful work. The print spooler sends some of the "spooled" data to the printer every time it sees an empty time slot. Using this technique makes it appear that the application printed all the data when it really hasn't. The end result is that you regain control of the computer faster than if you had to wait for the printer. It also means that you use machine resources more efficiently.

**printer control sequences** A set of special control character sequences that force a printer into a specific setup. For example, one set of control characters might select a special font while another set might change the print margins. The manual that comes with your printer will provide further details about what these control character sequences are, and how to use them.

**protocol analyzer** A device used to interpret the communication packets sent between nodes on a network. Think of the protocol analyzer as a spy reading a letter addressed to someone else before the addressee get to see it. A protocol analyzer allows consultants and network administrators to find communication errors on the network quickly.

**RAID (redundant array of inexpensive disks) systems** A set of interconnected drives that reside outside the file server, in most cases. There are several levels of RAID. Each level defines precisely how the data is placed on each of the drives. In all cases, all the drives in a group share responsibility for storing the data. They act in parallel to both read and write the data. In addition, there is a special drive in most of these systems devoted to helping the network recover when one drive fails. In most cases, the user never even knows that anything happened, because the "spare drive" takes over for the failed drive without any noticeable degradation in network operation. RAID systems increase network reliability and throughput.

**real mode** A Windows operating mode that supports the capabilities of the 8088/8086 processor. This essentially limits you to loading one application within the confines of conventional memory. Windows versions after 3.0 do not support this mode. You must use these versions with workstations containing an 80286 or higher processor.

**router** A device used to connect two LANs together. The router moves signals from one LAN to the other.

**SCSI (Small Computer System Interface) adapter (controller)** A computer interface card that allows you to connect up to seven devices to the computer system. The current SCSI standard is SCSI-2. Typical SCSI devices include tape drives, hard disk drives, and CD ROM drives. SCSI devices typically provide high transfer rates (10 to 15 Mb/s) and access times (device-type dependent).

**SDLC** *See* synchronous data link control.

**shell** A command processor that allows you to directly interact with the operating system. For example, COMMAND.COM is the command processor for DOS. This also refers to menuing systems or environments that perform essentially the same task as the command processor.

**sort order** A method of classifying and ordering a list of items. For example, you could place them in alphabetic order. A would come before B and so forth.

**SPX (sequential packet exchange)** This is the part of the NetWare shell that guarantees delivery of a message sent from one node to another. Think of SPX as the postal clerk who delivers a certified letter. In network terms, each page of the letter is called a packet. SPX delivers the letter one page at a time to the intended party.

**standard mode** A Windows operating mode that supports the capabilities of the 80286 processor. This means that Windows will use any extended memory found in the workstation by using the processor's protected mode. You might also load more than one application at a time (up to the limits imposed by physical RAM). This mode does not support virtual memory or page swapping. It also does not support the multitasking features of the 80386.

**static interface** A menu that does not automatically change to reflect the current machine configuration or operating system environment.

**synchronous data link control (SDLC)** A standard communication line protocol developed by International Business Machines (IBM). The protocol defines how two devices talk to each other. Think of the protocol as a type of language used by the two devices. This particular protocol was designed to work with Systems Network Architecture (SNA) a network architecture developed by IBM.

**TCP/IP** *See* transmission control protocol/Internet protocol.

**terminal emulation software** A form of communications software used to connect a PC to a host. The host can take the form of a LAN, a mainframe, or a minicomputer. Terminal emulation software might consist of a specially designed program or a standard, off-the-shelf package such as Procomm Plus.

**terminate and stay resident (TSR) program** An application that loads itself into memory and stays there once you execute it. The program usually returns you directly to the DOS prompt after loading. Pressing a hot key combination activates the application, allowing you to use it. In most cases, TSRs provide some type of utility, such as print spooling or another short-term function.

**transmission control protocol/Internet protocol (TCP/IP)** A standard communication line protocol developed by the United States Department of Defense. The protocol defines how two devices talk to each other. Think of the protocol as a type of language used by the two devices.

**troubleshooting procedures** *See* policies and procedures document.

**TSR** *See* terminate and stay resident program.

**Upsizing** The process of linking stand-alone PCs together into a LAN. Upsizing usually results when a business grows beyond the capacity to use a "sneaker" net for exchanging files. Upsizing might require the addition of a mainframe or minicomputer for storage/data manipulation purposes when using database management applications.

**value added process (VAP)** An executable file that loads on a NetWare 2.x file server during file server initialization. A VAP usually adds some capability that the entire network shares. Examples of VAPs include tape backup software, virus protection, UPS detection/management, and database servers. You must load a VAP during file server startup. NetWare 2.x does not allow you to unload the VAP while the file server is active. The NLM provided with NetWare 3.x alleviates this problem.

**VAP** *See* value added process.

**virtual memory** The memory provided by an 80386 or above processor. It appears as physical RAM to both the operating system and any applications running on the system, but might or might not reside within physical memory. A special part of the operating system (known as the swapping mechanism) manages the memory that appears in physical RAM and within a swap file on disk. If the processor runs out of physical memory, the swapping mechanism removes the oldest data from physical memory insegments (you can think of them as memory containers) known as pages, and replaces it with blank pages from the swap file on disk. When the swap file runs out of blank pages the virtual memory area is full and you must stop any unnecessary applications. If the processor requires access to data that appears on disk, the swapping mechanism removes the oldest data from physical memory, places it in the swap file, then moves the requested data from the swap file to physical memory.

**WAN** *See* wide area network.

**wide area network (WAN)** An extension of the LAN, a WAN connects two or more LANs together using a variety of methods. A WAN usually encompasses more than one physical site, such as a building. Most WANs rely on microwave communications, fiber optic connections, or leased telephone lines to provide the internetwork connections required to keep all nodes in the network talking with each other.

**Workstation**   The terminal provided to a user. It provides access to application programs, hardware devices, and the network. A workstation usually resides at the user's desk, but it can appear in a centralized location as well. For example, some companies provide one or more advanced technology stations in centralized locations. These workstations serve occasional graphics or engineering needs.

**WORM (write once, read many) drive**   A device that uses CD-ROM technology, coupled with a multiple power level laser, to allow the user to write to the drive one time. Once you write to the drive, you may read the data imprinted on it multiple times. Some drives allow you to correct errors by overwriting the area of the mistake and writing the corrected data to a new area of the disk. (Of course, this assumes there is additional room on the drive for the corrected data.) The main reason to use a WORM drive is archival of data. For example, a law office could use a WORM drive to store records of old cases. Like the CD-ROM drive, most WORM drives limit you to 650 MB of data storage. Some use a proprietary encoding technique to allow you to store up to 1 GB of data.

# Index

Illustrations are in **boldface**.

# About the authors

John Paul Mueller, a Certified NetWare Engineer, is a systems programmer, computer consultant, technical editor of *Data Based Advisor* magazine, and author of *The Novell CNA/CNE Study Guide*, 2nd edition.

Robert A. Williams is a Certified NetWare Instructor who teaches CNE courses nationwide, and co-author of *The Novell CNA/CNE Study Guide*, 2nd edition.